WELCOME TO BURMA

WELCOME TO BURMA

and enjoy the totalitarian experience

TIMOTHY SYROTA

Orchid Press
Bangkok 2001

Timothy Syrota
WELCOME TO BURMA
and enjoy the totalitarian experience

First published 2001

© Orchid Press 2001

ORCHID PRESS
P.O. Box 19
Yuttitham Post Office
Bangkok 10907, Thailand

Cover design: Timothy Syrota

Chapter heading page design and photographs: Timothy Syrota

This book is printed on acid-free long life paper
which meets the specifications of ISO 9706/1994

ISBN 974-524-008-7

TABLE OF CONTENTS

ACKNOWLEDGMENTS

To Dr Michael Aris and Mr Hal Kuløy, both now deceased, whose encouragement and positive comments concerning my work have been inspirational. Their wisdom, sense of humanity, and committment to helping the people of Burma have set an example to be followed.

To Mr David Murray, House Editor of Orchid Press, whose editorial comments have transformed 'Welcome to Burma' from a rambling manuscript into a book worthy of print.

To Mum for taking me through Asia as a child, thereby setting a foundation for my future work in the region.

To Granny, an honest and often harsh critic of literature, but whose comments have always been positive and helpful.

To Sarah and Duncan who, more than any other people, have been exposed to the day to day trials and tribulations of an author working on his first book.

To Mr Bruce Allardice, a mentor throughout, for his ongoing interest and friendship.

To a number of friends who have continued to ask how things were proceeding. I am sure that they do not realize the motivational significance of what to them would seem simple questions.

Finally, but perhaps most importantly, to my friends in Burma. Almost all of these people are anonymous in the book, their identities changed so as to protect them from military recriminations. But these are the people who have told me their stories, treated me with the utmost generosity and hospitality, advised me, looked after me, extended their friendship to me and, at times, protected me. They have taught me about their country and at the same time taught me about myself. For this I will be always grateful. I hope that these people as well as all of the others who suffer because of the nature of the current regime in Burma will live to see the end of military rule and enjoy the freedom for which they have waited so long.

Timothy Syrota
Bangkok
August 2001

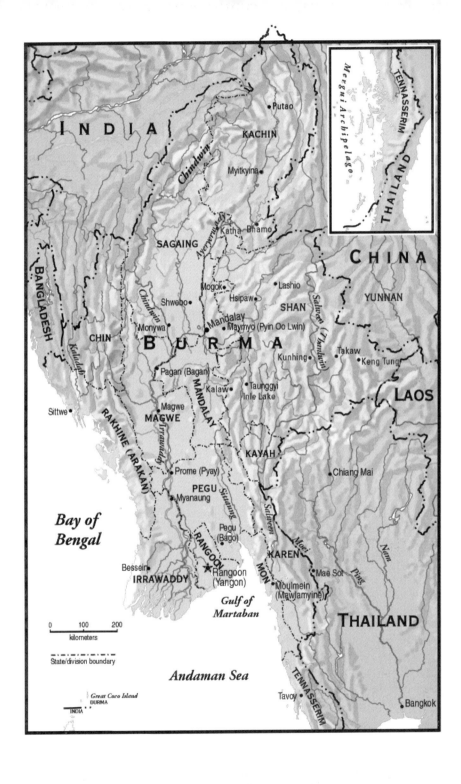

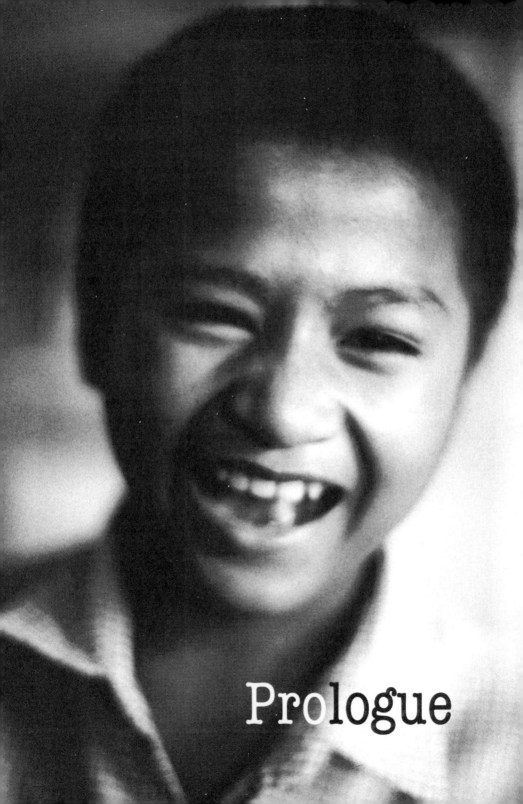

Prologue

In 1962 the Burmese military, led by General Ne Win, staged a military coup that wrested power from a civilian government led by Prime Minster U Nu. For the first seven years of this regime the longest visa available for entry into Burma was seventy-two hours. Visits were restricted to Rangoon. This was part of a policy imposed by General Ne Win intended to physically isolate Burma from the rest of the world. By 1988, the year in which hundreds of thousands of students, monks and democracy activists took to the streets to protest against continuing military rule, visas had been extended to seven days and visitors were allowed to travel to Rangoon, Mandalay, and the ruins of the ancient capital in Pagan.

Over the following decade the availability and duration of visas into Burma reflected a military dilemma. On one hand they wanted to bolster their faltering economy with tourist dollars and international investment. On the other they wanted to conceal the condition of the Burmese nation. As such, visas fluctuated between not being available at all to being available for up to four weeks.

In the mid-1990s, in a bid to attract the tourist dollars which were benefiting other developing countries in the South-East Asia region, the Burmese military decided to launch a promotional campaign called 'Visit Myanmar Year 1996'. By November 1995 the necessary 'cleaning up' of Burma had been completed and at the official opening Lieutenant General Khin Nyunt made a speech. At the time Lieut Gen. Khin Nyunt was Secretary One of the ruling State Law and Order Council (SLORC), the head of Burmese Military Intelligence, and the Chairman of the Burmese Board of Education. He was also (and still is) the godson of the former Burmese military dictator, General Ne Win. In his address, Lieutenant General Khin Nyunt had this to say:

> *Fabrications and biased stories of some foreign news agencies have made false impressions of Myanmar [Burma] on those who have not been here. The main purpose of Visit Myanmar Year 1996 is to enable many tourists to visit Myanmar and see the facts. On their return they will explain the true situation they experienced and all the fabrication will be rebutted.*

❑ ❑ ❑ ❑ ❑

Lieutenant General Khin Nyunt, I am a tourist who has come to Burma more likely than not because of an interest arising out of its colonial heritage. I know almost nothing of its status as a military dictatorship. I do not know who Daw Aung San Suu Kyi is. When I arrive I obtain a one-month visa and extend this for a further two months. Lieutenant General Khin Nyunt, what follows is an account of the situation that I have experienced in Burma.

chapter 1

Ramshackle
Rangoon

Burmese Under an Azure Sky' by Byatti, *The New Light of Myanmar*, 23 May 1996. *The New Light of Myanmar* is Burma's premier English language daily newspaper.

> The existing Government which is the State Law and Order Restoration Council Government is making all round efforts unwaveringly and without hesitation in keeping with the times to fulfill all the needs of the country for it to become a new developed modern nation which would practise a democratic system. To tell the bare truth, Myanmar Naing-Ngan (Burma) has experienced a complete change. There are different kinds of changes. The changes experienced now can be firmly remarked as good and progressive ones. However, the democracy sayagyis and sayamagyis (wizards) who tell fortunes with cowrie shells and are descendants of Devadat (the devil) are afraid to tell the truth so much so that they even criticize the Lord of Nats who had assumed the form of a buffalo which has its horns spread out.
>
> The Tatmadaw leaders who are today leading the State are imbued with leadership skills and well experienced in administrative and management tasks. Hence in changing over from one system to another there are situations where prompt measures have to be taken day and night without wasting time, while at times steps can be taken by taking time. This cannot be done by digging the well and wanting to drink clean water at once.
>
> Instant democracy cannot be obtained just by slinging on the pasoe and girding of woman's apparel and uttering mystic words. It would be totally unnatural to climb the stairs two or three steps at a time to get on top in a hurry. Climbing the stairs one by one is the proper way to get to the destination. Otherwise, if running up the stairs in haste, one is liable to get a broken head or a broken knee. Although there is no need to use a ladder to get to the moon or the universe, there is still the need of a ladder to climb up a house. Just as it is impossible to get to the moon or the universe by putting up a ladder so also is it impossible to climb a house using rocket power. It is now realized that the National League for Democracy are so stupid that they cannot understand this simple reasoning.

❑ ❑ ❑ ❑ ❑

Travelling to Burma, Bangkok to Rangoon, Flight BG 060, Bangladesh Airlines, Biman Air. My luggage is almost nominal but includes a book of Buddhist teachings, *War and Peace*, and an array of camera equipment.

Biman Air. The cheapest of the cheap. On the aeroplane sitars twang until someone flicks the wrong switch in the captain's cabin and the Bangkok control tower can be heard throughout the plane. Then the sitars resume. An air-conditioning unit drips onto a seat, a dinner table collapses, a chair reclines so far back that it rests on the seat behind, and the flight hostess demonstrates cabin safety using a Malaysian Airlines hand-me-down life jacket. Then, once we are airborne, one of the cabin crew emerges. 'Could some of the passengers from the back please move to the seats at the front so as to reduce aeroplane drag.' His comments add to what is already a jovial mood on the plane.

Looking out of the window, the land below is a patchwork of verdant rice paddies. They could be the fields of England except where they are brown and muddy because of flooding. Such areas become more and more extensive as the flight progresses. Streams become ponds, ponds become lakes and in the middle of the lakes stand isolated houses on stilts. It's the rainy season and this particular season is particularly rainy. El Nino is doing his business.

True to form, when we arrive in Rangoon the sky is grey and the rains tumble down. This would not be so much of a problem but for the fact that we wait on the tarmac outside the plane for a bus to take us to the terminal. El Nino gets us wet.

Rangoon International Airport – it is a thriving metropolis of aeronautic craft. One 737, four smaller planes, two military jets, one runway. One of the military jets departs as our bus ferries us to the terminal.

In the terminal and filling out customs declaration forms. Under 'occupation' I write photographer and writer. Suddenly, without even knowing from whence they came, uniformed officials surround me. Questions come chatter-chattering at me from all sides. 'Why are you here?' 'Who do you work for?' 'You write for a news agency?' 'Who do you write for?'

'I am a tourist.'

'You are a journalist!' 'Which news agency do you write for?' 'From England?' 'Which newspaper?'

I don't understand what is happening. Papers are produced, questions continue. I say that I write short stories for children but this answer is not satisfactory. Then one of the officials says, 'I think maybe you are an entertainer, maybe actor, maybe in movies.' 'Yes, yes,' I say, 'in the movies.' There is some shuffling of papers and I am allowed to proceed.

The next counter is the Foreign Exchange Certificate (FEC) counter and, like customs, it brings with it a precursory glimpse of life in Burma. Ahead of me in the queue are three Canadians – Shane with his spiky hair and guitar, Darryl with his black goatee and backwards cap, and peroxide Chris with four dog collars around his neck. These three are here because they have twelve days to fill before going to Australia on a surfing safari. They had heard that Burma was cheap but what they hadn't heard was that at the FEC counter it is necessary to exchange US$300 for 300 FECs. Shane tries to explain that he will use his VISA card but the customs official does not accept this. They talk at crossed purposes for a few minutes but then the official says, 'You give me present.' Shane follows her meaning, takes US$3 from his wallet and slides it across the desk. From where I stand I watch the official as she slips the money straight up the sleeve of her blouse. Thereafter, each of the Canadians offers a 'present' and they are allowed to pass.

❑ ❑ ❑ ❑ ❑

A digression concerning FECs. The first thing to recognize is that at the FEC counter US$300 cash is taken from a tourist and placed safely into a military pocket. This means that the real money is with the military. The tourist, in return, is given a handful of paper. FECs or 'Monopoly money' as many travellers call it. Thereafter, the military objective is to see how little it must give up in order to recoup the FECs.

And this they achieve in the following ways.

In scenario one the tourist enters a temple, a museum, or any other designated tourist destination. Payment of entrance fees must be in FECs or US$; payment in local currency (the *kyat*) is not allowed. This money goes straight to the military via Myanmar Tours and Travel (the MTT). This is a military department which employs military appointees and the head of which is Brigadier General Aye Myint Kyu.

In a second scenario, when a tourist obtains a visa extension or catches an aeroplane, train or boat, payment again goes directly to a military department, either Immigration or the Department of Transport. Again payment must be in FECs or US$ and in the transport cases, tourist prices are fixed up to two thousand per cent higher than local prices. This ensures that FECs are returned to the military as fast as possible.

An aside. The head of the Department of Transport is Brigadier General Kyaw Myint.

A third scenario involves hotels. For an hotel to be allowed to have tourists on the premises it must buy an annual licence from the military. This must be paid for in US$ or FECs. Furthermore, on the basis of having access to tourist money, the hotel must also pay its amenities fees, service fees and taxes in US$ or FECs. In order to meet their increased overheads, proprietors typically raise their prices from the standard 300–500 kyat (which is the price that local Burmese pay to stay in local hotels) to 2,000 kyat which is the tourist price to stay in equivalent hotels. This latter figure must, of course, be paid by tourists in US$ or FECs.

Tourist souvenir shops, like hotels, operate under military government-imposed licensing structures and must pay fees in US$ or FECs. As a result prices for goods are higher than local prices and must be paid for by tourists in US$ or FECs. Trade is guaranteed because, in theory at least, for a tourist to take gems, antiques, sculptures, and paintings out of Burma they must have a certificate saying that the goods were purchased from a military government-licensed shop. Without this, customs can confiscate the goods upon departure.

In yet another scenario, when a tourist pays FECs for unlicensed goods and services or changes FECs with black market money-changers, these FECs go into regular circulation. They will do this until such time as someone wants to exchange them on the black market either for local currency or US$. Ultimately this will occur at a military government-licensed shop or hotel. These premises exchange FECs because they need them to pay their military government bills.

Finally, in all of the above scenarios the common denominator is that for the FEC scheme to work, the one thing that can never happen is for an individual to be able to walk into a bank and exchange FECs for hard currency. The military regime prohibits this and hence currency exchange in Burma remains almost exclusively the domain of the black market.

FECs, they are the State Peace and Development Council's* scheme to monopolize tourist money. What it really comes down to is inflating prices and forcing people to pay the inflated prices in US$ or FECs.

❑ ❑ ❑ ❑ ❑

Out of the airport and ushered to a taxi by two friendly Burmese women. Then I am off and riding through Rangoon's outer suburbs. The overwhelming impression is one of green; green lakes and green trees. Lush, large-leafed, deep green tropical trees. Palms, teak, banyans, and banana trees. In outer Rangoon the buildings are small, the trees are tall and it is the buildings that sprout amid the trees, not vice versa.

As we drive, Charlie, the driver, requests, 'If we are pulled over, please do not say that this is a taxi. Please say that you are a friend and that this is a company car that is picking you up. I do not have the registration plates of a taxi and there will be a problem if I am caught.' 'Okay,' and we drive on.

Near the centre of downtown we reach the hotel at which I am to stay. Four smiling Burmese women greet me, show me a room, and then give me forms to fill in which are to be forwarded to immigration. It's like filling in more customs declarations except that the people at the hotel are friendlier than at the airport.

---

* In November 1997 the State Law and Order Restoration Council (SLORC) officially changed its name to the State Peace and Development Council (SPDC). The makeup of the membership, however, remains much the same, and the more benign name fools no one. Many Burmese continue to refer to the junta's repressive governing body as the SLORC.

Up to my room. It is the size of the bed, no bigger. A dog box. It doesn't matter. I'm here.

Off, out and into downtown Rangoon. Maybe nine, ten, eleven buildings over twelve stories in height. More predominant are the run-down, pastel coloured colonial buildings. Light blues, greens, yellows, and greys. Washed out, faded, mould encrusted. Buildings full of character with spider ferns and weeds sprouting between the colonnades and arches.

The main street is chaotic and higgledy-piggledy. No real sense of order as cars, bicycles, trishaws, trucks, and carts drawn by people form their own lanes. There are potholes in the road and a 1950s bus has stopped where it broke down. Passengers hang off the back even as two men change its wheel. Traffic negotiates the obstacle. Slowly.

Nearby, on the footpaths of the city centre are triangular barbed wire barricades, kept on hand in case of military emergency. But today they are being used for hanging washing out to dry. Soldiers posted on corners with automatic weapons survey the scene.

Into the side-streets cluttered with tucked-away shops and teahouses. Some overflow onto the streets, others are recessed into dark holes between buildings. One street is full of stationery shops, another of pipes and plumbing supply shops, and another has typists clattering away on clackety key-jamming typewriters. In one street large black scorpions and snakes are for sale on the pavement. Upon purchase, the creatures are duly executed on a wooden chopping board. In another street egrets, white falcons and squirrels are for sale. The squirrels are crushing each other in their cages and have bloody paws.

Off the side-streets and into the back lanes and the back lanes off the back lanes where chickens scratch and peck, crows circle looking for scraps, and rats scurry off down the open drains. Cats sit in windows and oversee the scenes below, waiting for night to emerge and hunt and fight.

Squalid in a run-down sense, neglected. Ramshackle Rangoon.

❏ ❏ ❏ ❏ ❏

One of my first points of call is the US Café and Richard, a renowned figure amongst Burma travellers for the information that he provides about the country. Almost all backpackers speak to him in their first days. 'Where should I go, how should I get there, where should I stay?' Richard used to be a teacher in America but now he runs a café, restaurant, and guesthouse in Rangoon. He also organizes travel to Mandalay and Pagan.

In the Café I sit, talk, and eat with an Englishman called Peter. He is a friend of Richard's who used to work with refugee orphans in Malaysia but now helps street children and orphans in Rangoon. We talk about work, both his and mine. 'Photography?' Peter enquires. 'Be careful. Photos of road works, hospitals, schools, labour gangs, soldiers, bridges, beggars, and barbed wire, photos of all of these are not allowed. And if you are caught taking such photos, the military will take your film and try to confiscate your equipment.' Peter's advice is to steadfastly refuse to relinquish it.

'Writers and photographers are a strictly monitored group in Burma,' explains Peter. 'There is a white list and a black list of media friends and enemies of the state and the general rule is "No Entry Allowed!" And did you know that in Burma you are not allowed to own a fax machine without military government authorization? The penalty for sending unauthorized faxes out of the country is up to fifteen years' imprisonment.'

Later on I discover that this law is imposed by the Wireless Act of 1933. It was introduced into Burma by the British during the colonial era because they feared that the wireless could be used to transmit state secrets to enemies. Now the Military Government uses it to punish people for sending information out of the country by fax, letter, or e-mail.

❑ ❑ ❑ ❑ ❑

Bribery, black markets, fifteen-year jail sentences, 'What newsagency you write for?', taxi licence plates, barbed wire in the streets, soldiers with automatic weapons, all in my first hours. I don't know what my expectations were when I touched down in Burma but these were not they.

❑ ❑ ❑ ❑ ❑

The evening, 9.30 p.m. in the largest city in Burma and the streets are almost completely deserted except for a football match which is taking place in the middle of Rangoon High Street. There are almost no cars on the roads. The shops and the restaurants are all shut. The lights are off. It's a hangover from the curfew days. Only the nightclub area is open – one street with some restaurants, karaoke bars, and a disco. Inside the latter a handful of local Burmese unrhythmically jiggle about to contemporary beats. A number of patrons are drunken sailors about to embark on their maiden voyage out of Burma. Two American women and I become the focus of their attention and they drag us on to the dance floor to do circle dances, our arms firmly grasped as we are spun around and around in manic country and western twirls to the techno grooves. Closing time is 2 a.m., the army enters and the patrons leave.

COMIC BOOKS AND CRUSHED STOOGES

Burma. I'm here but I don't know where I am going to go or what I am going to do, so I try to formulate a Burma travel plan. I look at a map and think that I would like to head as far north as possible, up to a wedge of Burma which is flanked by India to the west, China to the east, and has the tail end of the Himalayas running through the centre. I start to make inquiries and soon learn that very few travellers go to this region. It's hard to get to and most of the towns are off limits. 'There are very many interesting places to go in Burma,' observes a Burmese gentleman to whom I talk. 'But you are a tourist and are not allowed to go to them. They are restricted areas.'

Despite these comments, my mind is to go north, perhaps to Putao, the Switzerland of the East. There is a 6,000-metre mountain nearby and the cross-cultural mix would surely be fascinating. The trouble is that reports about the north are sketchy, contradictory, and what I hear makes it sound more expensive all the time. At Myanmar Tours and Travel (MTT) I am told that if I want to go to this area of Burma then I must fly there at tourist rates priced five times higher than local airfares. Furthermore, once I am there I must have a licensed tour guide which will cost me US$250 for three days. Although they are very friendly at the Tourist Authority, it becomes increasingly obvious as I talk to them that they cater for 'government-friendly travellers'.

Very quickly it becomes apparent that four weeks is not going to be long enough to make any sort of journey to the north of Burma so I apply for a visa extension. At MTT they ask, 'Please give us US$1 and then we will give you the form to fill in.' Okay, done. 'Now go to the hokey-pokey little shop across the street and make five copies of the form, five copies of each of three pages of your passport and one copy of your official FEC exchange document from the airport. Then bring them back to us.' Okay. 'Now come back on Tuesday and we'll have a signed form for you to take to the Department of Immigration.' What a palaver.

❑ ❑ ❑ ❑ ❑

The Department of Immigration. It is a decaying six-storey colonial building with slouching soldiers with their automatic rifles erect at the doorway. Inside it is dark and dusty, mildewy and musty with many Burmese people and no apparent sense of order to proceedings. Upon entering I ask 'Visa, Visa?' and determine that the right way is to the left and through a small doorway which opens between some prison bars. Beside these is a small room with worn wooden tables and officials sitting in cages receiving forms and money. I go straight ahead, ducking to pass through the bars. Beyond is a large room, an examination room from a second-rate high school from an age gone by. The room is concrete and along the back wall, ceiling-high and three-deep, are pile upon pile of aged browned pieces of paper that have been bound together with twine and stacked. The filing system for the last fifty years. Along another wall is a row of wooden cupboards and in the centre of the room there are rows of wooden desks. Behind these sit military personnel and immigration officials, mainly women in blue and white uniforms. At the front and facing the class is a stern looking soldier with lots of plastic badges safety-pinned onto his tunic. Overhead, fans whirr and vibrate. It's the administration bureau that time forgot, the Myanmar Department of Immigration.

Much of my time spent at immigration involves standing around and waiting for nothing to happen. I sit in front of the military official and he stands up and leaves. I give my passport to someone else who then tells me to go away. So I stand and do nothing, then do nothing for a bit longer, then ask what I should be doing, and then sit down and do nothing as my passport sits idle on various desks. Then it begins to make its way through three separate sets of hands, including those of the military official. I am told to buy new departure forms in the caged money room. I give the soldier some money. Then I pay for my visa extension. Whilst this is occurring everyone gets up and leaves the hall. Fifty people, all gone, all at once. It is as if the plug is pulled on immigration and they all go down the drain except for me, so I am left standing in the middle of an empty hall, passportless. After a few seconds I am escorted outside by a not unfriendly soldier who tells me to wait. So I wait. Ten minutes later everyone comes filing back to their desks and, with prompting, my visa extension is finalized.

Out of the Department of Immigration and on to the streets of Rangoon. El Nino is at it again. Yet again wet again.

❑ ❑ ❑ ❑ ❑

Down by the river there are many staring Burmese fisherman and assorted dockside scruffs. They follow me out of curiosity. I stop and they gather round. They laugh when I say something in Burmese. With an active vocabulary of *mingala baa* (hello), *kaun deh* (good), and *chey zu dem bah deh* (thank you), we strike up quite a conversation. But at least it's an amusing one.

Funny language, Burmese. One English word seems to equate to a whole sentence. And the writing, it's all a variation on circles. Full circles, circles with half circles inside them, circles with bits missing, circles with tails, circles with dots, crests, scoops and squiggles. I see a sign writer painting a sign and for the basic outline of each letter he uses the circular end of a tin can. Later, a Burmese friend says to me that the key to being able to write Burmese neatly is to practice drawing good circles.

Near the river two young men are reading a comic full of circles and squiggles. It looks interesting and I ask if I can buy it from them. 'No, no; present,' they exclaim and they give it to me for free. Later two second-generation Pakistanis to whom I had earlier said good morning stop me. They ask me to join them for a cup of tea, which I do. Then, when I offer to pay, they too declare, 'No, no; present.' Further down the street I watch a man rolling a wad of beetle nut. He gives me some to try. 'Present,' he says. It tastes like aniseed. Raises the heart beat. 'Don't swallow it, spit it,' I am told. 'Bad for the head, bad for the stomach to swallow it.' Too late. It's already on its way down through my digestive tract.

Back at the hotel I take time to look at the comic. It's full of children's cartoon stories disguised as paternalistic propaganda from Burma's military government. Or vice versa. Anyway, the stories are simple: hard work brings rewards, everyone must be prepared to contribute labour, don't skive school, don't want a big bike when you have already got a small bike (or you will crash), do your work and only then will you have time to rest. The message on the back, in bold, white, Burmese script on a red background, is even clearer:

PEOPLE'S DESIRES.

OPPOSE THOSE RELYING ON EXTERNAL ELEMENTS, ACTING AS STOOGES, HOLDING NEGATIVE VIEWS.

OPPOSE THOSE TRYING TO JEOPARDIZE THE STABILITY OF THE STATE AND PROGRESS OF THE NATION.

OPPOSE FOREIGN NATIONS INTERFERING IN INTERNAL AFFAIRS OF THE STATE.

CRUSH ALL INTERNAL AND EXTERNAL DESTRUCTIVE ELEMENTS AS THE COMMON ENEMY.

Such messages don't leave too much to the imagination. Children's comics, yes, but *The Incredible Hulk* or *The Adventures of Mickey Mouse*, not likely.

Meanwhile, at a meeting not far outside Rangoon, a more extended version of the 'crush all internal and external destructive elements' dictum is being expounded at a regional meeting of the Union Solidarity and Development Association. This organization, known as the USDA, is the popular front of the State Peace and Development Council (SPDC). It is a body reminiscent of the fascist youth movements of the first half of the twentieth century. Members are granted financial, employment and educational benefits by the military. In return, USDA members act as SLORC/SPDC spies and informers as well as acting as civilian enforcers.

At this particular meeting in November 1997, an alleged 43,000 USDA members sit cross legged on a football ground in what look like cohorts of the Roman army drawn up for battle. Before them, on a podium, U Thom Tun, the 'meeting chairman' of the Irrawaddy Division of the USDA delivers a speech.

Esteemed members of the Union Solidarity and Development Association, first I wish all of the USDA members present at this plenary meeting on the USDA's implementation of community welfare tasks both physical and spiritual health.

At a time when we are striving for all round development of Myanmar, some big nations could not bear to see the positive developments in the country and as such they are scheming and creating conditions to destabilize the nation with the excuse of human rights to secure power for their cohorts, lackeys and adopted children while at the same time minions of the colonialists and internal destructive elements are inciting riots to disrupt stability and peace in the country with the aim of seizing power. All must be wary of such attempts and guard against them.

Today, the Tatmadaw (Army, Navy, Air), the people, and patriotic nationalities groups are trying to achieve from regional to national progress with added momentum. As we, the national races, are working for all round development of the country, axe handles holding negative views and relying on external elements on the other hand are committing dastardly acts through their evil and treacherous schemes to destabilize the nation. Those destructive elements, being stooges of the colonialists, are colluding with the neo colonialists in disregard of national interests and their traitorous nature is thus evident.

Esteemed association members, neo colonialists are found to be blatantly interfering in the internal affairs of small nations all over the world in pursuit of their hegemonism. Internal traitorous maggots are enabling them to interfere in our internal affairs.

We have no reason to forgive the attempts to cause conflicts between one race and another and one religion and another, and arouse suspicion among religions and incite conflicts.

I would like to emphatically state that in the world today it is necessary to establish a global political system to destroy super power hegemonism.

Esteemed association members, in conclusion at this plenary meeting I urge all to oppose and crush the hegemonism, neo colonialists and axe handles holding negative views and relying on external elements in accordance with the four points in the people's

desire:
　　Oppose those relying on external elements, acting as stooges,
holding negative views.
　　Oppose those trying to jeopardize stability of the state and
progress of the nation.
　　Oppose foreign nations interfering in internal affairs of the state.
　　Crush all internal and external destructive elements as the
common enemy.

❏ ❏ ❏ ❏ ❏

Welcome to Burma and enjoy the totalitarian experience.

BEWARE THE CIA BACKPACKER IN THE HINDU TEMPLE

Rangoon, renamed by the SLORC as Yangon. Rangoon, full on. Bearded Indians sit on stools on the pavement, corn on the cob for sale by the side of the road, golden stupas, bus horns from leftover World War II trucks that squeak instead of toot. Almost-black skins, almost-white skins, crash helmets, military helmets, a cowboy hat, monks in brown, monks in yellow, monks in orange, poppadums, samosas, sweet tea with carnation milk, fritters, buckets of water with ice dripping down through funnels to be served as drinks to passers-by. Kyat, FECs, US dollars, black marketeers, 'You want to change money' coming from every corner, kissing sounds to attract attention, the Rock and Roll Café, shaved heads, heads with plates on them, a head with a monument of fifteen brightly coloured plastic rubbish bins on it. People stare and people smile.

Rangoon. Full on.

Next to Sule Pagoda, in the centre of downtown Rangoon, is the militaristic, ready-for-a-battle-in-the-streets City Hall. In front of it, a bevy of armed guards, heavy barbed wire, and military vehicles. It looks like something that the allies might have come across in Central Europe in 1945. Imposing. Authoritarian. It's presence keeps downtown well and truly in perspective.

In the middle of 1998 the image of City Hall was complete. Trying to deter any possible civil unrest that may have arisen with the approach of the tenth anniversary of the 8 August 1988 massacres, the junta ordered tanks to be positioned around the periphery. A precautionary measure, but it was a precautionary measure Burmese military junta style.

❏ ❏ ❏ ❏ ❏

Two blocks from City Hall is an Indian temple. As I walk past people pour out through its entrances. Inside, madness, mayhem and frenetic commotion. There are loud clashing cymbals, smashing drums, and shrieking woodwinds. Hundreds of Indian people crushed together. An old man is flinging himself around, out of control. People shout for the music to stop, the old man slows down, stops when the music stops, crumples on to the floor and four people stretcher him out, his face contorted, sweat pouring off him.

Off the street, into an Indian temple and into this.

They are fanning the old man. The music starts up again. An oboe-like instrument, a horn. The air is full of smoke, smoke from hundreds of sticks of incense, smoke from fires. Another man is shuddering. A man who can speak English and is called Lawrence is scabby and scaly-headed and drunk. Another man, a leader, is vibrating.

The Indians carry a statue of a tiger on their shoulders. They go into the temple and set it down. Money is placed on it. One of the men, the gyrator, takes the money and flings it into the crowd who grabble and scrabble with their hands to catch a hold of it as it flies into the air and then onto the ground. People in a fiscal frenzy.

Men dance around the periphery of the temple with silver urns containing coconut milk on their heads. They take the urns inside the temple and the milk is poured over the head of the icons of 'The Mothers'. A festival for the mothers; for the mother of Shiva and also for Shiva's wife, the mother of Shiva's sons. There is a third woman, a third mother, but I don't know who she is. But each of the mothers is represented by a statue, side by side. And the priests in the festival, they are the symbolic sons of the mothers.

The music again reaches a crescendo. Smoke, incense, fire. People come up to the flames, scoop up handfuls and then brush this over their foreheads, through their hair, over the faces and heads of their children. More money is thrown into the air. The gathered throng grabs for it. The chief priest screams into the ear of an icon of the mother. Money grabbing continues. It is as frenetic as the music. Possessed. Naked flames are waved around and around.

The heat inside the temple is intense, the heat of many bodies crushed together. The musicians are soaked to the skin as are many of the devotees. Me, I am a walking puddle.

A darkly-lit, smoky corner. In front, the coconut milk urns have been lined up. A curtain is pulled back. Clouds of smoke billow out. Burning lamps of incense. The priests are all there, stripped to the waist, painted markings on their bodies. Some are the men who were not long ago shuddering on the ground. A lady is in a trance, eyes closed, arms flailing in the air. Some people support her, others hit her on the head many times. Hard, hard to watch, almost brutal. She loses her footing, falls over, and is dragged outside. A young man in a trance is held up as he stumbles around outside the temple. He is throwing his head around too violently and one person supports his neck. Two other people hold him up by the arms, one supports his waist, two more make sure that he does not drop his urn of coconut milk. It is as if placing the urn on his head transports him to some different, chaotic, far-away place. A chant goes up, yes, maybe a chant, or maybe more of a mad, manic shout.

In the evening I see little children praying. Three and four-year-olds on their knees, distracted by their surroundings but nonetheless with hands clasped together, bowing before statues, going through the motions as they have observed others doing. One particular four-year-old is holding the arms of a two-year-old, leading her around the outer compound, placing her hands together at each of the images. Primary instruction by physical coercion. A mother comes looking for them and rescues the toddler.

There is a statue of a God with nine heads, nine legs and many arms. There is a poster which depicts a supreme being, a lion, and a blood-spattered person who has been torn violently apart.

The tempo rises again. A confused cacophony. Three bands playing simultaneously. One group thrashes drums and symbols, beating a powerful and basic rhythm that only stops when the priest holds up his arms. In a separate troupe there are three musicians, one with a small oboe, two with drums. They play their own tune. Wild staring eyes, a hooked wooden stick that stabs at the taut skin of a drum. Another group is led by a man with a long oboe. I try to take a photo of him but he stares at me and I back away.

Two young men move to the front of the temple where they hold aloft flaming torches. A dancer, stripped to the waist and with a painted upper body, bells on his feet and a jug of something unsecured on his head, starts a stamping dance in the flame-lit courtyard. His head, shoulders and neck are motionless whilst his arms twist, gyrate and curl like snakes and his feet jangle as he stomps the ground beneath him, eyes glaring intensely.

The tempo reaches yet another level. An icon of a rat is borne on the shoulders of ten carriers into the courtyard where it is walked round and round a central shrine. The dancer dances before it. Then the lion god emerges. Once it reaches the courtyard it starts to swing, twenty people supporting it, many with eyes closed, many with no sense of where they are going but following the pushes and pulls of the other bearers. It moves almost out of control in one direction until a counter-pull sends it reeling in a different direction. Bystanders scatter to avoid collision. Bearers stumble and fall, pick themselves up and retake their places. It is intense, manic, mad. Music, heat, bodies; and the drunken, lurching, crashing dance of the lion.

A man ascends the lion's platform with a bow and arrows. He is the favourite son of the 'Mother' because he can shoot arrows the furthest and the straightest. He begins to fire arrows blindly over the temple wall. Some are fired across the grounds sending scores of people charging off in a bid to grab these sacred items. Others are fired at the feet of the platform-bearers. People wrestle to try to get them. The final arrow is fired into a young palm. At the same instant as the arrow hits the trunk, people slash madly at the palm with machetes, hacking it down within seconds. The lion is taken back into the temple and people, including the musicians, cram in after it. A tightly-packed circle of three hundred dance, jump, and wave their arms in the air. Trances, raves, oblivion. Drums beat, oboes screech, and horns swoon and hypnotize.

The heat, the intensity, the claustrophobia. This festival is like a turbulent river that catches hold of you and then burls you along with it.

I break away and talk with a smartly-dressed Burmese gentleman with good English. His name is Charles and he is a lawyer. We talk about the festival and then we talk about the law, his family, his wife and his English speaking. I am tired and I forget many of the details, but before departing Charles gives me a number to call if I would like to meet him again in Rangoon. He explains that it is a secret number. 'When you call, only say, "I would like to speak to Charles please," don't say any more. Don't say that you are a tourist. No tourists are allowed to call. My boss does not allow it. Call in working hours, between 9.30 and 4.30, not later. Don't give the number to anyone. It's very secret. Where I work is not just a law office but also a secret detective service.' Then he asks me whether I know who Bogyoke Aung San was? This question is approaching sensitive ground – a question that skirts the periphery of political talk about Burma. For while Bogyoke Aung San is a National Hero in Burma because of his role in bringing independence to the country, his daughter, Daw Aung San Suu Kyi is the figure most hated by the military regime. It is she who is the leader of the democratic opposition. So to Charles I venture, 'Yes, I know a little about Bogyoke Aung San,' but then leave it at that. Finally, before departing, Charles asks me, 'Do you work for the CIA?'

Do I work for the CIA? What a ludicrous question.

With the benefit of hindsight, it is not difficult to understand why Charles had asked about the CIA and my potential involvement. Firstly, in Burma spies and informers are an omnipresent part of day-to-day life. In addition to this, the daily newspapers of Burma constantly warn the population about the infiltration of their country by spies from overseas. These spies, they say, are seeking to overthrow the country and install a puppet democratic regime. An example of such media is found in the article 'Adrift and Washed Ashore' written by Po Yaygyan and which appeared in *The New Light of Myanmar*, 11 May 1997.

Before referring to the article, it should be noted that the leader of the Burmese democracy movement and winner of a Nobel Peace Prize, Daw Aung San Suu Kyi, is referred to throughout as the *Bogadaw*. This is a derogatory Burmese term which was used to describe the British in the colonial and immediate post-colonial eras. Its strict definition is 'big nose' but in context, calling Daw Aung San Suu Kyi *Bogadaw* in the national press is something like *The Times* of London referring to Nelson Mandela as a nigger.

From: 'Adrift and Washed Ashore' by Po Yaygyan, *The New Light of Myanmar*, 11 May 1997.

> During the period of the disturbances, the Bogadaw had been used in turns by the leftist and rightist neo colonialists so much that she had to shunt to and fro like a shuttle loom. But from the 1990 onwards, one of the execution organizations of the West bloc, the American CIA was able to hold a firm hand on the Bogadaw. As an advance payment she received the Nobel Peace Prize award of one million dollars.
>
> Throughout the cold war period, Nobel Awards for peace and literature were given to those whom the American CIA wanted them given. In 1991, as Suu Kyi indulged in direct confrontations, defying all authority and breaching of law, an order on restricting of movement was imposed on her. Bogadaw Suu Kyi won the Nobel Peace prize. Well, the world has come to know that Nobel Peace Prize which carries a cheque for one million dollars is won by those who act according to the wishes of the West bloc to destroy their own country, dissidents and disturbance makers.
>
> The Bogadaw has now accumulated about 40 million dollars for trying to destroy the country. It is rather difficult to estimate how many million dollars she gets from the CIA pay roll. Here it would be necessary to be aware of the methods employed by the CIA to raise people by throwing a lot of cash in their direction. The CIA has made use of would be diplomats, journalists, intellectuals and scholars, businessmen and tourists and has spread them out in the international sphere. They entice and lure the traitorous elements in all countries with dollars. The CIA is in the habit of organizing politicians and informers. These people act according to the bidding of the CIA. If they don't accept what is offered by the CIA, then investigations of their old sores are made and files opened. These files are then shown to the people who are made to act according to their bidding.
>
> The sons and daughters of top notch personalities, State leaders, kings, ministers and political leaders who come to pursue education in Western countries, especially the United States, the CIA organizes

them through the respective University professors. Later on the CIA
uses them as their men.

The Bogadaw, through one of the methods employed by the CIA
in organizing people, is being used. Whatever Suu Kyi does is never
in the interests of Myanmar and its people, but it is quite obvious
that she is trying to place the State in the hands of neo colonialists
for the people to become poor and suffer a lot of trouble. Suu Kyi's
democracy is a potato democracy and a fake one. They are merely
defining the democracy just for them to get state power and for
their colonialist masters to bully and have influence over the
country. Suu Kyi has assumed the role of a single party dictator
under name sake democracy.

A SWIMMING-POOL, A CHURCH, AND AN HOTEL

Having breakfast in the US Café one morning I take the opportunity to
read through a book which contains notes, information, and obser-
vations made by travellers who have been through Burma. One of these is
written by a German gentleman, Torsch, and comments,

> Be careful with what you say to which person. You never know
> which person you can trust. And always keep in mind that you
> yourself never get into trouble when talking in open places about
> politics or for whatever you do but the people of Myanmar can get
> in big trouble. Even when you don't mean it – for example if you
> are talking to a person about what another person told you about
> politics in Myanmar etc.
>
> Myanmar is very interesting because it is an unspoilt country to
> travel. So are the people. But not everything that shines is gold
> and not everyone who smiles is happy. Have a look under the
> table, behind the curtain. Many people are oppressed by the mili-
> tary regime which is a dictatorship. It is not a legitimate govern-
> ment. You won't see or realize it if you are only walking on the
> beautiful paths. Ask who cleaned the cities and the towns. Ask
> who has to pay for the restoring or beautifying of the pagodas. Ask
> who lived before near the pagodas! Go to University Avenue and
> find out why you can't go on a certain part of the Avenue? What
> happens to the three hundred dollars that you had to change at the
> airport? Why are there people in front of the Myanmar bank who
> are changing money on the black market rate two or three kyat
> more than elsewhere? Maybe because they are from the bank itself.
>
> If you start asking such questions you will have more and more
> questions. Make up your own opinion of this country. But do not
> only scratch on the surface.
>
> Torsch – Germany

Thank you Torsch, you as much as anyone are responsible for the direction in which my travels in Burma are to take. Thank you for your message and I hope that every traveller to Burma reads your words.

An immediate change of plan on the basis of the comments I have read. I want to go to University Avenue and see what is there. In order to do this, I meet with a Burmese gentleman, Wai Lin to whom I have spoken on a number of occasions, and ask him if he can take me. Yes, he says, and we board a bus that will take us there. But on the way he tells me that if anyone asks where I am going I must say that I am going to a swimming pool, not to the University.

We disembark from the bus three stops beyond the University and then walk back to it along the edge of Inya Lake. As we do so Wai Lin tells me that he had studied chemistry as an undergraduate at Rangoon University. He was on a scholarship, he said, 35 kyat a month, but that was in 1982. In addition to this he was given a job in a government office so he could work during the day and then study in the evening. He was very poor, he explains. Now Wai Lin works by talking to tourists on the street and seeing if he can take them anywhere or show them anything. He also changes small amounts of money on the black market. These jobs earn him US$1-2 a day.

When we arrive at the University I cannot go on to the campus. No one can. It is deserted and the gates are padlocked and guarded by soldiers. Wai Lin says that this has been the situation since December 1996. It was then that students last demonstrated against the military regime. The response was swift and harsh. Student leaders fled to Thailand and the military shut down all tertiary institutions across Burma. Good policy really; close all the universities and you kill three birds with one stone. One, keeping Burma uneducated is an important element of keeping the SPDC in power. Two, no universities means no need for military government tertiary education expenditure. Three, no universities removes the threat posed by students by no longer having any students. No universities means no students and no students means no student democratic movement. Sensible. Why pay money to maintain a system that only brings together young, intelligent, people who oppose your particular approach to the maintenance of totalitarian power?

'Shut 'em down, that'll learn yez all.'

❑   ❑   ❑   ❑   ❑

Wai Lin and I walk along the periphery of the campus and as we do so we meet Matthew, a law student from Oxford. We continue towards University Avenue, but as we get closer Wai Lin says that he cannot come with us and instead he stays in a teashop five minutes walk away. Matthew and I continue to University Avenue. We are hoping to see the house of Daw Aung San Suu Kyi.

No go. Wrong way, go back. There is a roadblock on University Avenue manned by a stern looking posse made up of a government official, two policemen, someone else, and some soldiers. We try to explain that we want to go to a church further down the street. We even put our hands together and bow our heads to try to communicate this message. Not a chance and as we persist one of the soldiers, three metres away, puts his gun up to his shoulder and points it straight at us. This is his way of expressing, 'Go away, now!' Intimidating. I've never experienced this before.

Returning to the teashop, there is a man who is clearly watching us. We do not speak to Wai Lin but instead sit and have tea and then leave together. Only then does Wai Lin explain that he could not be seen with us at the roadblock. Big trouble for him. We can act like stupid tourists but he can not do this. There is no excuse for him to be there.

'Informers everywhere,' Wai Lin declares, 'sitting in coffee shops, watching everyone, everywhere and what they are doing in this quarter (district). The University is here, the house where Daw Aung San Suu Kyi lives is here, the embassies are here, and the houses of the top military officials are here. Many important things are here so there are many military intelligence here also.'

It is a pleasant district, this district of Military Intelligence and important people, a green district with many trees, luscious and expensive. All buildings have maximum security entrances. Some have armed guards. A Volvo pulls out of an embassy. And nearby two boys try to catch fish and freshwater crabs in a fifteen-centimetre-deep, thirty-centimetre-wide muddy trench by the side of the road. They are having some success and one fish that they have is about thirteen centimetres long. They catch them by dangling their bait in the small holes in the mud.

A car pulls up. Wai Lin is questioned. He cuts a meek and fawning figure. He explains that he is taking us to an hotel. He is asked his name and address. The man questioning him stays in the passenger seat of the car but two others get out from the back seats. I take out my juggling sticks which amuses them greatly. I am sure they have never seen anything like them before. I got them out on a street corner in downtown yesterday and within minutes there was a crowd of sixty people watching what I was doing.

'Quickly, quickly', exclaims Wai Lin when the car has pulled away, 'C'mon, c'mon,' and we beat a cracking pace off down the street.

We hurry past the Rangoon headquarters of the National League for

Democracy. It looks run down and dead, no sign of life. We don't stop –
it's under constant surveillance from the teashop across the street where
military intelligence sit and wait and watch anyone who goes in or out. I
snap off a photo under my arm as we go by.

Wai Lin says, 'I am not afraid of people, only the military. If I go to
prison I will be beaten and maybe killed.' As Torsch writes, dangerous for
him but not so much for me. Foreigners at least have their consulates and
the Burmese military prefers not to rouse the possible ire of the international community. It wants tourists, it wants economic investment, it wants
a good international image and consequently it tries to minimize bad pub-
licity. This said, being an overly inquisitive tourist can still be dangerous.
But for the Burmese, there is no recourse to embassies and international
policy issues. Do the wrong thing and there is no one to step in and
save you.

I go to the University but I am actually going to the swimming pool. I go
for a walk down University Avenue but I am actually going to a church. I
wander through a suburb but I am actually looking for an hotel. I go to
Burma but I am actually venturing into some time-warped, totalitarian
lunatic asylum. How does the military regime get to do what it does? How
can you imprison someone for fifteen years for sending a fax? How can
you close down tertiary education for three years as if it were the local
corner shop that has just been condemned by the city council? I go to
Burma but actually end up in an evil Wonderland. It's a land called Myanmar.

Rains teem down and the road becomes a river. Within ten minutes
people are wading ankle deep along it. Whitened figures continue to load
bags of cement into a truck. A football game is postponed. The rain does
not relent for two hours.

❑ ❑ ❑ ❑ ❑

Daw Aung San Suu Kyi. The first time I've really heard or taken note of
her name was today. One week ago I didn't know who she was.

> I vow to stay in my motherland and work unceasingly with all
> nationalities in accordance with the guidelines laid down by my
> father to maintain the sovereignty of our country, to bring devel-
> opment to all nationalities, and to establish democracy. Daw Aung
> San Suu Kyi, August 1988.

Daw Aung San Suu Kyi, Burmese democracy leader and figurehead, the
daughter of the revered Burmese independence hero and leader Bogyoke
Aung San. He was assassinated shortly before Burma achieved the independence that he had striven to broker. Implicated in his murder was an

officer by the name of Ne Win.

After his death, Daw Aung San Suu Kyi left Burma and was educated in India. She later studied philosophy, politics, and economics at St Hugh's College, Oxford University. She went on to work for the United Nations in New York and in 1972 she married an Oxford academic, giving birth to two sons.

In March 1988 Daw Aung San Suu Kyi returned to Burma from England to take care of her mother who had suffered a serious stroke. Her arrival coincided with increasing civil unrest and demonstrations against the repressive military dictatorship of General Ne Win. These demonstrations culminated in the massive pro-democracy demonstrations of the 8 August 1988 (also known as '8888' or 'the four eights massacres') in which millions of students, citizens, and monks nationwide took to the streets and demanded an end to military oppression. At one rally on 26 August 1988, Daw Aung San Suu Kyi announced in front of an audience of half a million supporters her decision to enter the struggle for democracy in Burma. The demonstrations, however, were ruthlessly suppressed by the military and between three and eight thousand demonstrators were shot and bayoneted. Many more were wounded, imprisoned, and tortured and tens of thousands either fled to the borders to continue their struggle or fled the country completely.

Daw Aung San Suu Kyi remained in Rangoon as the leader of the National League for Democracy. On 29 July 1989, in a bid to curb her continuing popularity, the military placed her under house arrest. Even so, when general elections were held on 27 May 1990, the National League of Democracy won 392 of the 485 seats. Only 10 seats, 2 per cent of the vote, were won by the military. Power, however, was not and still has not been transferred to the NLD.

Why were the 1990 elections held? Perhaps because the military was arrogant enough to believe that it would be able to win. Perhaps not. An alternative explanation is that the 1990 elections were announced to give the military some breathing space in its bid to quell the revolutionary spirit that was so strong in 1988. Consequently, during 1989 steps were taken to undermine the democracy movement. Not only was Daw Aung San Suu Kyi placed under house arrest, but in excess of 500,000 NLD supporters are reported to have been forcibly relocated out of urban centres and into satellite townships. New laws were introduced which further restricted freedom of movement, freedom of press and freedom of association. High schools and tertiary institutions throughout Burma were shut down. And all of these measures took place whilst the carrot of democratic elections was dangled before the Burmese population. By the time the elections took place, the Burmese military had already done the work that it needed to do and the actual results were immaterial. In fact, perhaps the most telling immediate consequence of the elections was that it allowed the military to clearly identify its opposition. Certainly it was the case that after the 1990 elections many members elect were imprisoned. Some were tortured and some were killed.

Daw Aung San Suu Kyi, meanwhile, continued to actively promote democracy in Burma during her period of house arrest. In 1990 she was awarded the Thorolf Rafto Prize for Human Rights in Norway. In January 1991 she was awarded the Sakharov Prize for freedom of thought by the European Parliament and in October of the same year she was awarded the Nobel Peace Prize. At the presentation of this award, the Norwegian Nobel Committee stated that it wanted to 'honour this woman for her unflagging efforts and to show its support for the many people throughout the world who are striving to attain democracy, human rights and ethnic conciliation by peaceful means'.

On 11 July 1995 Daw Aung San Suu Kyi was released from arrest. It was a token gesture rather than an actual release, amounting to no more than the granting of some privileges of movement and association in a bid to satisfy ASEAN and Western pressure. But it backfired for the junta when Daw Aung San Suu Kyi proved to be as popular amongst the Burmese people as she had been prior to her isolation. Every weekend she delivered speeches from her house in University Avenue, speeches that were well attended by Burmese citizens who would then face the prospects of incarceration on the basis of their attendance.

Today Daw Aung San Suu Kyi is once again almost permanently confined to her residence. There are no speeches, her freedom of movement and association have been almost completely curtailed, and she is under constant surveillance. The National League for Democracy has been branded an organization of terrorists and in the year 2000 moves were afoot by the military regime to criminalize the party. Daw Aung San Suu Kyi is encouraged to leave the country but she knows that once she does she will never be able to return to Burma. Thus she stays on in Rangoon.

This predicament led to the impossibility of Daw Aung San Suu Kyi being reunited with her terminally ill husband, Dr Michael Aris, whom she had not seen for three years. A tragedy, but as Daw Aung San Suu Kyi says, just one of the many tragedies of Burma.

Daw Aung San Suu Kyi. The SLORC/SPDC expend a lot of energy trying to discredit her. The Council members wish she would die but would never dare kill her themselves.

The official Burmese media paints a very different picture of Daw Aung San Suu Kyi. She is referred to as an ogre, a whore, a spy, a dog, a rodent, a puppet mistress, a stooge, and a stool pigeon. She is accused of everything from being a bad Buddhist to being a CIA agent trying to undermine the peace and stability of Burma. The Nobel Peace Prize was no more than a bribe to win her over to the side of the West. Every day there are different allegations, different calumnies, and different slanders. According to the military she is a blight upon her country. Extracted below is an article featured in *The New Light of Myanmar* which discusses the effects that studying at Oxford had upon Daw Aung San Suu Kyi.

From: 'Let's Tell the Truth' by Myo Chit, *The New Light of Myanmar*, July 1996.

Today I would like to say the truth about Boo Yoo person who thinks highly of Europeans and tries to imitate them. It is because the disease of Boo Yoo has spread at a certain speed. The disease is quite evident when we switch on the TV in the morning. They are neatly dressed. The man is in European attire with pants, coat, necktie and shoes. The woman wears a blouse keeping most part of the chest bare with sleeves neither long nor short. In fact, the blouse has no sleeve at all. The skirt edge ends above the knee nearly exposing half of the thigh. She also wears lady shoes with high heels. They appear to be a couple entertaining at a modern restaurant in London's Picadilly Square. Only when they shout into the microphone do they reveal their true identity. Indeed, they are totally crazy.

This is the Boo Yoo who entertains regularly on Saturdays and Sundays. She stages a soap box opera. After only a brief study of the tune of music and her movements it becomes clear that she is a Boo Yoo puppet dancer whose strings are manipulated from behind and what she chants are the language, the ideas, the thinking and the outlook of foreigners which she longs for, regarding whatever they do as good. Oh, very good. Her being Boo Yoo is quite obvious.

Her grandfather was Arzani, Bo Min Yaung, who was amongst the initial leaders in the anti colonialist struggle. Her father was Bogyoke Aung San who wrested independence back for Myanmar. The blood from the paternal side is indeed red. But even so the puppet doll should be classified Boo Yoo, person who is crazy about Europeans and looks down on her own nation and race.

Boo Yoo spirit developed in her due to the environment in which she grew up, overshadowing her origin.

The environment, physical and spiritual, in which the puppet princess has grown up from teenage to a grown up maiden is greatly different from that of Myanmar. Science testifies to the fact that she has been made different from her origin by what she had felt, seen and heard in this strange environment. Images etched in her mind were the features, styles, attitude and behaviour of aliens which impressed upon her then.

Her years at Oxford coincided with the sex revolution around 1960-70. It was before the gun culture when youths playfully shot at random at persons or groups in England and America. It was the beginning of the sex liberation when people of the same sex or different sexes joined hands freely without let or hindrance to go all out after free sex. Hippy culture, in which people were without order or discipline and behaved in a haphazard, disjointed or nonsensical manner was also in vogue.

The experiences of these days would remain unforgettable to the puppet doll. She would recall again and again memories of the Oxford pasture where those who could change partners as often as they would their dresses were popular and said to be sociable and dignified and where she had enjoyed the company of enchanting mates while rowing a boat on the Isis river. In a letter sent to the editor of an English paper in 1989 (whilst political campaigning was taking place) the puppet doll mused,

'The last trip was rather gruelling travelling by bullock cart and small boats in the blazing sun. Alas, your Suu is getting weather beat, none of that pampered elegance left as she tramps the countryside spattered with mud, straggly haired, breathing in dust and pouring with sweat. I need a few months in grey damp Oxford to restore my complexion.'

Due to these facts it is obvious that she has lost her Myanmar blood and psyche. She became so badly inflicted by the Boo Yoo malady that she got to the stage of declaring she had nothing to do with Myanmar. It is found that she lacks patriotic spirit. It is really her Boo Yoo spirit by which she says with rashness what she wrongly thinks is right.

At the time when restrictions were imposed on the puppet girl the State Leaders felt love and pity towards her as the daughter of their (former) leader and called her and had preliminary discussions with her. After holding discussions with her twice, it is a fact that the State Leaders must have taken into consideration all aspects about the role to be played by her and deliberated.

The clear political sky overhead became dark and cloudy not long after and gradually the black clouds began to roll and gather momentum. The loving kindness and affection placed on her by State Leaders as a real daughter was not reciprocated. All who could perceive it knew it.

I recently discovered that the puppet princess would not be the true Golden Princess but one with feet of clay who had fallen from the sky and that she was bereft of original Myanmar thought, Myanmar aims, Myanmar action, and that she simply was a puppet dancing as manipulated. She was embellished with the ornaments called the Nobel Prize, the anointments of human rights groups, elation over her Olympic Speech sent to Spain, her address to the Women's Conference in Beijing, and the Nehru prize - all these seem to add to her glamour as a puppet princess but glancing down one would day by day realize she has feet of clay.

Myo Chit would like to say again that all party members and the entire public should ponder whether it is appropriate or not to give the

role of a national leader and elect as the head of state such a traitor
puppet who is blatantly betraying the national cause and dancing to
the delight of neo colonialists. I would also like to urge all to be
mindful of the fact that state secrets and national security will be in
great danger if such an axe handle and alien who will become a Fifth
Columnist is elected as a leader.

As I have told the truth thus, we have only to face the facts.

Articles such as this would almost be laughable were they not such an
indictment upon the conditions under which people exist in the Burma.

NOTHING GOLDEN ABOUT THE STREET CHILDREN OF RANGOON

The contrasts of Rangoon. An afternoon spent at one of the most
beautiful monuments to Buddhism in Burma and an evening spent
with the street children of Rangoon.

❑ ❑ ❑ ❑ ❑

The traditional name for a Burmese temple is *paya*, and a *zedi* is the
central, tapered, cone-like structure around which the *paya* is built. In
Burma, one of the most spectacular *paya*s with the most spectacular *zedi*s
is Shwedagon in Rangoon.

Legend has it that Shwedagon *Paya* was originally built to house eight
hairs from the head of Buddha. Today it is a Disneyland of golden spires,
both tall and small, and the tallest is topped by a *hti* encrusted with emer-
alds, diamonds and other assorted gemstones. On the ground, polished
white and black marble tiles pave the walkways and open areas. These are
constantly swept clean by women in broad-brimmed hats employed only
for this purpose. And throughout the *paya* worshippers kneel and bow or
sit and meditate, passing meditation beads through their fingers. Offerings of money and flowers and incense are made, gold leaf is stuck on to
the *zedi*s, and people wish for health, wealth and happiness. Garishly-
painted, sometimes almost clown-like statues watch over proceedings and
two great lions stand beside each of the four entrances to protect the *paya*.

Shwedagon, sitting on top of a hill overlooking Rangoon. A glittering,
shimmering, golden embodiment of peace and calm. Loud noise is incongruous and people talk in hushed tones. Bells jingle-jangle and the dull
reverberation of a gong echoes around the *paya*.

But if Shwedagon *Paya* is one of the most opulent, magnificent sights
in Burma, the street children of Rangoon are one of its most destitute. At

9.30 p.m., once the streets are dark and almost deserted, Peter from the US Café introduces me to some of the children that he looks after.

Kyaw Lin Aung is Mr Lucky. He is not actually a street kid but comes from a poor family in a village. Now he has a job at the US Café, is fed, given board, paid 500 kyat a month (US$1.70), and Peter is teaching him to read and write English. With his earnings he has bought himself jeans, a watch, and gym shoes.

Also at the US Café is Ne Win Htun, only off the streets for four weeks and struggling with his new surroundings. Insecure, demanding attention, smashing things, throwing tantrums. I watch him as he dances in front of a mirror and then combs and re-combs his hair. He often sleeps in Peter's room and when he does he has a habit of crawling into Peter's bed half-way through the night and cuddling in like a baby. Then, yesterday, in a pique of anger, he smashed the guitar of one of the other employees at the US Café. Peter says it's borderline whether he will run off, stay, or do something so destructive that it will no longer be possible for him to remain where he is.

Difficult, unstable, no confidence, socially inadequate, self-destructive; the characteristics of young children who live on the streets without having had the support of a family. Same problems that you see with street children everywhere, says Peter.

We leave the US Café and see the children who are not quite as fortunate as Kyaw Lin Aung and Ne Win Tun. These are the scruffy, barefoot, rag-tag, tatty little street urchins of the night that come out of their hiding spots once downtown Rangoon is deserted. They loiter, argue, scrounge, hang around, sometimes steal. Orphans, street kids, children with faces and heads often scarred from beatings, the poorest of the poor in one of the world's poorest countries.

We meet Noisy Boy, Cheeky Monkey, and Indy whose name comes from the cap he wears and which makes him look like the boy from Indiana Jones. Peter has names for them all. These are real street children, not so lucky, the sleeping under bridges and in doorways brigade, aged anything from six to the mid-teens. At the moment many of them are sporting tufty, patchwork haircuts. Last night people came along and shaved off chunks and strips of their hair making them look ludicrous. The children don't say who did it and claim that they slept through the event. Peter thinks they are too scared to say that it was the army who was responsible.

That makes sense.

Peter looks after these children to the best of his ability. He makes sure that they eat, he tries to help them find work and foster families, he sees them every day, and he organizes donations for them from travellers, often odd things that travellers no longer need like mirrors or combs or toys or caps or washing items. But sometimes the donations are money – leftover kyat or FECs which it is illegal to change back into US dollars or to take out of the country.

Peter's ultimate goal, however, is to establish a home for these children, a refuge in which they can stay for as long as they want or need, somewhere that they can be safe. As it stands, the streets are full of bad influences. Theft, bullying, alcoholism, sexual promiscuity, sexual abuse, and harassment are all rife on the streets, particularly amongst the older street children who abuse the younger ones.

'You have to get to the young ones before the older ones have too much influence,' says Peter.

Whilst eating at a roadside food stall I meet Door Wimp U. He collects plastic bottles to make money and earns two kyat or one-third of a US cent per bottle. He can usually collect twenty a day. Last night an older child took his bottles so tonight Peter buys Door food and gives him twenty-five kyat along with the message that if he still has the money in the morning then Peter will buy him breakfast. Poor little fellow with his patchwork head. He likes to walk along and hold your hand for security.

Eight-year-olds, ten-year-olds, twelve-year-olds, scavenging an existence.

It's so as to be able to curb incidents such as the bottle-stealing that Peter wants some sort of shelter for these children. But the military regime does not appreciate this Western interference in Burmese affairs and police officers hassle Peter on an almost daily basis. When they catch up with him they pull him over and question him about his activities. They tell him to leave the children alone, they tell him that if he continues they will round up the children and take them to orphanages. This, says Peter, is a fate worse than the streets. Burmese orphanages are playgrounds for paedophilia, maltreatment, and forced child labour.

Yesterday military intelligence pulled Peter over and gave him the sternest warning that he has yet received. Stop, they said, or you will be deported. Then, that night, the mysterious tufty patchwork head shavings. One boy had one side of his head completely shaved. Another all but a tuft on the front. Others had streaks and random bald patches the size of saucers cut from their scalps. But the children maintain that they slept through this. Impossible. Peter thinks that this is the army's way of saying to him, 'We can do anything we like to these children and you can't do anything about it, so do as we say.' If this is the case, it is a bizarre and malicious way of getting a message across.

Peter tells the children that he will take them all to the barber tomorrow to have their heads completely shaved. He promises that he too will have his head shaved. 'I've been looking for an excuse to do it for years,' says Peter.

We eat, we have ice cream, we check on more children. Wandering through the streets, some of the older children tell Peter that military inspectors are out and about and looking for him.

We stop and I take photos of the children in doorways and the side streets of Rangoon. Eerie photos of small, dark, shadowy figures dressed in filthy rags. A car stops about forty metres away. The driver and passengers are clearly watching us. 'Military Intelligence,' observes Peter and beats a hasty retreat. I keep taking photos, almost baiting the military to take issue. It is an attitude borne of ignorance but on this occasion it does not land me in any trouble. The occupants of the car just continue to sit and watch me. Very soon I loose my nerve and rejoin Peter at the US Café.

Quite clearly the Burmese military does not want a Westerner seeing this side of Rangoon and equally clear is that it does not want a Westerner to be involved in helping these children. So for these little urchins of the most hopeless and destitute variety, bad luck.

Good bloke Peter, only twenty-one years old.

DODGY DEALERS

Three days ago I met an Englishman who was an international trader, buying on the Burmese black market and then shipping goods out of the country. Gems, motorbikes, antiques, these were his stock in trade. Over breakfast this morning I speak to a Californian who is in a similar line of business. He tells me about the motorbike trade in Burma. 'Old World War II BSAs and Triumphs, US$500 for a good bike in working order,' he says, 'Maybe US$500 to ship it out. Look for a '39 or a '45 model, antique bikes – a lot around, especially the BSA's. Try to buy the two-cylinder ones. Bigger bikes but worth a lot more. Should be able to sell a bike like that for Aust$10,000. Easy. Also look for gramophones, cameras, old photos, things like that left over from the British era. Closed doors in Burma for thirty years. There's a lot of stuff still around.'

I guess that's what happens if you lock off a country from the rest of the world since the first of the post-colonial years. Everything that was here still is.

I meet the Californian motorbike dealer again in the afternoon in the Rock 'n' Roll Cafe. It's a dive of a dark, musty-smelling bar that serves Western food and has pictures of Harley Davidsons and Elvis on the walls. The dealer is sitting by himself when Peter and I go in to have a hamburger, so we go and join him. 'I do my business in the morning and the

evening so what else is there to do in this country except sit here and
drink beer during the day?' he asks. We talk. It transpires that he not only
buys and sells motorbikes in Burma, but also prescription drugs which he
resells at the Chinese Hospital in Manila. 'Highest mark-ups are on rabies
inoculations, ampicillin, other penicillin based drugs, and the 'knock out'
drugs, the ones you take and are out cold for twelve hours. Usually between US$25,000 and $50,000 on a $5,000 investment.' The thing is,
buying and transporting pharmaceuticals is not illegal per se – they are
not narcotics but prescription drugs.

Dodgy dealer, this American. He tells us about the buying and selling of
work visas racket. US$15,000 for a Japanese visa, US$5,000 for an
American work permit. 'You better believe it,' he continues, 'This isn't the
only country where it's easy to bribe people. All you gotta do is find out
which consulate employee wants to make extra money. All they gotta do
is stamp a few forms for you. Easy as that. There are many people that
you can buy.' He laughs. 'Best deals in South-East Asia used to be bringing arms over the border from Cambodia into Thailand. Buy from the
Khmer Rouge. Big money.' But for the time being it's Burma and this is
his third visit this year, primarily because of the biannual international gem
fair. 'Gotta have contacts in gems, buy from the black market. Buy jade,
rubies, sapphires for almost nothing. These guys are stealing them from
the mines, smuggling them out, and then want to sell them. Not too many
people got the cash to buy them in this country except for people like me.
I come here with US$10,000 and my Filipino girl. She takes the stuff out
for me. Partners. She likes the money but mess with her and she'd cut my
hands off.' He laughs again. But the long term goal, 'There are nine
people hiding in Burma wanted by the CIA with a price tag on their heads
of one to five million. That's the biggest business here. Criminals. You
give people enough money and they don't care who you are or what you
do or what you want. Takes a lot of time and a lot of dollars to build up the
contacts to get close to these people. Maybe I've spent US$25,000 in
Burma already. You gotta get to the person, you gotta knock him out,
then you gotta pay enough people until you get him across the border
into Thailand. Set me up for life. My retirement plan. And in the mean-
time, I do other business.' More laughter and then he takes out a leather
case under the table. It is padded with purple velvet on the inside and
contains ampoules of the knock-out drug. 'Those are the ones you gotta
give 'em,' he explains. 'Half an hour and they're out cold and they're not
going to move for another twelve hours. Mix it with vodka and you'll
probably kill 'em straight up. Good for hookers as well. Slip one of these
into her drink, after about quarter of an hour she starts to think she's
drunk too much, you take her home. Then you can do anything you like

to her. Can't say no. Can't remember a thing in the morning. Had a Filipino hooker do it to me once. Thing was I woke up the next morning still in the bar with my clothes on but with no wallet.'

'Hookers here, you know one of these girls asked me for 50,000 kyat for one night. I tried to bargain with her but that was it, 50,000 kyat. Can you believe that? She's waiting for one big, stupid catch, maybe a rich Japanese or Chinese who's just gonna give her a year's income for one night. Maybe she's gonna get it. Not from me.'

As he talks I try to work out how much of what he is relating is rubbish and how much is true. I don't know. Funny bunch, these traders. They remind me of the sort of people seen in films set in Africa at the turn of the century, the boat owners who you hire to go up a river into the wilderness but who then either don't turn up or when things start to get difficult you discover have sold you to a tribe of colonial casserole-crunching tribesmen. Hardy and unscrupulous.

4 + 5 = *THE CURRENCY OF A DICTATOR*

Not a happy chappy. Flat, tired, stroppy and wallowing in a mire of conflicting information as to what can and can't be done in Burma. It seems like I am chasing myself around in circles. Richard says catch the train from Mandalay to Putao in the north. At my hotel they say the train from Mandalay only goes as far as Myikyina and then I have to catch an aeroplane. The MTT says I have to book everything in Rangoon and travel with a licensed tour guide if I want to get to Putao. I don't know which is correct but one thing is certain and that is that everything suggested by the MTT is the most expensive.

❑ ❑ ❑ ❑ ❑

Changing money in downtown Rangoon. Money exchange is almost exclusively the domain of the black market. Banks, such as the Myanmar Foreign Trade Bank, will change dollars into kyat but do so at the official military government rate of 6 kyat per dollar. On the black market, however, the rate is 260 kyat per dollar and by the time that I leave Burma it has risen to 300. With an annual inflation rate that wavers between 30 and 60 per cent it is not surprising that Burmese traders want the security of US$. The black market reflects the magnitude of this want with rates of exchange for the greenback going up on a week-by-week basis. In the first half of 1997 the black market rate almost reached 400 at which point in time the military executed an arbitrary crack down on the usually-tolerated traders. Many were arrested and the black market exchange rate dropped to 200 kyat almost overnight. Then it slowly crept back up again. Nothing stops the demand for hard currency.

For travellers, black market money-changers are not hard to find. Every time you walk past Sule Pagoda they try to attract your attention. Likewise they are not backward in coming forward outside the Myanmar Foreign Trade Bank.

For me, I change money in the back of a roofed pick-up parked not far from the bank. Someone watches up and down the street and the dealer is also on the lookout. A calculator comes out and figures are shown to me. Tens upon tens of thousands, bundle upon bundle of notes. Some are forty-five or ninety kyat notes; soft, smooth old notes like well worn leather. Nice to touch. The wads are either ten ninety kyat notes wrapped in a hundred, eleven nineties wrapped in a ten, or far-too-many-forty-fives-to-count wrapped in a ten or hundred. When I leave the back of the pick-up I have a plastic bag full of money squashed in with my camera equipment.

❏ ❏ ❏ ❏ ❏

Burma has had a number of currencies in the last two centuries. First it had local currency. Then, as a British colony, it had British currency. In World War II the Japanese invaded and so it had Japanese currency. Upon Independence in 1947 it reverted to a currency of its own, but then in 1962 there was the military coup which brought General Ne Win to power. With him came the most bizarre currency of all.

During his time in power, many of General Ne Win's policies were radical, bordering on absurd. He succeeded in almost completely isolating Burma from the outside world for decades. No one goes in, no one comes out. He also revolutionized the economy, reducing Burma from being one of the wealthiest countries in South-East Asia in the 1950s to being one of the poorest in the world in the year 2000. Along the way he announced that all notes in circulation of 500 kyat or greater denominations were to be devalued. This was the Ne Win road to socialism. But perhaps Ne Win's most ridiculous policy was his introduction of the forty-five and ninety kyat notes. The dictator had been told by his astrologer, a practitioner of Burmese 'Ya Da Ya Chein' magic, that number nine would be an auspicious number for him. Hence, in homage to his lucky number he introduced the forty-five kyat note because four plus five equals nine, and the ninety kyat note because nine plus zero equals nine. It is amazing the policies that you can get away with when the army is yours and you shoot people who object.

General Ne Win. An Eastern totalitarian dictator who maintained sole control of Burma for twenty-six years. Mad as a hatter, loopy as a piece of overcooked spaghetti but murderously clever when it came to maintaining power. He removed his unpopular self from the fore of Burmese politics in the face of mass civil unrest in July 1988. But it is widely held that after the massacres of 8 August 1988 he was at least partly responsible for the military coup that occurred the following month. The Ne Win shuffle. He had complete power, took a step back, shuffled forward again and it is suggested that he still maintains significant influence despite almost being dead.

General Ne Win, responsible for twenty-six years of oppression. Responsible also for the death of thousands of students, democracy activists, and ethnic peoples. Control them by killing them, the politics and diplomacy of the gun.

General Ne Win, he likes to keep a low profile nowadays although he is trying to ensure his posterity by building and dedicating *payas* to himself. And his current influence in the military regime? The truth is that no one really knows how much power he still wields. But if one thing is certain, it is that he still has his connections. Indeed, he is the godfather of Lieutenant General Khin Nyunt, Secretary One of the SLORC, Secretary One of the SPDC, Head of Burmese Military Intelligence, Chairman of the Board of Education.

It's a totally totalitarian family affair in Myanmar.

❑ ❑ ❑ ❑ ❑

Leaving Rangoon and once again the rains come bucketing down. It is as if there is a game being played in conjunction with El Nino by the people who live above the clouds. The object is to see who can dump the most water on Rangoon in the shortest period of time, thereby creating the largest amount of chaos. Streets flood, traffic jams, and vegetation is hurled around until it crashes to the ground. As I travel to the bus station from where I will catch a bus to Mandalay, a brief but tempestuous variation of the game is played. After an hour it is over.

I arrive at the bus station and the bus that I board for Mandalay is large, modern and air-conditioned. I am travelling again and I like that.

Outward bound, driving along the northern highway, just beyond Rangoon. There are rice paddies and huts with woven walls and thatched roofs, water buffalo in the fields, and children fishing in flooded streams with bamboo pole fishing rods. There are very few trees. It seems that it is only in the towns that they have not been cleared away.

I practise my Burmese with the behemoth of a Burmese man sitting next to me. Another man, a fellow traveller, is reading a book on Buddhism. I tell him that I want to head north and go up into the mountains. 'What did you lose there?' he asks. A good question but perhaps the answer lies in what I would like to try and find.

If you are looking for a path and then follow the path that you think is right, it might be that you don't even know the questions that you will stumble upon let alone the answers that you might find. A retrospective perspective.

At 4.53 p.m. I begin to play a game in which I see if we can travel for five minutes by the digital clock at the front of the bus without spotting a new *paya*. It is impossible. As I write in jiggled, bumped, and barely legible scribble, it is 5.16 p.m. and although we are in the middle of rice paddy territory with no evidence of towns or villages, I can still see three separate *payas* and we have just passed another two. Some are small single shrines in the middle of rice paddies, some are larger but still single structures, others are in compounds full of trees and comprise three, four, five, ten different *zedis*. Then there are the huge golden *zedis* that have been built in prominent places, like on the top of hills, and sparkle in the light.

An Irish friend in Thailand had observed to me that in Burma there is a *paya* on every vantage point and one in every beauty spot. It is hardly an exaggeration.

Eighty kilometres out of Rangoon, close to the town of Pegu and the traffic is thick as the sun goes down. We dodge trishaws, dogs, pedestrians, buffalo carts, cow carts, pony carts, people carts, logging trucks, chicken trucks, durian trucks, and rice trucks. Then there are the bicycles. One-person cycles, two-person cycles, little-person cycles, family cycles, and load-them-up-with-as-much-produce-as-you-can cycles. All of this on a one-and-a-half lane, bump-and-grind road laid by the British over fifty years ago and with little maintenance since their departure. I lie. There are some signs of progress. Beside the roads are piles of stones, gravel and sand, the materials for road works. This is Highway One in Burma, the road that links Mandalay and Rangoon. Basic. We move no faster than the traffic in which we are stuck.

Pegu at sunset. Character, atmosphere, a golden *zedi* gleaming in the middle of the town in the last light of a hot day, crowded streets, big red propaganda hoardings decrying the threat of external influence and internal instability. It's the same message as on the back of the comic which in turn is the same message that is on the back page of the daily newspapers. Crush, remove, destroy, stooges, external control. The message is very clear.

We brake abruptly for some water buffalo that are not paying heed to the give-way signs.

Highway One. Sometimes made, sometimes unmade, sometimes old and potholed. When buses and trucks approach in opposite directions, each vehicle proceeds half on and half off the road in a shuffling passing manoeuvre. Trucks stop where they will. We swerve around a decrepit machine with no bonnet that has broken down on the road and been left there. Other vehicles throw up clouds of dust so thick that our driver has to slow down and wait until they clear before he can see the road ahead. This is Highway One, Rangoon to Mandalay.

We pass through a military checkpoint with four people lounging around registering the movement of traffic and people. The bus attendant hands across a list of passengers and we proceed. We stop at many such points as we drive.

Night-time, a paradoxical journey. I sit in an air-conditioned bus and looking towards the front I see a digital clock and a television playing the film Dante's Peak. I forget where I am. But looking to the side I see exactly where I am, central Burma where the poor are poor and the rich are not quite as poor. Hollywood's film extravaganza world in front of me, and out of the window a world of dogs and fluorescent lights and candles and roadside shacks and cooking fires and Burmese people squatting and talking.

One film follows another on the bus. The man beside me is a video shop owner and he is bringing his new pirated copies up from Rangoon. He asks me which of the videos I think are the best and then puts them on for my benefit. I make the mistake of putting my boots on an overhead shelf. 'Please, no,' says the man in front. Sorry.

Night becomes dawn and dawn becomes day at six o'clock and the bus passes through the dry central plains of Burma. Very poor villages surrounded by thistle thicket hedges – it could be part of Africa. Large white-humped cows sleep in dirt forecourts or tethered under huts. Workers head off into the fields with their wooden bullock-team ploughs. In the distance, to the east, rising from the plains, are mountains. They are not very high but are the final bumps of the Himalayas which have descended from their lofty heights in Pakistan, Nepal, and India, down through the north of Burma and to here, where they have almost petered out. On some of the hilltops are payas looking out over the plains, further apart than they were last night but still they are almost always evident somewhere.

chapter 2

Central Burma

WANDERING WAYS IN MANDALAY

Mandalay, a city whose name everyone seems to have heard. Images of Britons in rattan sun hats and khaki clothes with canes tucked under arms and stiff, well clipped moustaches. A city which one associates with the height of the British colonial era.

More recent associations may be with a city fought over by the British and Japanese in World War II. Diggers and Tommies and older generations of Westerners have all heard of Mandalay. And now... now Mandalay is Burma's second largest city, an urban sprawl over the flat central plains. *Lonely Planet* calls it a boomtown. Certainly building proliferates. The local construction sites are small – houses and shops and businesses with four or five labourers working away. The large developments, hotels and multi-storey buildings are more likely to be owned by foreign investors.

❑ ❑ ❑ ❑ ❑

My journey from Rangoon ends at 9.00 a.m. There is a taxi driver waiting for me at the bus station with a name board. He approaches me and asks if I am Mr Tit. Yes, that will do, and he drives me off to a pre-booked room.

The hotel is simple, comfortable, and full of backpackers. A double room, a hot shower, bottles of Mandalay Bitter in an icebox downstairs and a rooftop sitting area with a view over the city.

Next to the hotel is Zegyo market. It is busy and people bustle and bump between people. Lots of bustle and lots of bump. Stalls are wooden, the walkways between them narrow, the ground is muddy and the sun filters through gaps in the iron roof. Hot and sticky, the food and the atmosphere. There are mounds of fish paste two metres high, ripe for the nostrils from fifteen metres. There are wicker trays of onions and garlic and chillies and spices, and vegetables both fresh and dried. In the meat area, not so fresh and rapidly drying, a platter of skinned, fly-infested goats' heads with dangling eyeballs. A visual treat. Epicurean optometry.

Beyond the food there is the domestic section, not so sensually engaging but quite a collection nonetheless. Steel pots and pans, knives and forks, mortars and pestles and various other vessels. Straw hats, sleeping mats, shirts and skirts. Jewellery, vinyl flooring, sewing machines, spanners, old suitcases, plates, and traditional blankets in strong cotton, black with purple and red rectangles. I buy two as I pass through. Sandals, Milo, rope, plastic tubes, nails, stainless steel water carrying pails. Every domestic knick-knack, odd and sod, bit and bob of which one can conceive.

Next to the market is the bicycle park. Hundreds upon hundreds of bicycles lined up in a vacant dirt allotment the size of two football pitches. Ten kyat for a day's parking.

Downtown, past the clock tower, a different atmosphere. Broad, empty, quiet streets which lead up to the old British fortress with its moat and two-kilometre-long walls. It is a serene sight although the most attractive thing about the fort is its appearance from the outside. Inside there really isn't much to see and the general consensus among backpackers is that it isn't worth giving US$5 to Brigadier General Aye Myint Kyu and the MTT for the privilege.

Back outside and there is a snake swimming in the moat of Mandalay Fort.

❑ ❑ ❑ ❑ ❑

In the northern quarters of Mandalay, beside the Irrawaddy, beyond the Mandalay fairground, the backstreets are unmade and bumpy, behind the times and not ideal for wheeled transport. Occasional bicycles clunk along but most of the traffic is pedestrian or horse-drawn carts. There have been floods recently, and puddles of black mud, brown mud, dried mud, and wet mud fill the potholes. There are woven-walled houses, scrappy dogs, horses and people at work. They are leisurely and unfussed in the way that they go about their business.

Monks walk by, purple monks, brown monks, orange monks, pink nuns. Fathers carrying children, mothers carrying children, others carrying children, children carrying children. Games of marbles played in the dust by the side of the road, games of flick counter pool played on wooden tables. Run-down, crotchety, rusty, grumbling old trucks. Ladies with shade umbrellas to keep the sun off their faces. Darker shades of skin are considered to be the sign of being a peasant. Paler complexions are much more desirable.

The dusty trails along the Irrawaddy and its levy bank, interesting if you like to observe life. A different type of life. Animals abound. Horses, cows, buffalo, ducks, chickens, dogs, pigs as big as Morris Minors. Not quite, but there are some monstrous pigs.

On one stretch of river there is a build-up of logs which have been floated downstream. Water buffalo, two to a harness, drag them through the mud and up the levee bank to where trucks wait to motor them away.

The people by the riverside are very poor. There are one-room shanties and shacks. There are scruffy people in dirty clothes and bare feet and there are children who are not at school. There also seem to be a disproportionately high number of disabled people in this area. People with legs bent at unnatural angles, a man with a deformed hip, another with a twisted face. People with a staring vacancy in their eyes that indicates mental disorder.

Up until now, in both Rangoon and Mandalay, I cannot recall having seen a disabled person. Strange in a very poor country. Yet here, in a one-kilometre stretch by the river, I see probably ten. Some are lolling on woven mats on the ground, some stare at me, and one hobbles after me, not to beg or to be intrusive, but only because he, like the children who run after me, is inquisitive.

There is an explanation as to why tourists do not see beggars and disabled people in the streets of Rangoon and Mandalay. But to understand it, one must also appreciate that the military government understands that tourists to Burma do not want to see deformity and abject poverty on the streets. Nor does the military want to show this off.

In the lead-up to the opening of Visit Myanmar Year the military undertook many projects that were intended to make Burma look presentable when it opened its doors to the international tourist market. These projects often involved the abuse of human rights; for example the use of slave labour on tourist infrastructure projects. The dredging of the moat of Mandalay Fort, the building of the road that goes up Mandalay Hill, the highway between Rangoon and Pegu, are just a few of the projects where the Burmese people have been forced to work without pay in the name of international tourism. Indeed, the prevalence of this practice in Burma has been acknowledged by the international community and each year Burma's military leaders are condemned by the United Nations and the International Labour Organization for its continuance.

Five years ago, in October 1995 when Burma was preparing for Visit Myanmar Year, the United Nations Commission's Special Rapporteur on Human Rights in Burma, Professor Yozo Yokota acknowledged the use of slave labour, enforced by the military, on tourist infrastructure projects.

Another part of the preparation for Visit Myanmar Year involved the 'cleaning up' of the poor and disabled from the city centres of Rangoon and Mandalay. These people were rounded up and relocated, often being taken to satellite townships outside the major cities and away from tourist eyes. One rumour has it that some were taken to areas where the Burmese army fights against ethnic minority groups. Here they were used to front army columns so as to protect soldiers from mines. Maybe, maybe not. But one thing for certain is that for a country as poor as Burma one is certainly not exposed to the most obvious reminders of poverty either in or around any of the major tourist destinations.

However, on the banks of the Irrawaddy a five-kilometre walk north-west of Mandalay Fort it is a different story. Perhaps by the time of reading, this area, too, will have been 'cleaned up'.

◻ ◻ ◻ ◻ ◻

East of Mandalay Fort is a very different type of neighbourhood; a neighbourhood of leafy, broad streets, huge trees, overhanging boughs, and uniforms. White uniforms, fawn uniforms, light green uniforms, dark green uniforms, pale blue uniforms, navy blue uniforms. The uniform district. The shops and many of the houses here are made of concrete, bricks and mortar. A corner shop boasts a large refrigerator full of Western-style ice creams in wrappers. The fridge alone is worth more than many of the dwellings along the Irrawaddy. Along one of the streets is a decrepit Bugatti that has not left its ditch for the past five years.

Whilst walking through this district I pass a building site and stop and talk to a round-faced, smiling Filipino overseer. He tells me that the site is the property of an Australian construction company. He also says that the labourers on the site are Burmese but the architects, the overseers, the site managers, the surveyors, the developers, in fact all the people with positions of responsibility including himself, have been imported from overseas.

The labourers are paid three to four dollars a month. This must mean that the cost of labour to build a hotel such as this one must be very little. Based on figures from equivalent hotels in Rangoon, once the hotel is finished cleaners and similar service staff will again be paid three to four dollars a month. Other staff will be paid six, seven, maybe eight dollars a month and a Burmese Night Manager is paid ten dollars. These figures mean that staffing the hotel will be very cheap. But when the hotel is finished, guests pay upwards of US$100 per night, the same as at any other luxury international hotel anywhere else. This must mean that the potential profit margins are very large. The only counterbalancing expense is the money paid to the military government in order to be able to gain permission to develop and invest. A Burmese friend later tells me that it is all about who you know in the military and how much you pay them. Development in Burma is based on corruption and without it you can't do anything.

In Mandalay a Chinese construction company paid for permission to bulldoze the Allied World War II cemetery and build a hotel on the site. Money handed over, permission granted. Do investors and developers care? About anything? Or are they just corporate suit-and-tie versions of the rogue traders whom I met in Rangoon?

Continuing through this district, a man sits by the side of the street with a canvas spread out on which there are animal souvenirs for sale. Hides, tusks, teeth, claws, skulls, feet, and jawbones of tigers, deer, boars, leopards, and monkeys. No thank you, not for me.

Mandalay General Hospital. I recognize it by an intravenous drip that is in the middle of the pavement outside, pulled out and left. People with assorted ailments, including one with an arm in bloody bandages, loiter with their relatives outside the main buildings. No waiting rooms here. No glass in the windows of the wards either, only shutters and bars.

Mandalay General Hospital. If this is an indication as to the standard of public health care in Burma then it is little wonder that in May 2000 the World Health Organization rated Burma as providing the second worst health care of 191 countries assessed. Only Sierra Leone was considered to provide a worse service to its citizens.

Near the hospital people are spreading rocks and gravel on the road. Road works, Burmese style, no money to spare. Rocks are spread over the road manually and then a steamroller rolls over them. This is a job that the men do; the women spread fine gravel over the crushed rock base. Beside the road three forty-five gallon drums stand on the pavement by a blazing fire, black smoke billowing around them. One man, naked from the waist up and with a cloth wrapped around his head, stokes the fire. Another ladles boiling pitch into buckets which are then carried off, smoke still wafting from the top, to be poured over the road. Primitive.

Back into Zegyo market at night. It's closed, slum-like, smelly, and dirty. Headlights filter through dust thrown up from the roads, silhouetting figures of people and dogs. People rummage through the debris of the day's buying and selling, looking for food even as garbage workers heap rubbish into a truck. Three young scruffs are playing in a pile of wood shavings in the mud as if it were snow, throwing handfuls at each other. One scruff runs towards me. I prepare to fend him off but someone else grabs him by the wrist and drags him away. Dark. Rats scurry to and fro; many, many rats. Sometimes I almost step on them before they make a dash for safety. The dogs are out as well, also looking for food.

Rats, dogs, people, all scrounging in the shadows of the deserted market. Squalid, surreal.

YANKIN HILL

I hire a bike for the day, a Mean Cruise Machine from Mandalay, a 'Forever-All-Steel-from-Shanghai-China-Express'. I jump on and dodge and weave and *mingala baa* my way through the jam-crammed, chaotic market backstreets and onto the drag strip that is the Fortress Road Expressway. I wait at the traffic lights and watch them count down until they turn in my favour. These particular traffic lights are the pride and joy of Burmese technology. When they are red, there is a number beside them which tells queuing passengers and drivers and riders how long it will be until the lights turn green.

I wipe my brow and loosen my grip on the handlebars. The other bicycle riders, all fifty of them, false start at the lights, taking off before they change. Before I know it half of them are ahead of me. I put my feet to the metal and pedal. First I overtake a family bike, husband, wife and baby pedalling along. Then it's past an old cruiser, fifty years old, on his trusty Chinese rattle machine, World War II GI helmet placed firmly on his head, false Ray Bans wrapped around his face to keep the wind out of his eyes. Easy Rider. I overtake two Burmese beauties, slowing a little to admire their upright, erect postures, so slender, so fine, pedalling bow legged to stop their *longiis* (the traditional Burmese cotton wraparounds, much like Indonesian sarongs) from flapping in the breeze. A young man overtakes me then relaxes once he has passed. '*Myan myan*', I shout after him, 'Quickly, quickly!' He looks back but does not smile. A challenge. We race. Extra effort, a burst of power, I catch him easily and go sailing out in front of the crowd. The Speed Demon from Down Under. The Tour de Mandalay. I fall into cruising mode, thinking that I have got him, but no, he comes charging back past me and this time he does not relent but keeps pedalling furiously. I try valiantly to rein him in but cannot make up the lost ground in time. The end of the Fortress Road Expressway approaches and he speeds around the corner.

I head towards the outskirts of Mandalay and the hills to the east at a more leisurely pace. The road changes into a bump-and-clatter, dirt, potholed affair before disappearing altogether.

A military chopper flies low overhead and then buzzes off, becoming nothing more than a black dragonfly in the distance. The military is a constant and pervasive presence in Burma.

A pony cart clip-clops down the road.

❑ ❑ ❑ ❑ ❑

Directly east of Mandalay is Yankin Hill, maybe six kilometres away. Like Mandalay Hill, it is strewn with *payas*, although they are smaller than those on its more glamorous neighbour. Cycling towards it I pass dogs fighting and an old lady fishing in a rice paddy. There is a house leaning over as if in a hurricane, boys tend herds of cows, there is a chalk pit with a very white, dusty person standing beside it and a policeman smiles and waves at me. In fact, as I cycle along I encounter more hellos, smiles and *mingala baas* than I know what to do with. They all combine to make me happier and happier and smile more and more as I go.

At Yankin Hill there are no US$ entrance fees. Instead one has the opportunity to give a donation at the entrance. Giving is much easier when one is not compelled to do it and the money is likely to go towards the upkeep of the temple.

Inside the entrance there are three two-metre-long concrete fish. They lie in parallel at the feet of a statue of Buddha. Before proceeding up the hill to the various shrines and *payas* a monk asks me to take a bowl and pour water over each of the fish.

Temples – it is not that I actually tiptoe around them but I almost do. They are like a pond in which one doesn't want to create any ripples.

Peaceful and relaxed, I sit down and fall asleep in a particularly secluded shrine on the top of Yankin Hill. When I wake up there is a young monk sitting and watching me and an old monk comes over and offers me water and palm sugar sweets. We sit together but he cannot speak English and my Burmese is no more than a few sentences. After a few minutes I take out my notebook and begin to write. As I do so members of a group of Burmese visitors see me and come and sit around to watch what I am doing. They touch me and smile and when they leave a young man puts his hands together and bows his head to me. I return the gesture.

Across the top of the hill there is a covered walkway that links the various shrines. Beside it are garishly coloured Humpty Dumpty gods and little gods with two bodies and one head. There is a god riding a *garuda*, and a menacing multi-coloured ogre god brandishing a large spiked club. There are also many statues of lions and elephants and pigeons.

At one point I come across four monkeys on long chains that leap and fight, stare and scowl, fall asleep, play, and rip up and eat the grass stalks and frangipani flowers which I give them. A monk comes along, picks one up and puts it on his knee. The monkey rolls onto its back, plays with a stick and has its tummy tickled at the same time. Monk and monkey.

I open my camera bag to take a photo. My sunblock cream bottle has burst over my camera lenses. I remove and begin to clean them just as the army comes along. I immediately worry about my array of equipment. It is the equipment of someone who could be a professional photographer and I envisage problems. But there are no problems and this makes me realize that I am falling into the trap of pre-judging soldiers and policemen. I think of them as power-wielding pawns in a totalitarian state. While this might be the case in instances of confrontation, on a day-to-day basis the reality is often different. They are shy, polite, curious, and they smile and laugh. In fact, they are very much like other Burmese people. To some soldiers, being in the army is just a job, perhaps the only job available in a country where there are few, if any, prospects of employment. Furthermore, there is informal conscription into the army and in some cases, particularly in the ethnic regions of Burma, there are people who join the army to be in a better position to protect their own families and villages from military abuse. As a further inducement, with tertiary education shut down across Burma, joining the army can mean that one's children have access to education, albeit education that takes place in military barracks with soldiers as teachers and schools that are not open to the general population. As such, joining the army may not be an indication of political inclination or attitude, merely an indication of some of life's necessities.

Anyway, a group of girls walk past where the soldiers and I are standing. I see that some of the soldiers watch them as they go. I raise my eyebrows at one particular soldier. He raises his eyebrows. We smile. I put my hand on his shoulder and say to him, 'Nah boo.' Laughter all round from soldiers, a drinks vendor, the old monk who is playing with the monkey; laughter even from the senior commander who had been maintaining the attitude of detached severity which I think he felt it necessary to maintain towards a Westerner. Nah boo means 'womanizer' or 'flirt'. Burmese men are shy when it comes to women and sexuality but they take 'nah boo' as an embarrassing compliment. 'Better to be nah boo than not to be nah boo,' says a Burmese friend. Here, now, the fact that a Westerner knows this phrase amuses everyone greatly.

Later, at the main shrine on Yankin Hill, I meet the most senior of the soldiers. He is amicable, helpful, speaks good English and asks where I am from and what do I think of Burma. Then, before he departs, he says that should I have any problems in Mandalay, I should come and speak to him.

❏ ❏ ❏ ❏ ❏

Burmese soldiers, normal Burmese citizens except that they are disliked and distrusted by Burmese people, ostracized because of the part that they play in maintaining the current regime. They also have a reputation for corruption and a stigma attached to them because of the brutal and unquestioning way in which they carry out orders.

Four o'clock and I have walked to the final temple on the ridge of Yankin Hill. It is an old, whitewashed structure with squirrels in the trees and a 270 degree view of the surrounding countryside. Below me is the greenness of the patchwork paddies that surround Mandalay, vibrant in the late afternoon light.

Down the steps from the temple and a young Burmese man offers me a lift on the back of his bike. No end to the politeness of these people although I don't think he realizes how much heavier Westerners are than the Burmese. Nor do I realize how uncomfortable it can be to sit on a steel pack rack on an unmade road whilst holding your legs out at right angles so as to keep them from dragging on the ground.

Before returning to Mandalay I have a wash in a communal concrete wash trough where twenty Burmese have gathered to wash after coming in from the day's work. They are surprised to see me in their midst, a half-naked Westerner. They are half-naked as well but that is beside the point. We wash, I buy a drink and then sit and talk to an ever-increasing group of Burmese people. By the time I leave I am in the midst of a gathering of thirty.

If it doesn't involve the offering of food straight away, conversations with Burmese seem to follow the same format: 'Hello mister, Where you come from? Where you go? Where you stay? How much does it cost? Do you like Burma? How old are you? Are you married? Do you like Burma girls? What is your name? (well down the list of vital information). What is your job? How much do you earn?' People prefer it if you keep the answers short so that they can ask the next question. They are more comfortable asking questions than listening to the answers. Questions in longer conversations are usually about the prices of things, for example the price of my boots, my sunglasses, and my camera. I halve them at least. To tell them that my sunglasses cost the equivalent of two years of their salary is not right.

Burmanized English. A mixture of politeness and odd, often outdated, expressions left over from the colonial days. You can hear students reciting them when you walk past schools or houses in the early morning or mid-afternoon, a monotonous recited drone that some tourists have mistaken for religious incantations. All learning is by rote, not uncommon in South-East Asia. This means that if you break from the accepted manner in which a conversation should evolve, then any Burmese party soon finds him or herself in murky waters. For example, the following is a quaint extract from the book, *Conversational English*, an English textbook for Burmese students:

A *Morning Walk*

-Oh, isn't it wonderful?
-*Yes, it is always nice to get up early.*
-Fresh arr (sic) is so good to our health.
-*You'd better take plenty of deep breaths.*
-Don't worry. I won't miss the chance.
-*Everything is so quiet.*
-Listen the birds are singing. It is such beautiful scenery around us.
-*Yes, you would write many beautiful poems if you were a poet.*
-Certainly. Hey! Don't walk so fast.

❑ ❑ ❑ ❑ ❑

There is a festival in Mandalay in the evening. It is the pagoda festival of the Eidawya *Paya* next to the hotel in which I am staying. I go with a Burmese friend and as we walk through the temple compound he taps me on the arm, grins and raises his eyebrows as a pretty woman walks past, one that he feels should not escape my notice. *Nah boo!*

The festival is low key compared with the Indian madness in Rangoon. There are hundreds of platters of food laid out before various shrines and tomorrow morning there will be between one and four thousand monks in the temple at five in the morning. Other than this, however, the festival is more like a fair for local people. Two large, temporary stages have been set up and on both of these dance and theatre are being performed. Actors stand in front of microphones blaring out their lines to an enraptured audience seated on the ground. It is a different theatrical tradition, boring if you don't understand Burmese. Not so, at least to me, is a highly skilful game of *chin lon*. *Chin lon* is a game played throughout Burma. It is played in a number of ways and in this instance five men are standing in a circle and using everything but their hands to keep a small wicker ball in the air. This is not too difficult but the trick is to execute fancy manoeuvres in order to achieve this feat. The players that I watch are particularly good and perform jumping kicks, behind the back kicks, kicks with knees and thighs as well as kicks with the tops, sides and heels of feet. Head kicks, elbow kicks, toe pokes and sole-of-the-feet-under-the-armpit scoops. Sometimes the players contort themselves into awkward shapes so as to be able to execute a particular manoeuvre. And all of this takes place to the music of an accompanying Burmese orchestra.

In a different part of the temple there are shooting galleries where participants fire rubber bands at packs of cigarettes. Not only must you hit the pack but you must also knock it off the shelf. Difficult. In another game, it is a case of hoop the cigarette box. Again, difficult but I do see one winner, a monk who happily walks off with his packet of London cigarettes. Arcade games in Burma, not quite Sony Playstations.

On the following evening, at the same temple, the stages have been dismantled and the main attraction is films which are being projected onto a large piece of canvas. The projector is from the 1930s and whirrs away. It looks like a cross between a boiler and a tractor engine and it smokes profusely whilst running film over a two-metre distance from the contraption itself to a piece of rotating bamboo which acts as a spool. The film is a crinkle cut, scratchy, Burmese slapstick martial arts film with all of the action sequences in fast motion so as to make them look more... I don't know, snappy? Compelling? Whatever. Braveheart, eat your heart out.

A little boy runs up to me pointing and laughing at a middle-aged man who has fallen asleep on the flagstones around the main *zedi*. What do Burmese men wear under their *longiis*? About as much as Scotsmen purportedly wear under their kilts and in the case of this gentleman his attire is not adequately covering the required parts of his anatomy. Nearby children are squealing with delight.

TAH MA TAAH – A BUDDHIST ENCOUNTER

My travel plan has firmed in my mind. I will depart for Bhamo, a town in northern Burma, by boat tomorrow. The idea of taking a leisurely cruise up the Irrawaddy has great appeal.

One of the employees at the hotel tells me that the price for the boat is 255 kyat, marginally less than one dollar. At the booking centre, an official in army uniform states, 'No, you are a foreigner. There are three classes – first class, US$72, second class US$36, third class US$9 to sleep on the deck.' For me, third class it will be.

On the way back to the hotel I see a photo that I would like to take. It is of a man who is sitting on a trishaw. Beside him is an Indian in a turban and the two are framed by a tree and a colonial-style yellow building. As I take the photo another man in a turban comes up to me and asks, 'Why are you taking a photo of this? Why are you taking a photo of the Sikh temple? Are you working for an embassy?' 'No.' 'Please do not show this photo. Please do not put it on display. Please do not give it to the Burmese.' 'Okay.'

There are a number of instances in Burma when I am confronted by people or situations the significance of which I can hardly even begin to understand. One such thing is the need to maintain some sort of secrecy about the Sikh temple.

❑ ❑ ❑ ❑ ❑

4.30 p.m. and I take to my bicycle again, heading off to another temple festival – this one is at the base of Mandalay Hill. Ridiculously happy, a crazy tourist, calling out to people as I cycle past them, 'Mingala baa, mingala baa!'

When I arrive I put my bicycle in one of the bicycle 'car' parks and walk through streets full of people and past stalls selling food, drink, and shiny trinkets. An elephant walks by in search of her own parking spot.

I soon escape from the throng and make my way along a small, litter-bestrewn path that leads into the trees and up Mandalay Hill on the non-tourist route. I pass a communal washing well where ten people wash and I help a Burmese woman lift a pail of water onto her head, much to the amusement of a fellow pail carrier. A little further on the path leads to a wide awning that has been fixed to the side of one of the zedis. This a place where families cluster together with their belongings, like the denizens of caves, like the dwellers that might have existed in the corners and holes at the foot of medieval castles, living lives in darkness and shadows. Little fires for cooking, children playing, chickens scratching around in the perpetual dark. I can't see any faces, merely outlines that I know are looking at me and wondering why I am here.

At the top of the hill I take photos of the sun setting over Mandalay. I do not go any further, not tonight. It is almost dark. I will go about trying to conquer Mandalay Hill without paying fees another day.

I proceed down some steps but then a monk comes across to me, sits me cross-legged in front of a statue of Buddha with a row of candles burning in front of it, and begins to talk to me in Burmese about Buddhism. I do not understand why he does this.

It is completely dark and I am sitting in the flickering candle light of a temple on the side of Mandalay Hill. Me, the monk, and a forty-year-old lady who is reclining half asleep in a chair behind us. No one else. The monk continues talking to me in Burmese, I don't understand but he keeps talking anyway. When he finishes we meditate in silence for ten minutes, maybe more as the candles burn down. I sit with my eyes closed, head bowed, and although I try to relax I become more and more conscious of being bitten by mosquitoes. They bite my legs, my arms, my shoulders, my neck, even my ears. I start sweating and then break my position, swat at one of them, and return to sitting still. After a few more minutes we stop and the monk talks to me, again in Burmese. Something about breathing. Then he slaps the ground hard with his hand and says 'No!' He thrusts his chest forward and his shoulders back. Then he sucks in his stomach, sits rigidly upright, legs in the lotus position, puts one finger on his forehead and then points directly to the eyes of Buddha. *Thah ma taah.* Focus. Concentration. Power in his eyes, strength. He slaps an imaginary mosquito on his arm but almost before he has finished the gesture he slaps the ground again, 'No!' Chest, shoulders, stomach, strong, straight, finger on his forehead, points at Buddha, '*Tah ma taah!*' He lolls his head slightly to one side and closes his eyes. Slap! 'No!' Not head down. Not eyes closed, head straight up, no slapping mosquitoes, eyes focused, one thing, Buddha. Breathing is one sharp exhale through the nose then five further exhalations. Then, after this, breathing is relaxed.

In between his slapping and his strictness the monk smiles beautifully, effusively, and continues to talk and gesture with animation. Then his manner changes in an instant. *Tah ma taah.* He takes a candle and puts it out on the back of his hand. He takes five candles and puts them out on his tongue and then breaks into his smile again. He gives me the five candles and re-lights them. I don't want to try this. But no, he takes the candles and puts them in a row in front of the Buddha.

U Ti Law Ka is the monk's name. Maybe I led him astray by speaking to him in Burmese to start with. Maybe not. He speaks to me continuously in Burmese but watches closely to see if I understand. Sometimes I do.

We meditate a second time, sitting in a half-lotus position as the candles burn down. It is painful but I keep my body taut and try to focus on a single candle flame. To watch U Ti Law Ka meditate is to see, simultaneously, strength in both body and mind and also complete relaxation.

Finishing, we head down the steps to the base of Mandalay Hill and into Kyauktawgyi *Paya*. More meditation, this time in public and in the full-lotus position. As I meditate I lose visual focus. Sometimes everything except the face or even one eye of Buddha becomes a blur. Sometimes, by focusing completely on breathing and Buddha, I overcome the pain in my lower back, hips and ankles. But then, as soon as I think, 'Ahh, no pain,' or 'I'm doing it,' this breaks the singularity of thought and the pain comes back.

After a few minutes the discomfort is too great and I am almost crying in pain and frustration. My forehead and upturned palms are hot and sweaty. I try to move my legs into a more comfortable position but they are locked where they are. I break my position and use my hands to manually unhook my legs. U Ti Law Ka smiles at me, clasps my hand and thanks me. But still we are not finished.

We go into the foyer of the *paya*. U Ti Law Ka takes a candle, points to his forehead, points at Buddha and then puts the candle out on the back of his hand. He then re-lights the candle, points to my forehead, points at Buddha, takes the candle and puts it out on the back of my hand. The candle burns and a blister appears. U Ti Law Ka repeats his lesson, sucking in his breath and pointing again to my forehead and again to Buddha. *Tah ma taah*. Concentrate. Focus. He re-lights the candle, puts it out on my hand and it burns me again. But I understand what he means. There must be no tension in body or mind, no anticipation of the candle burning, not even of its being put out on the back of my hand. Thoughts must be completely focused on a single object and even the slightest consideration of pain must not enter the consciousness. More candles are stubbed out on the back of my hand and there is no burn and no blister.

Leaving the *paya* U Ti Law Ka keeps talking to me in Burmese. Now he is happy and smiling all the time. He gives me a gift, his monk's belt, and wraps a piece of yellow tape around my wrist. Then we part company.

Riding back to the hotel I feel very strange. Things seem other-worldly, almost unreal. It is after midnight and I must pack my bags. My wake-up call is in only a few hours time. A boat to Bhamo tomorrow. Everything feels like a dream.

❑ ❑ ❑ ❑ ❑

A note on Buddhism, Burma, and Daw Aung San Suu Kyi, from 'Arati, Unhappiness About Others' Well Being' by Pe Kan Kaung, *The New Light of Myanmar*, 7 May 1997.

> Myanmar Buddhists accept four cardinal virtues and practise them. Every Buddhist knows that the four virtues are 'metta', 'karuna', mudita', 'upekkha'. 'Metta' means loving kindness, 'karuna' compassion, 'mudita' sympathy for others' welfare and 'upkkha' indifference or freedom from sorrow, happiness, love and hatred under any situation.
>
> It is said 'dutto atthan nazanatti' (an angry person cannot see the effect) and at the same time it is also said 'dutto dhammam napassati' (an angry person cannot see the cause). Because of anger the person tends to commit various acts such as wronging persons whom he should not, breaching laws and committing sins verbally or mentally. Sympathetic people, on the other hand, should sympathize with

persons who are suffering from the hardships with the feeling that they are sharing the sufferings of the latter. It will not be enough for them just to say that there are people who are suffering and that they are truly wretched.

It cannot be over emphasized the delicate mentality of Myanmar people who adhere to and practise the four cardinal virtues.

Since she does not understand how to preserve the prestige of being Myanmar and Myanmar character or noble Myanmar mentality, the Oxford graduate, the one who has forsaken her people, the Bogadaw is drowning in the shallow water.

According to reports appearing these days, I have noticed that the United States of America has taken measures including economic sanctions based on one sided allegations.

The Bogadaw, who has forsaken her people and become a million-aire during her brief stay in Myanmar, hastily supported the measures taken by the American Government. In delight, she said that one sided action of the US was what she had expected for quite some time. She was overwhelmed by joy in telling foreign correspondents her satisfac-tion. She alleged again that those investing in Myanmar from outside were giving their support to injustice and unfairness.

No one can deny the fact that there is economic progress in Myanmar. It is obvious that the Bogadaw who has forsaken her people is jealous of the well being and rising standard of living of Myanmar people. To study her acts from a Buddhist point of view, it is seen that she is jealous of the progress of the people who have improved their positions. By doing so she is gaining demerit at her own expense. She cannot sleep or eat well because of unhappiness. She tends to be aggressive, utters inuendos and indulges in gossips. If the extent of jealousy becomes too great the person may vomit blood. Such a state of mentality is called 'arati' in literary terms. It means unhappiness about others well being. In Abhidhamma term, it is 'issa' or an evil tendency.

If we compare the difference between democratic practises of the West and the four cardinal Buddhist values in Myanmar and their ability to bring peace to the world, the truth is that Myanmar does not need to import the Western Democracy.

An afternote. In 1998 it was purported that the author of this article, Mr Pe Kan Kaun, was taken into detention at Insein Prison because it was alleged that he was a democracy sympathizer who was using his position to write pro-democracy articles. Such is the paranoia and the fragility of the Burmese military psyche.

chapter 3
The Boat to Bhamo

The journey to Bhamo, a fitting epilogue to my candle and hand burning experience of last night.

Four hours sleep. A wake-up knock on the door at 4.30 a.m. Downstairs with my bag. A taxi drive through the deserted streets of Mandalay, cold and dark in the hours before dawn. We stop near the river because of the build-up of cars, wagons, horses and trishaws that are ferrying people and cargo to the river bank. Beyond these, the boat. Three tiers of fluorescent lights that beam through the darkness. A procession of bodies file along a gangplank loading crates, sacks of rice and vegetables, wicker baskets, cardboard boxes and hessian bags. I join them, onto the boat, body to body, so many people, almost on top of each other with no room to move yet everyone moves. And beyond us, the darkness and the mists that are rising from the Irrawaddy.

I pick my way through the cargo and then through the people and up to the front of the boat. Five in the morning, still dark and still cold. I stand outside the ticket master's pokey, dimly-lit office – a small office, a small desk but with a big man sitting behind it. My taxi driver, an hotel employee, tries to negotiate the purchase of a ticket. The ticketmaster talks to him but then turns his back and listens to other appeals for places. The taxi driver and I stand waiting outside the office. Then I am told that there are no tickets left.

Further negotiations occur. An agreement is reached. A place becomes available on the second deck. The price, however, is US$9 for the boat fare and US$1 for the ticket master.

Up to the second deck to find my space. It is already occupied by an old lady. Down stairs again to the ticket master's office and then it is back upstairs to the space that will be mine for the next three days. It is an eye opener. White painted lines divide the floor of the second deck into two-metre by sixty-centimetre allotments. One of these allotments is my space. It's body to body, myself and sixty Burmese. I am lucky that my spot is on this deck and not the one below. There are a hundred people down there. Bribed third class is definitely more civilized than regular third class.

I lay down a sleeping mat, a blanket and then put my rucksack at the head of my space. A very old lady and two younger women watch me as I organize myself. In fact, almost everyone on the deck is staring at me.

The sun rises, yellow light bringing out the browns of the Irrawaddy River, the browns of the surrounding countryside, of the tree-cleared hills, of the stilted, wooden riverside shacks, of the sand islands that form in the centre of flood plains, and of the fisherman with their nets and boats. The Irrawaddy, one kilometre wide, sometimes two or more where it has flooded the flats. Sometimes, looking to the horizon, all that can be seen are expanses of its water. The Irrawaddy, a sluggish, sun-drenched, drowsy, flood plain of a river that cuts Burma in two, gathering water from the whole of the country north of Rangoon.

Ahead there is a silhouette of a woman on an island with a basket on her head. On another island there is a solitary house on stilts. Four barges pass and in the distance there is a splash of colour, a red Manchester United football shirt worn by someone in a dugout canoe.

Manchester United, more pervasive than the British Empire ever was.

❏ ❏ ❏ ❏ ❏

The upper reaches of the Irrawaddy are part of Kachin State, a state which extends to Burma's northernmost borders. It is a mountainous region flanked by India and China and boasting Burma's highest peak, Hkakabo Razi which stands at 5,889 metres. Myikyina is the largest town in the state. Almost 200 kilometres south is Bhamo, Kachin State's second largest town. It sits on the banks of the Irrawaddy at the foot of the hills that lead to China which is only 25 kilometres away.

❏ ❏ ❏ ❏ ❏

We move steadily upstream with the sun rising and a gentle breeze blowing, only the whirr of the engine and the sound of water slapping against the bow. There are hazy mountains in the distance. The mountains, 'What did you lose there?'

Payas dot the hills, too many to count. One is the spectacular Mingun *Paya*, ten kilometres up the river from Mandalay. King Bodawpaya had intended that this *paya* would be one of the most impressive in Burma. But the King died in 1819 and all that was completed was the fifty-metre-high, seventy-metre-wide base upon which the rounded *zedi* was to be built.

Mingun *Paya*, dusky red bricks, more shades of brown. A king's grandiose dream that proved to be grander than he.

I move to the back of the boat and sit and write my notes. As I do so people gather around to watch. I speak to them in Burmese but they do not answer. I try to encourage answers by answering my own questions on their behalf and this ultimately brings some responses. Many, however, are more comfortable staring.

A cabin door opens next to me, a head pops out, a guttural clearing of passages, then a spit overboard.

I take my copy of *War and Peace* and show the assembled crowd the picture on the front. It is a picture by a classic artist of the Russian winter with soldiers marching through it. They take it and pass it around, pointing and talking. Then I give them my Burmese guidebook which they

MAYMYO ↵

thumb through finding the pictures. I hear them exclaim, 'Ahhh! Pyin U May Mu Lwin' or 'Ahhh, Mandalay' as they recognize the locations that have been photographed. When they do not know I read them the caption and then they nod as acknowledgement of the place. I run through my Burmese vocabulary again, reading it directly from a list of sentences that I have compiled over the last few weeks. Now everything is more relaxed and the people around me laugh and smile and correct my mispronunciations. The best at this is a ten-year-old girl. She is often the first to understand what I am trying to say. She repeats my sentence with a smile on her face and then explains to the group the error of my ways. I hear them laughing and repeating the sentence, 'Ahhh, that is what he was trying to say, ahhh, *now mah tweh tcha meh.*'

I meet an Engineering student, Ko Thi Ha, who is travelling home to his family in Bhamo. He is currently studying English at a private language school in Rangoon while he waits for the universities to reopen. So far he has waited for three years to be able to resume his third year of study.

Two months later I visit Ko Thi Ha at the language school. It is located in a narrow building squeezed into downtown Rangoon. There are five floors in the building. The first is a shop with a staircase that leads up to the language school above. All subsequent floors are made up of one main room which is used as a classroom during teaching times but is otherwise a meeting and study area. There is only one office and it is occupied by the lady who runs the school. There are six other teachers and 120 students who attend part time classes in the morning, afternoon and evening depending on their other commitments. Many of these students, like Ko Thi Ha, were formerly at university and have had their studies interrupted by the current policy of the military regime. Small though it is, the school is well set up with an appropriately studious atmosphere. This said, it is far from an adequate substitute for a functioning university system.

❑ ❑ ❑ ❑ ❑

On the boat Ko Thi Ha introduces me to some other students. They are all travelling in first class cabins on the top deck and wonder why I am travelling third class. I explain that first class would cost me 18,500 kyat. They did not know this, and tell me that they are paying 1,500. Ko Thi Ha also tells me that there is a two-mile (three-kilometre) limit around Bhamo beyond which tourists are not permitted to go. He also informs me that when I arrive in Bhamo military intelligence will be watching me. 'Too many military intelligence, too many immigration, too many police in Bhamo,' he explains. The town is very close to the Chinese border and there is much illicit trade. Black market logging and opium smuggling are the biggest problems but there is a constant stream of all sorts of goods crossing the border.

As we continue talking, rice paddies and tiny settlements of two, three, five houses pass us by. There are mountains to the east. One of them reaches up into the clouds.

I leave the top deck. The crowd around me has grown too big and after three hours I feel the need to escape. This is easier said than done and as soon as I sit myself down in my spot on the second deck, a teashop owner from Bhamo comes across and begins to talk to me. He tells me that sometimes there are up to four or five tourists in Bhamo, but now there are none. He is a friendly man, a Muslim Bangladeshi born and bred in Burma.

Twelve o'clock and the boat pulls up at Kyauk Myaung, a small town with a pagoda, a gathering of shacks by the river, and a docked barge that serves as a jetty. People on both our boat and the barge squeeze and push along the adjacent sides of the respective vessels like two boarding parties about to engage one another. But rather than prepare with swords and fisticuffs, people instead brandish bunches of bananas, whisky, dried fish, bags of rice, cakes, and other goods necessary for an afternoon's boat ride. Trading takes place between hands that reach out to each other over the water as people cry out their pitches and their orders. A frenetic five minutes ensue. Then the whistle blows and the boat begins to pull away. Hands reach further and further across the water in last desperate trans-actions until people must throw things at each other in order to receive money or merchandise. We depart, continuing up river.

The little ten-year-old from this morning is called Ma Aye Hla. She follows me around with her smile and her pink-varnished thumbnails.

It is hot in the mid-afternoon when we arrive at the first narrowing of the Irrawaddy. The river narrows in three places as it winds its way down through Upper Burma and this is the first, the shores being only a few hundred metres apart. Being closer to the banks it is possible to see life along the river more distinctly. There are wooden huts in clearings set beside small beaches, water buffalo, chickens, fishermen, dense scrub and the hills behind. Often the hills have been logged, and felled trunks can be seen secured in the river waiting to be floated down to Mandalay. In some areas saplings have been replanted on the cleared land but in most cases the hills are left bald.

No cars, no roads, no bridges, no motorbikes, no electricity; only little clearings by the side of the river – a buffalo, a pig, a hut, a dugout boat, and the water-bound traffic that plies the river. The Irrawaddy, a lazy brown

river with its dusky banks and its dusky settlements; a lazy brown river
which eddies and boils up from the depths of somewhere.

The sun goes down and the river widens into a vast expanse of water.
A full moon rises over the countryside. From the light of the sun to the
light of the moon, two pictures of the same landscape.

The boat from Mandalay used to travel at night but two passenger
boats sank in quick succession. According to the passengers on this boat
many people drowned but in the newspapers there were no reports of
these events. Such news is considered subversive to national interests.
Now the boats don't travel at night.

The boat stops at Che Nye, an oversized river village. There is a sandy
foreshore beyond which is a long row of wooden buildings facing the
river. It is the Festival of Lights at the moment and each building has rows
of candles on its balconies, verandahs, along roof lines, and on window-
sills. Thousands of tiny candles along the shore. Fairyland. And at the end
of the row of buildings is the village pagoda. It too is lit up with tiny lights
and candles.

I go on shore with Het Moo and Het Oo, two of my neighbours on the
boat. These are different young men from the students, much poorer and
with limited education but big smiles. Het Moo is a toy salesman from
Mandalay who is taking a sack of cheap plastic toys to Bhamo to sell at a
festival. When we go on shore a friend stays behind to look after our
luggage. Now that we are docked it is important to be more protective of
belongings as people from the shore can wander on and off the boat as
they please.

Behind the foreshore houses are a deep-rutted dirt track and four or
five half-full teahouses. These are lit by oil lamps and candles and some
have diesel generators that chug along. But otherwise it is almost pitch
black. There is no central electricity in Che Nye.

The toy salesmen and I stop for tea and cake. Everyone stares. Why is
this white person here?

Down to the river bank and children rush after each other, wrestle and
hurl themselves off a ledge and onto the sand below. Other children,
smaller ones, run up behind me, touch me, and then run off. As their
confidence grows, they form a waist-high throng that follows me around.
In front of us is the boat with all of its deck lights on, a beaming carousel
in the stillness of the night. But it is not part of this scene, it is only
passing through.

Back on the board I talk to Daw Htar Yi, a woman who I had met briefly
during the afternoon. She is an ethnic Kachin from Bhamo but no longer
lives in Kachin State. Instead she teaches English and looks after orphans
in Taunggyi, Shan State. Sometimes she takes up to twenty orphans into

her house at once. She explains that money is a constant problem. As a high school English teacher her salary is 1,200 kyat per month, US$4. She admits that it is impossible to live on this amount and so English teachers must supplement their incomes. Many teachers give private tutoring lessons but these are often associated with the corruption that is rife in the education system. Tutored students are given higher grades which justifies continued extra tuition. But Daw Htar Yi does not give private classes. Instead she knits jumpers and then, during her holidays, she travels to Bhamo to sell them at the market and to friends. Her brother, also an English teacher, goes to the market every morning before school to sell slabs of pork fat. 'We do not make much money,' Daw Htar continues. 'To live, it is necessary to earn 10,000 kyat each month (US$36) but even the headmaster of our school only earns 1,600 kyat.'

Daw Htar Yi tells me that English teaching is a profession in which many Kachin people are employed. This is a legacy of the Christian missionaries who worked throughout Kachin State in the nineteenth and early twentieth centuries. Not only did they teach English but they also codified the Kachin language using the Roman alphabet. Daw Htar Yi illustrates this when she shows me her hymn and prayer book.

But life in Burma has not been easy for the Kachin people. As Daw Htat Yi's brother observes, 'We are not a democracy in Burma, we are not free people. The Kachin people hide in the hills. The Burmese army watch us because we are not Burmese. We are Kachin.'

After Ne Win's military coup in 1962, the Kachin people fought for secession – Burma under General Ne Win was not the Burma that Kachin leaders had agreed to be part of during the negotiations which had occurred in the lead up to Independence in 1947. The Kachin Army, which at times numbered up to 10,000 troops, received support from both the CIA and the Kuomintang. This, combined with the remoteness of the region with its mountains and jungles, saw this secessionist movement continue with some success for almost three decades. In the late 1980s and early 1990s, however, the Burmese military launched a number of large-scale offensives against the Kachin people and by 1993 the Kachin Independence Organization and the Kachin Independence Army were forced to sign a treaty with the military regime. But there are still many problems. 'This is not a country of equal rights,' says Daw Htar Yi.

As we sit, Daw Htar Yi tells her nephew to go and buy me a drink. When he returns she gives him a fan and he proceeds to sit and fan me while Daw Htar Yi continues, 'You will not be able to travel out of Bhamo,' echoing what I had heard from the students earlier in the day. I ask her about the next leg of my journey, from Bhamo to Lashio in Shan State. The journey is about 175 kilometres and both towns are open to tourists so I had presumed that travel between the two would be permitted. 'It is not possible,' states Daw Htar Yi, 'the army will not let you do this. They say that it is not safe for you to go.' But then she admits that perhaps I would be able to make the trip under a blanket in the back of her uncle's car. Then, before going to bed Daw Htar Yi makes an appeal. It won't be the first that I receive whilst travelling in Burma. 'Can you please help me', she asks. 'Please get my nephew and niece out of this country. They have finished school. They have passed their exams. They can work. Please help me to get them to Australia. They can go to college in Australia. They can do any work. I am a good Catholic. Please talk to the Catholic Church in your country. They will be able to help them. Please help. They have no future in Burma. This is not a good country.'

What can I say? Price, emigration laws out of Burma, immigration laws into Australia, they don't speak any English, they are not from a rich family. It is impossible. I respond that I think it is very difficult and that I do not think it is possible. 'I am a good Christian,' she says, 'Maybe God will help me. Please try to help me.'

❑ ❑ ❑ ❑ ❑

Everything leads to something and being on this boat, being surrounded at all times by these people, having them constantly so close to me, sometimes suffocatingly close, this is part of something. Western culture and the security that it lends is a very long way away.

I set up for the night, unravelling my sleeping bag. It is the laughing-stock of my neighbours. Every time they look at it they start laughing again. Then, despite my fatigue, I cannot sleep. The floor is undeniably steel, my space is undeniably no bigger than a half a metre wide, and there is undeniably a baby who indulges in regular nocturnal wailing fits.

❑ ❑ ❑ ❑ ❑

IN THE MIDDLE OF NOWHERE

To the military government of Burma: 'Backpackers and travellers would like to see your country. Why do you hide it from us? You say that it is for our own protection but I do not believe you. What are you hiding? What is so important to you that we should not see? What is the real reason that I am not allowed out of Bhamo township?'

❑ ❑ ❑ ❑ ❑

The first light that heralds the new day is purple. There are low-lying clouds and thick mists that make the dawn light weak. The sun tries to show itself above the horizon, pastel hues of orange radiating into a pale blue sky. It is a half-light, a soft beginning. To the east there is the bank of the river which can be seen clearly but from there each row of trees, each row of hills becomes more indistinct until physical existence fuses with the dawn mists – the hills become the mist and the mist becomes the hills.

The light becomes stronger, the yellows and oranges and reds of awakening, fantasy streaks through the sky. And the land becomes foggy green and foggy brown, smudged colours that are all variations of one colour, the colour of the earth rather than the colour of the sky.

The sun is briefly visible as it climbs above a mountain. Too early, too vivid, too harsh, and a cloud intervenes to mask its brightness. The sun burns from behind and the upper rim of the cloud becomes a strip of glowing white light, like an angelic halo. The cloud is saying to the sun, 'No, not yet. Let the land, let the river wake up slowly, gently, let the mists rise. There will be plenty of time for you to burn down later, but not now.'

It feels as if we are travelling to somewhere very far away, an outpost buried in the primitive wilderness. In one sense we will be days away from Mandalay but in another we are only travelling a few hundred kilometres. But in this instance, perhaps days are the better measure of distance.

❑ ❑ ❑ ❑ ❑

My second day on the boat. Long days in a relaxed, easy sense. Days which give me plenty of time to do the few things that there are to do – watch the banks go by, talk to people, and write about what I see and hear.

Early in the morning the top deck is cold and wet from the overnight dew. Ma Aye Hla, the ten-year-old interpreter from yesterday is playing with a Rubik's Cube-like puzzle. She is an unabashed, inquisitive, vivacious, little whirlwind who is likely to come charging up behind me and grab my hand and then follow me everywhere. 'Okay Ma Aye Hla, this time you stay there, I'm going to the toilet.' She stands and waits for me. Then, when I sit and clean or change my camera lenses, she holds on to the one that I am not using. And she particularly likes my books, flicking through them and looking very serious one moment and then laughing or smiling the next. Good company, this cheeky little ten-year-old.

Ma Aye Hla disembarks with her family half-way through the day at Ti Jaq Township. Like Che Nye and Kyawk Maung yesterday it is a very simple town with dirt roads, few cars, and no electricity. Colourfully-clothed throngs line the banks awaiting our arrival. Behind them there are the whitewashed walls of the *paya* with a procession of monks filing monk style, largest to smallest, in front of it. A row of horse and trap taxis queue up waiting for fares. On a mud flat there are people pulling carts from the water's edge. There are small boats. There are bigger boats. There are dugout boats. There are boats aground and there are boats afloat. A river township.

There is little evidence of development in these towns and villages, no contact with the West, no contact with tourists. Poor. The forces at work instigating change or progress are nominal.

Military officials board the boat as Ma Aye Hla waves goodbye to me from the shore. Then she coordinates the removal of her family's baggage. When this is done, she runs off to a group of friends who are waiting for her.

We pull out of the town and back into the river and its flood plains. There are fields covered in tall white-headed grasses that sway in the breeze. Sometimes there are desolate looking plains with thatch houses, solitary, isolated, in the middle of them.

Nearby a pig is groinking from a hut and I look to see what is going on. It is head to head with a chicken, arguing about grain distribution. A Burmese 'Babe' on the banks of the Irrawaddy.

❑ ❑ ❑ ❑ ❑

On board the boat there is a man with a video camera who has been filming our passage up the Irrawaddy. He is a Mandalay magazine journalist and documentary producer who has been travelling in a first class cabin with a senior military official from the town of Katha. I had noted his camera as he filmed. It is a Panasonic NTSC camera that films on to a videotape recorder. Big, bulky, and twenty years out of date. Something one would pick up in a pawnshop for fifty dollars and definitely not a camera with which one would make documentaries for national television. At least, not anywhere but in a country like Burma.

When we arrive at Katha the two leave the boat. The military official, overweight as many senior officials in Burma seem to be, disembarks in his white shirt and Ray Bans. He is followed by attendant soldiers who have come from the shore to carry his bags for him. This courtesy is not extended to the video man who follows behind carrying his own bags and equipment. It is a fitting image. In Burma, media representatives are little more than followers of their military masters. Everything that is written or produced in Burma's media is controlled by the military. The media is censored by the military, the media is the mouthpiece of the army, the media may as well be a military department. All news is good news and reflects the military regime in the best possible light. Articles in the newspapers, news reports on television, they are little more than listings of the day-to-day doings of Burma's armed forces.

The New Light of Myanmar, 17 November 1997. The front page boasts four articles which are extracted in full.

Secretary 1 receives ASEAN Secretary-General Dato Ajit Singh
Secretary 1 of the State Peace and Development Council Lieutenant General Khin Nyunt received Secretary General of South East Asian Nations Dato Ajit Singh at Dagon Yeiktha of the Ministry of Defence at 10 am today. Also present together with the Secretary 1 were Minister of Foreign Affairs U Ohn Gyaw, Minister for National Planning and Economic Development Brigadier General Abel and Director General Thura U Aung Htet of Protocol Department of the Ministry of Foreign Affairs.

Chinese Medical Delegation Arrives
A medical delegation led by Major General Li Chaolin of the People's Liberation Army of the People's Republic of China arrived here by air this morning. They were welcomed at Yangon International Airport by Deputy Director of Medical Services Colonel Aung Naing and Officials. Director of Medical Services Brigadier General Mya Thein Han met the medical delegation at Tatmadaw (army, airforce, navy) Guest House at 11 am. The delegation visited the Shweddagon Pagoda at 4 pm. Major-General Li Chaolin signed in the visitors book and donated cash towards the pagoda funds. Brigadier General Mya Thein Han hosted dinner in honour of Major General Li Chaolin and party at the People's Park Restaurant.

Foundation Laid for Construction of Hlawga Combined Cycle Plant
A foundation ceremony for construction of Hlawga Combined Cycle Plant of Myanmar Electric Power Enterprise of the Ministry of Electric Power was held at the project site this morning. It was attended by Deputy Prime Minister Vice Admiral Maung Maung Khin, Minister for Rail Transportation U Win Sein, Minister for Energy U Khin Maung Thein, Minister for Education U Pan Aung, Minister for Communications, Posts and Telegraphs U Soe Tha, Minister at the Office of the Chairman of the State Peace and Development Council Bigadier General Maung Maung, Ministers at the Office of the Prime Minister Brigadier General Lun Maung and U Than Shwe, Chairman of Yangon City Development Committee Mayor U Ko Lay, and officials of departments and Marubeni Corporation Japan. Minister U Khin Maung Thein spoke about the 100 mega-watt Combined Cycle Plant Project to generate 60 mega-watt. The General Manager of Marubeni Corporation Mr Murai also spoke. Vice Admiral Maung Maung Khin, ministers and officials laid the corner stones.

Deputy Prime Minister, Ministers Lay Cornerstone for Construction of Yadana Gas Planning Office Training School
A foundation ceremony for the construction of the Myanmar Offshore Yadana Gas Planning Office and Training School of Myanmar Oil and Gas Enterprise of the Ministry of Energy was held at the construction site near the Buddha's Tooth Relic Pagoda on Mayangon

Township this morning. Present also were member of the State Peace and Development Council Commander of Yangon Command Major General Kin Maung Than, Deputy Prime Minister Vice Admiral Maung Maung Khin, Minister for Rail Transportation U Win Sein, Minister for Energy U Khin Maung Thein, Minister for Education U Pan Aung, Minister for Communications, Posts and Telegraphs U Soe Tha, Minister at the Office of the Chairman of the State Peace and Development Council Bigadier General Maung Maung, Ministers at the Office of the Prime Minister Brigadier General Lun Maung and U Than Shwe, and Chairman of Yangon City Development Committee Mayor U Ko Lay.

Also on the front page, in clear, bold letters and taking up a quarter of the page are the stated objectives of the ruling military government. These appear every day.

Four Political Objectives
- Stability of the State, community peace and tranquility, prevalence of law and order.
- National reconsolidation.
- Emergence of a new enduring State Constitution.
- Building of a new modern developed nation in accord with the new State Constitution.

Four Economic Objectives
- Development of agriculture as the base and all-round development of other sectors of the economy as well.
- Proper evolution of the market-orientated economic system.
- Development of the economy inviting participation in terms of technical know-how and investments from sources inside the country and abroad.
- The initiative to shape the national economy must be kept in the hands of the State and the national peoples.

Four Social Objectives
- Uplift of national prestige and integrity and preservation and safeguarding of cultural heritage and national character.
- Uplift of the morale and morality of the entire nation.
- Uplift of dynamism of patriotic spirit.
- Uplift of health, fitness and education standards of the entire nation.

Every day the content and format of the Burmese daily newspapers is the same: lists of names of military figures being associated with progress in the areas for which the military government is universally condemned. Education, economic development, health, acceptance by the international community. The one that is missing from the front page on 17 November 1997 is the unsuccessful handling of Burma's burgeoning drug problem. These are the issues about which the military government is most sensitive. Read the front pages, however, and the active and ongoing involvement of the military in tackling these issues is clear for all to see.

Not too hard to see right through as far as I am concerned.

Behind the front pages are spreads and editorials equally predictable in their conent. Either they praise the progress of the military or they vilify and slander Daw Aung San Suu Kyi, the National League for Democracy, and those who support them. Typically, these articles are written in prosaic language and attempt to gain credibility through analogies with Buddhist or Burmese history, or by claiming to have been written by independent observers such as housewives, people in the street, or respected elders.

From: 'Adrift and Washed Ashore' by Po Yaygyan, *The New Light of Myanmar*, 11 May 1997.

If we look at the dispute for the child in the *Mahawthahta Jataka*, the ogre, in order to eat the child assumed the form of a human being and snatched the baby saying that it was her child. The real mother could not permit the child to be taken away by the ogre and thus a dispute arose between the two. The case was brought before Mahawthahta. When Mahawthahta perceived with wisdom, he knew which was the ogre and which was the real mother of the child. He then made them place the child in the middle and made the two of them struggle to get the child. The child being her food, the ogre could not let go and snatched the child with force without minding whether the child's limbs were torn apart or not. The real mother, not wanting the child to get hurt, relaxed her grip and let go of the child. At this, a decision was given that the one who spared the child from getting hurt was the real mother and the one who did not care whether the child died or not was the ogre.

The State does not want the people to be affected and suffer losses. As for the Bogadaw group (the NLD) they don't care for the people as long as they get things to eat and drink. History is like the wise Mahawthahta. History has decided today that the Bogadaw is the ogre.

Suu Kyi is a person who arrived to give trouble to Myanmar. In rivers and streams it is usual for rubbish, weeds and carcasses to be carried down by the current. With the tides some of them are washed ashore. This is known as adrift and washed ashore. Those who cross the river or stream lengthwise or breadthwise in boats and ships or by swimming, they do so with an aim. For those who get adrift and washed ashore they have no aim. They are in the habit of pushing the rubbish, weeds and carcasses ashore with bamboo poles into the water and the swift current usually carries them further down.

Suu Kyi is a person who has drifted aimlessly in the western countries. She accidentally drifted to Myanmar and was washed ashore during the period of the four eights. Now the people have come to see Suu Kyi as English Bogadaw, axe handle, power crazy dictator and CIA person. As Suu Kyi is not entitled to place Aung San in her name, so also is she not entitled to the name Suu which was taken from the name of Ahmay Suu, mother of Independence hero Bogyoke Aung San. After she got drifted and washed ashore in Myanmar the

Bogadaw, relying on the relatives of her husband to give various kinds
of trouble to Myanmar, is now looked upon by the people as a rubbish
dump and pile of weeds. No person would want rubbish, weeds and
decaying carcasses to accumulate on the shore near the respective
houses, villages and towns. If the swift current does not take them
along with it, then it is always the case with the people to use a long
bamboo pole (mask the nose with cloth) and push them from the
shore and set them adrift again.

Such articles as this evidence the ridiculous lengths to which the military
government goes to try to discredit the opposition. The vehemence of the
rhetoric and the outright stupidity of the tales reflect the military's own
perception of its tenuous grip on power. They also evidence the fear the
military has of the popularity of the opposition.

❏ ❏ ❏ ❏ ❏

The video man leaves the boat, loaded down with his bags, at the back of
the military entourage. In many ways I feel sorry for him. Meanwhile,
onshore, there is a military welcoming party of thirty people for the overweight military officer. I do not like this army turnout. It is repugnant and
reeks of people feeding off their own sense of self-importance.

As it transpires, Katha is to be our overnight stop and we arrive well
before dark. It is bigger than previous towns, a major river trading station
between the North and Mandalay. Its size may be measured by the fact
that, unlike Che Nye, it has three roads that are not dirt tracks, there are
some cars and trucks and electricity, although this is still only produced by
generator. In addition, Katha boasts a cinema. Well, a cinema of sorts.

Walking through Katha, I am invited to play *chin lon*, the game that
involves keeping a wicker ball in the air. As I play, someone comes up to
me and gives me a bunch of bananas. 'Present,' he says. Then someone
else gives me four large avocados. More presents. Then Ko Thi Ha and
Ko Tin Hlaing, the students from the boat, see me and ask if I will join
them at the local film house. Okay. We arrive. It costs four cents to enter.
The screen is small and housed in a dirt-floored wooden barn with rows of
benches for seating. Screening, in black and white, is Michael Jackson's
Thriller video from 1984. This is a preview, followed by the final of the
women's football from the South-East Asian Games, between the People's
Republic of Myanmar and Thailand. There are ninety people in the cinema, all men, all watching eagerly.

In the middle of nowhere, sitting in a barn with an enraptured audience
watching black and white coverage of a woman's football match.

The Burmese goalkeeper makes a save and the crowd cheers and claps
enthusiastically. A Thai woman is tripped and sprawls face forward on the

ground. The crowd laughs. Then there is a Burmese foray into the Thai forward line. Clapping and oooohing builds up as the Burmese winger dashes down the wing, looks towards the goal, crosses, and then a loud aaaahhhh and some commiseratory claps as the cross is missed. There is a missed bicycle kick from a Burmese defender. More laughter. Then there is a collision between two players. Still more laughter. And then a Burmese player kicks the ball into the face of a team-mate who crumples to the ground. This incident brings hoots of continuing laughter from all who are assembled. They do not care that it is a Burmese player being stretchered off, the farcical slapstick of the situation is side-splittingly funny as far as the audience is concerned and they laugh until play resumes.

By half-time Thailand is two goals to one up and eventually wins comfortably. In a way I am glad – a Burmese victory would only have made it into *The New Light of Myanmar* as an indication of the success of the military regime.

DO YOU LIKE THIS BOAT?

Awake before dawn as the decks of the boat become a hive of activity. People come and go on and off shore to buy their day's provisions. New passengers board, snack sellers wander the decks, and cargo loaded into the hold below. Last night the boat was half empty but now it is full again.

Under way, travelling further up the Irrawaddy. Occasionally on the banks there are trees that tower over other species in height and girth, magnificent trees. There are flat lands of the tall, elegant, shimmering and swaying grasses. There are the thatched huts and primitive villages. I take many photographs. All that I want are some that might capture the softness, the browns, the simplicity and the stillness.

❑ ❑ ❑ ❑ ❑

I know many people on the boat now and despite sometimes being overwhelmed by the constant attention there are many good mornings to be said when I wake up, many people with whom to smile. There are my neighbours, Het Oo and Het Moo, the young Bhamo toy stall salesmen. There is the old lady behind me who was in the original spot that I was given and the middle-aged lady with whom she is travelling. They are the ones who could not stop laughing at my sleeping bag. We don't talk. We haven't all trip. We just nod at each other, smile and sometimes laugh. There is Daw Htar Yi, the Kachin English teacher and there is the man of Bangladeshi heritage, a teashop owner in Bhamo whom I suspect would not stop talking to me all trip if I gave him the opportunity, head wobbling from side to side in caricatured Indian fashion. There is Ko Htin Hlaing the friendly round-faced maths student from Mandalay and there is Ko Thi Ha, the Engineering student and son of a Bhamo goldsmith, best English speaker on the boat and my go-between translator. He explains to people who I am, what I am thinking, where I come from, and what my work is. I now tell people that I work with computers. It is a safe thing to say. Then there is the old monk whom I cannot understand and a young monk who is perpetually fascinated by me. Maybe it's because of the monk's belt that I was given in Mandalay. Finally, there is the lady who sleeps directly behind me and my bag. We are virtually head-to-head. I have noticed that sometimes when I come back from the upper deck she has gone to sleep with her arm hooked around part of my bag to make sure that it is safe.

These are my friends on the boat.

There are mountains and jungles in the distance. My Bangladeshi friend tells me that there are elephants and tigers in the jungles. He also tells me that we will reach Bhamo today at three, four, perhaps five o'clock. He is not sure.

At 10.30 we reach the second narrowing of the Irrawaddy. The river is only 200 metres wide which means that it must be very deep. Cliffs drop down into the river and I imagine them continuing for hundreds of metres with their caves and crags and precipitous drop-offs all below the surface. And beside the cliffs there is dense, untouched jungle, a mass of intertwining vines and creepers and bamboo and leaves and palms and trees. I keep my eyes open for signs of movement, signs of life, but nothing makes itself apparent.

There are shacks in the jungle. Little structures in little clearings. There is a dirt road, still being made, only sometimes visible, that leads to a remote military outpost. Four small buildings, a flag, and 614 Engineers written in white stones on a lawn next to the gate. And even here, in the middle of the jungle, there are monuments to the Lord Buddha. There is a *paya* at the base of a cliff with no visible paths leading to it. Another is closer to the water and another is on top of a large boulder in the river. There are no people to be seen.

Passage through the narrowing does not take long, only an hour, but during this time the upper deck fills with people who pose to have their photos taken against the scenic backdrop.

A photographer comes over and talks to me. We had spoken two nights ago about camera equipment and now he asks me, 'Do you like this ship?' 'Yes,' I respond. He replies 'I do not like it. This ship is made in China.' He points to his *longii*, 'My *longii*, traditional Burmese dress, it is also made in China. And my shirt, made in Thailand. My camera, it is made in Japan. In Burma we do not make anything. This is very bad.' With that, he shakes his head and looks down at the deck. Then he asks, 'How much does your camera cost?' I undervalue it significantly and say US$300. He says that his cost him US$100. 'How much do you earn?' he continues. This is a common question in Burma and can be asked in order to gain a rough gauge of the status of a person, something like asking what ones profession is. To me, however, it is always a bit difficult and now it is particularly so because the photographer is asking me in the context of a conversation that touches on issues concerning the state of Burma's economy. It is a dangerous subject to broach in public.

The gentleman with whom I am talking is a professional photographer with his own laboratory and shop. He is twenty years my senior and he earns 30,000 kyat in two months. It is what I earn in two days but I do not tell him this. Instead I try to explain costs of living in Australia relative to costs of living in Burma. I write down the price of eggs, bread and housing but this does not work. In fact, I think that it only makes him believe us to be even richer in the West because of the prices that we pay for basic foodstuffs.

As we talk one thing becomes clear. What the poorest people in Australia call 'poor' is a long way removed from what 'poor' is in Burma. Poverty in Australia is relative and a measure of commodity possession. In Burma it is absolute.

❑ ❑ ❑ ❑ ❑

Burma – a professional photographer with his own lab earns US$50 per month. A teacher earns US$4 per month. A video producer, documentariest, and magazine writer films for national broadcast on a video camera that I would buy for a twelve-year-old child to play with. The roads are built by press gangs who break rocks with hammers, lay gravel and stones by hand, and then ladle boiling pitch from twenty-gallon (170 litre) drums that have been set up on bonfires by the roadside. Yet under British colonial rule Burma was one of the largest rice producers in the world. Furthermore, shortly after Independence, Burma had the strongest economy in South-East Asia. The foundation of this had been its abundance of natural resources and even today the gem mines are open, natural gas and oil fields are being developed, hotels are being built, and timber is being cut and sold. But the problem is this: Burma's wealth is no longer Burma's wealth. Instead it is wealth divided between international investors and the private bank accounts of the military élite.

An example: Burma's natural gas and oil reserves. As a result of thirty-eight years of military policy, Burma currently has neither the intellectual nor the physical means to utilize its abundant fuel resources. Instead it sells them to international concerns. A case in point is the US$1.2 billion Yadana pipeline. This pipeline is a joint venture – TOTAL of France owns 31.2 per cent, UNOCAL of America owns 28.3 per cent, the Thailand Petroleum Authority (PTT) owns 25.5 per cent and the State-owned Myanmar Oil and Gas Enterprise (MOGE) owns 15.0 per cent. The natural gas is extracted from production fields in Burmese territorial waters in the Andaman Sea and then transported through a pipeline directly out of the country and into an electrical power generation plant in Thailand. The product doesn't even touch Burma and the MOGE's 15 per cent interest is no more than a reflection of the fact that the natural product originally came from Burma.

And what of this fifteen per cent? Forty per cent of it is spent on an army and equipment that is used to keep the military government in power.

Like TOTAL, UNOCAL, and the PTT, British, Malaysian, Chinese and Japanese companies have entered into similar trade agreements in order to access oil and natural gas reserves. There are also agreements concerning other raw materials such as ruby and sapphire mines, timber, construction and development contracts. They all share similar characteristics.

Pay us the money and you can take it away. It is economic mismanagement such as this which threatens to permanently condemn Burma as one of the world's poorest countries.

And the personal aggrandizement and private bank accounts of the military élite? An example. International trade is channelled through companies run by the military, the most significant of which is the Union of Myanmar Economic Holdings Limited (UMEHL). This is the largest company in Burma and is 40 per cent owned by the Defence Ministry's Directorate of Defence Procurement. The remaining stock is privately owned by military officials, many of whom fill senior positions in the military government including positions in the Defence Ministry's Directorate of Defence Procurement. The military government then forces foreign companies wanting to invest in Burma to enter into partnership deals with UMEHL. An example of this was the dealings between UMEHL and Heineken of Holland. Wanting to build a brewery in Burma, Heineken was placed under pressure not to proceed with this venture. One area of criticism was its dealings with UMEHL. In a letter concerning Heineken's partnership with this company, the Manager of External Affairs and

Corporate Communication, Peter Van Westrhenen wrote:

> Our partner in Myanmar is the Union of Myanmar Economic Hold-
> ings Limited (UMEHL) which is controlled by the country's mili-
> tary regime... The only way for us to invest in Myanmar was through
> cooperation with the government-controlled company UMEHL. The
> military regime would accept no other agreement. Consequently,
> we were not at liberty to choose our partner.

Heineken withdrew from this partnership on 10 July 1996.

A further point of interest – UMEHL also manages the army, navy, and airforce pension funds and owns the Myawady Bank.

Burma, it is not in the asset creation business but the asset liquidation business. After the Chinese and the Thais and the Singaporeans and the Malaysians and the French and the British and everyone else have taken out their share of the profits there is barely enough to fill the pockets of the local generals and the colonels and the lieutenant-colonels and the brigadiers and the chief commanders and the commanders-in-chief.

And for the Burmese people, like the photographer? In 1996, after thirty-four years of military rule, the United Nations rated Burma, for-merly such a prosperous country, one of the ten least developed nations in the world.

❏ ❏ ❏ ❏ ❏

I have been talking with the photographer and Ko Thi Ha for an hour when a group of three men comes up to me and asks for my passport. Immigration, they declare and show me their papers, all written in Bur-mese. I do not have my passport and so go and retrieve it from the lower deck. By the time I return the people with whom I had been talking have disappeared. In fact the whole of the top deck is completely deserted except for the officials and myself. I hand my passport over. 'What is your father's name,' they ask. 'Where do you come from? Where are you go-ing? What is your job? Where did you stay in Mandalay?' They write the answers down. Then they start thumbing through my passport and taking notes. They tell me that I am not allowed out of Bhamo township and that I must stay at the Friendship Hotel.

When I next see Ko Thi Ha I ask him about this incident. 'The people that came to look at your passport, they were not from immigration. They are military intelligence and they have been told that you are on the boat and going to Bhamo. They are watching you. This is why everyone left the top deck. And the Friendship Hotel, it is owned by a Chinese opium dealer. Everyone knows. The owner, he is like this with the military,' and with that Ko Thi Ha, puts the fore fingers of each hand next to each other, so close that they touch. 'It is the same with many of the Chinese businesses in Bhamo.'

Arrival at Shwegu, another town on the Irrawaddy, and the decks once again become a trading place. Frantic, noisy – the noise of selling and competing with other sales people. Someone is using a rattle to attract attention. A loud, grating sound. A moment ago I had been asleep and dreaming but then this abrupt awakening.

There has been little peace on the boat and no privacy. If I am not being offered bananas and dried fish and cakes then people are taking their turn to come to talk to me. Eating, writing, going to bed, waking up, falling asleep, these things do not deter the procession from coming across and sitting on my mat and asking me what my name is and where I come from. The old lady next to me has borne witness and she nods in understanding when I catch her eye.

The gentleman who has occupied the spot directly to my right on the boat is a gruff-looking man, large and grumpy. He stands and stares at me from behind his sun-glasses and often is to be found sprawled asleep over both his own and my spot. He is always disgruntled if I ask him to move. Yesterday he had pointed at a boat passing on the other side of the river and wanted me to take a photo. I had not done so. Again he was unimpressed.

As it transpires, this neighbour is a low-ranking officer in the Burmese army and he changes into his uniform as we approach Bhamo township. I think, Mr Grumpy has probably had thirty years in the army, thirty years of propaganda, never risen above the few badges and bars on his uniform, never risen above sleeping on the deck in third class, never made it to the paunchy stomach and the first class cabins. Now he is wondering how this Western tourist, also in third class, sitting in the middle of sixty Burmese people and battling through some basics of the Burmese language, fits into the picture of anti-Western sentiment with which he has been inculcated. Perhaps this explains something of the way that he is and why he watches me so carefully. Perhaps it also explains why he wanted me to take the photo of the boat. He saw it as an indication of the progress being made in his country.

After three days next to each other Mr Grumpy, now in military uniform, gives me a banana leaf with sticky rice in it. I thank him. It is funny how things have worked out between us. No friendship; just acknowledgement.

Very different to Mr Grumpy is an important-looking man with whom I speak on the top deck. He is in his forties and is part of the overweight, neatly-dressed-and-wearing-Ray-Bans brigade. He tells me that he is travelling from Rangoon to visit Bhamo for the first time. He asks me what I will be doing in Bhamo. I mention my intentions of going directly to Lashio and he says that I should have no trouble with immigration in doing so. I do not pay a lot of attention to what he is saying on account of his not being from this region.

Late in the afternoon I see the dock at Bhamo in the distance. Behind are the mountains on the other side of which is China. It is quite a concept. China, just over there. The boat pulls up to the bank of the river and the milling throngs descend across a plank and onto the mud. I am amongst them.

On shore the Bhamo military is out in force to meet the Ray Bans man to whom I had been speaking on the top deck. One soldier holds an umbrella over his head to shade him whilst another takes his baggage and yet another opens a door for him to get into a car. I should have realized earlier that he was something to do with the military. It is not that they all dress in the same fashion, it is just that white shirts and blue *longiis* are common. It is not that they are all overweight, it is just that their stomachs more often than not paunch out over their *longiis*. It is not that they all wear Ray Bans, it's just that there is something about high-ranking military officialdom which necessitates their eyes not being seen. Nor is the give-away necessarily the fawning deference of the people who surround them, nor their sense of self-importance, nor their aura of power and untouchability. It is just that there is something about these people which makes them look as if they feel themselves to be innately superior.

I leave the boat and catch a horse and trap into town, arriving at Central Hotel. It is cheap, scrotty, and occupies the two floors above a shop opposite the Bhamo market. I check in and give my passport to the manager, Mr U Cho Wen. He takes down the details, confirms them with me, and then gives it back. I move my bags into my room. It is small, has three-millimetre plywood walls that separate me from the next room, and contains a bed, a mosquito net, a desk, and a fan that is dragged in from a room being used by a Burmese resident. As I unpack I hear Mr U Cho Wen spelling out my personal details over the phone to various people. Then, in the evening, Mr U Cho Wen tells me that immigration has come to talk to him. I am not allowed more than two miles out of town. Okay, I already know.

I ask where to eat and Sein Sein, a nearby restaurant, is recommended.

Choices on the menu include fried pork stomach, fried large intestine, fried small intestine, fried liver, fried tongue, pig's tongue salad, large and small intestine salad, hot and sour large or small intestines, fried chicken liver and fried gizzard. I opt for sweet and sour potatoes, rice, fried mixed vegetables and a beer. As I eat an elderly gentleman walks over to me, sits down, asks me who I am, where I come from, where I stay, and what my work is before excusing himself to go and watch the football. I meet this same man two days later and he tells me that he had thought that I was a spy from the British Consulate.

Coinciding with the end of the Festival of Lights is the *paya* festival of the main temple in Bhamo. As in Mandalay, it is like a fair but here it is a rural affair. The temple compound is full of stalls selling trinkets and plastic toys and cheap jewellery and food. Het Oo and Het Moo, the two toy salesmen from the boat, are there with their wares spread out on hessian sacks next to the entrance to the temple compound. Inside there is a small portable Ferris wheel with an attendant who swings around from seat to seat like a money-collecting gibbon as the wheel turns. There are food donations at the main *paya*, there are palm readers' tents and a photographer's tent which boasts a scenic canvas backdrop upon which trees, a river and a small waterfall and lake have been painted. Next door there is a nightclub – a temporary bamboo hall with a singer and a band. And there are many people; many, many people. They come up to me, say one word and then run off and talk with their friends. Some people touch me and run away, and some stare or laugh. Some people look at me and say, 'Very big.'

A young monk comes up to me, introduces himself, and invites me to his novitation ceremony, the ceremony in which he will go from being a novice to being a monk. It is in a village outside Bhamo, so immigration and the police will be a problem if I am to go. I ask the monk for a note, written in Burmese, explaining where I am going. Perhaps I will be able to give this to the police if they question me about my activities.

Back in my hotel room, I wonder why I am here. Is it so that I can say that I have been where most people do not go? That's part of it. Is it to prove something to myself? That also is part of it. Is it because I like to go somewhere and see what I can see? Is it in search of adventure? Again, these are a part of it. But now that I am here I am not quite so sure about it all. I am staying in a dingy hotel, the mountains are off limits, I'm not allowed out of town, I can't go to Lashio, and there are no other travellers around. So I think to myself, why am I here?

As I go to sleep, music from the festival resounds through the still night air. They are playing a Burmese dubbed version of a dance song by Sweden's Ace of Bass.

chapter 4

The President
of North
and South
America
is ...

Northern Burma

NORTHERN BURMA, NORTHERN EXPOSURE

Bhamo at six o'clock in the morning. Cold. People cycle along the main street towards the market next to Central Hotel. Teashops begin serving sweet carnation milk tea to their first customers of the morning, fires burn under charcoaled steel plates with *chappatis* toasting on top. In the *paya*, trustees and employees clean up after last night's festivities, and amongst the eucalyptus trees children run around in woollen hats. Near the eastern limits of town, on the golf course, a man practises his putting. Each ball he hits leaves a streak across the green as it flicks up dew in its wake. Further to the east, a vivid orange light emanates from behind the mountains that form the border with China.

Bhamo is not a big town. One side to the other is a forty-minute walk.

At one of the teashops a rugged-up three-year-old Eric Cantona boots a miniature football between table leg goalposts. A woolly ball playing football. I stop for breakfast and soon after, Ko Thi Ha, the student from the boat, joins me. I am pleased to see him. We talk and he tells me that the people who asked for my passport yesterday were military intelligence. There was also someone listening to our conversations and a man had followed Ko Thi Ha into his cabin and asked why we had been talking about the Golden Triangle. 'We were talking about the Golden Dragon Hotel,' Ko Thi Ha had explained. Now, reiterating the sentiments of the other students on the boat, Ko Thi Ha says, 'In Bhamo there are too many people from intelligence, too many military, too many police. There are many problems.' I think, 'Yes, maybe there are many police and military in Bhamo but are they here to cut down on opium trading and illegal transportation of goods over the border or are they here to ensure that these trades are not disrupted?' Who knows?

The topic changes to something more light-hearted. With a smile on his face, Ko Thi Ha asks if I slept with a Burmese girl last night. 'No,' I reply. Then he explains that he thought that I was staying at Central Hotel because it doubles as the Bhamo brothel. I had wanted to stay there rather than the Friendship Hotel because I wanted a Burmese girl, or so he thought. I reassure him that this was not the case but still he smiles at me with a look of mischief in his eyes. He smiles even more when I tell him that I will be spending the morning with a Chinese/Burmese woman and her family. Clearly he is not convinced as to my moral fortitude.

❑   ❑   ❑   ❑   ❑

'I am very angry with you because you did not come to see me last night. I think you do not like me,' complains Nyein Thu when I arrive at her house. I had been introduced to her by Mr U Cho Wen (the hotel owner) the night before and I had said that I might come to her house to meet her family. However, I had been too tired and had gone to bed instead. 'I waited up for you. Why did you not come?' I try to explain as I am ushered into the living room and offered a seat but the explanation falls on deaf ears. 'My house is always welcome to you. You can come here any time,' continues Nyein Thu. Then a string of questions follow. 'How long will you be in Bhamo? Do you think my sister is beautiful? Do you think that I am beautiful? Will you come and see me tomorrow? What are you doing tonight?' 'I might go to see my friend Ko Thi Ha.' 'We can go together.'

The walls in the living room are covered with family photos. One person who figures prominently is Nyein Thu's grandfather, a handsome, dark-browed man in military uniform. 'He was a senior Chinese military officer,' says Nyein Thu. 'An officer in the Kuomintang. Do you know the Kuomintang?'

Yes, I know a little about the Kuomintang (KMT) and later I learn more. The KMT retreated from China into northern Burma in 1948. Whilst in this territory they were supported in their fight against the Communists of China by Taiwan, the United States and the CIA. At the same time as they enjoyed this support, so too were the KMT heavily involved in the opium trade of north-eastern Burma. During the 1950s and 60s they fought against both the Chinese and the Burmese leadership and in the early 1970s they joined forces with the secessionist Kachin Independence Army. After the Vietnam War, however, the KMT lost their support from America and began to lose their grip on the drug trade. By the early 1980s the KMT had been all but completely wiped out, not by the Burmese military but by their rivals in the opium trade, the Shan drug lords.

The Kuomintang, an army with a history of involvement in the drug trade in Burma.

As I look at the photos, Nyein Thu asks if I am hungry and thirsty and then goes off into the kitchen to bring me refreshments. A cheeky little sister comes bouncing up to Nyein Thu singing, 'I love you, I love you.' When I finish my drink, Nyein Thu pours me another and then another. 'I would like to come to Australia,' she says, 'I have family in Australia. My uncle is a doctor. Is it hard to get work?' 'Yes,' I answer, 'It is hard to find work. You should use your family contacts.' Then Nyein Thu says, 'Can I work for you in Australia? You can be my family.'

No, no, no, I cannot and I can see what you are doing and none of this is going to work. Please stop running around after me, I'm fine for snacks, I'm fine for tea, and I'm...

'When will you see me again? Will you give me a gift when you leave?

What will you give me? Will you write to me at Christmas?' 'Yes.' 'I don't believe you. How much did you earn last year? Do you want to see around the house?'

Nyein Thu's house is a large, double-storey, stone, Chinese-style house with two courtyards, one used for cooking and another used for washing. Around these are many rooms including a schoolroom with tables and a blackboard. Written on one of these are the sayings, 'The world is a comedy to those who think, a tragedy to those who feel' and 'Hope for the best and prepare for the worst.' Upstairs there are bedrooms for grandparents, uncles, cousins, brothers and sisters.

I am invited to stay for lunch. Thank you. There is a large spread of food on the table, eight different platters of very good food. Fish, vegetables, chicken, beef, pork. I am given the seat of honour beside the father. He serves me my dinner, he peels my grapefruit for me, he pours my drinks. Meanwhile Nyein Thu asks me, 'Is my mother a good cook? Is she better than at Sein Sein Restaurant? Could she be a cook in Australia? I can cook like my mother.' Then little sister runs in again, 'I love you, I love you,' she sings. Mother watches me from the other side of the table with Mother-in-Law eyes. Nyein Thu's father oversees her progress. Out of interest I ask what his job is. Nyein Thu says that he used to work in shipping but for the last six years she does not know. Hmmm. He is clearly a wealthy man with a big house, fifteen relatives living here, three outdoor toilets, all sorts of rooms, but no apparent job. Suppositions and circumstantial evidence: the Kuomintang were heavily involved in the drug trade in this part of Burma, grandfather was a senior Kuomintang officer, father is wealthy but has no distinguishable trade in a town known for its wealthy Chinese opium traders.

I depart after lunch. Nyein Thu sees me to the door and as I walk away from the house I smile at images of myself as the next drug lord of Bhamo.

Now this is the way things are. I have chosen to come to Burma, I have chosen to come to Bhamo, I know that there are restrictions on tourists, I know these things and have made the choices that I have made. Certainly there are some things about which I have not known – the two-mile limit around the town and the inability to travel directly from Bhamo to Lashio. So be it, but in the last twenty-four hours I have had to relinquish my passport three times. I have been confronted by two people who claimed to be from immigration but were not, I have given my personal details to the hotel manager and on a number of occasions have overheard him spelling these out over the phone.

Upon returning from Nyein Thu's house I overhear Mr U Cho Wen giving my details to someone else, in person this time. It is an elderly gentleman from immigration who wants my passport. I give it to him. He takes down the details. He asks me where I live, how old I am, what my job is, where I am going to go, and what did I do this morning?

A few minutes later and again my name is being spelt out over the phone. Ten minutes pass and there is a knock on my door. Someone else has come to look at my passport. I give it to Mr U Cho Wen although I am totally unimpressed by this succession of people to whom information about me is being given. When he returns I tell him, 'I am a good person. I come to your country and I am treated like a criminal. I am always asked questions. Always people make notes about me. No good, *makauw boo!*' The people at the hotel look at me strangely. All they see is a string of military and immigration personnel asking after me.

The manager has kind eyes and as I let my sentiments be heard he offers me a seat. When I have finished he looks down at the table and shakes his head. 'The Government,' he sighs sadly. Even so, I do not trust him.

Travelling in Burma: from the moment that you step through customs in Rangoon a neck brace is locked on to you, on to everyone, backpacker, first-class traveller, it doesn't matter, and this neck brace allows you to look in only one direction. You see many beautiful sights and encounter many delightful people but this does not alter the fact that you cannot turn your head freely and the more that you try to do so, the further afield that you try to travel, the tighter the brace becomes. So it is fine to travel to Burma if you like to follow the path which has been clearly defined by the military government – Mandalay, Rangoon, Lake Inle, Pagan. But if you go elsewhere, to the towns which have only recently been opened, your freedom will be restricted and when you arrive you and your movement will be closely monitored. There are too many things in Burma that you are not allowed to see, too many things that the military wants to hide from you.

Back in my room I worry about being caught with the notes that I am making about Burma. I do not think the military would appreciate their contents and I have already written over one hundred pages. I take these and tuck them away into a discreet part of my camera bag. Better hidden there than nowhere.

❏ ❏ ❏ ❏ ❏

Bhamo in the late afternoon as the sun begins to set. The streets are quiet, easy-paced and peaceful. Simple sights and simple pleasures. Antiquated, rustic, charismatic. Little dirt lanes lead off into the fields. Towering trees are home to hundreds of birds and home also to ferns that grow like mistletoe in every fork of every major bough. Young men play football in High School Number Two and they call me over to join them. On another football field, the Bhamo sports stadium, the grazing cows are up six goals to two over the snoozing water buffalo with an attentive audience of chickens pecking and scratching in the grandstand. I run into a member of the military who recognizes me from the boat. He stops his bicycle and we exchange civilities. Further on a gentleman calls out to me, a smiley man who is holding his young daughter. He invites me for dinner but I say no so he invites me for breakfast instead. He offers me the use of his bicycle to cycle around Bhamo if I want to. Thank you.

Further on and I meet Ko Thi Ha again. I tell him about my experiences – the good, the bad and the intrusive. He laughs about Nyein Thu and shakes his head when I tell him about the constant questioning. It is good to be able to talk with him. He is my first Burmese friend and right now I am not sure that he can understand how important that is to me. Today's questioning has been quite affronting.

□ □ □ □ □

Central Hotel, the hotel in which I am staying, has character, noisy character. There is the resident prostitute, a tiny girl, and an assortment of layabout Burmese patrons who loiter on the second floor. It is the communal meeting area. Noisy. In my room plywood walls separate me from the radio next door. At the top of the walls there is a thirty-centimetre piece of wire mesh that extends to the ceiling. The floors are wooden. More noise. Then there is the television set in the hall next to my room. The volume is always on high and the TV stays on until the hotel's generator goes off at 10 p.m.

The bathrooms, four of them, have a pervasive moldy, mildewy, slippery character although each one also has its own individual traits. There is the mosquito hole, dark, small, and with a dirty green window which does not open and against which a squadron of mosquitoes are always bumping and bouncing trying to get out. There is the throne room in which to go to the toilet one must ascend three steps and then, from there, it is possible to look through a little window at the people in the corridor and so too can they look straight in at you. Then there is the dungeon. It has no windows and nor does it have a light. Always a dark experience. And finally there is the luxury suite so named because it is spacious enough to wash and go to the toilet without having to touch the walls.

Central Hotel. Mould, grime, noise, prostitutes, Burmese larrikins, and the ever-grinning Mr U Cho Wen. Yes, character.

OUT OF BOUNDS

Arriving for breakfast at the house of the smiley man who had yesterday offered me his bicycle, I find an assortment of children assembled in the front room. They are aged from four to ten and sit on the floor behind makeshift desks while a school holiday class takes place. Those in the front rows have their heads tilted at obtuse angles as they copy English words into their workbooks. Meanwhile, in the back row, two boys roll a ball to each other under a table whilst their pencils lie idle. When Ko Lay Nyo, the smiley man who is also the father of one of the boys, enters the room the ball is hastily hidden and the students resume work.

The class is being taught by Ko Lay Nyo's mother-in-law, one of many English teachers in the family. Both Ko Lay Nyo's wife and sister are also English teachers and an uncle is a high school teacher. As we eat breakfast Ko Lay Nyo asks me what my work is. Computers, I say. Then I ask what his work is, expecting him to say teacher by association with his family or immigration or soldier because he lives in a part of Bhamo in which many military officials live. But no, he studied Biology at university and now works in Mandalay as a middleman in business dealings, introducing jade buyers to jade sellers. It is not such a good job, he says, and he does not earn much money. As a consequence his wife and two children live in Bhamo in this house, the house of her parents, while he works in Mandalay. When he makes some money he comes back to Bhamo to be with his family.

As we continue to talk and eat, Ko Lay Nyo reminisces about his times at Mandalay University when he used to go on field trips into the forests doing research and collecting data. 'But now there is no work for biologists in Burma,' sighs Ko Lay Nyo regretfully.

❑ ❑ ❑ ❑ ❑

Ko Lay Nyo, a member of the Burmese professional middle class. What professional middle class? A student goes to school, studies, and gains entrance to university either because he or she succeeds academically or because his or her family is sufficiently well connected or wealthy to pay the relevant bribes. What then? The student studies and obtains a degree. Obtains a degree, that is, if the schools and universities remain open for a sufficiently long period of time for the student to achieve this improbable feat. And what then? Nothing. This is where the professional middle class road in Burma becomes a cul-de-sac and students must do an about-face and return from whence they came. Ko Lay Nyo tells me stories of his field trips but now he ekes out a living from commissions obtained in the jade industry. Ko Thi Ha from the boat was at university studying Engineering, but even if he has the opportunity to finish his degree he will work as a goldsmith in his family business. Wai Lin who took me to the University in Rangoon has a degree in chemistry but earns an income by asking for money from tourists and from the small percentages that he receives changing tourist dollars on the black market. Hotel receptionists with university degrees, trishaw drivers with university degrees, tourist touts with university degrees. Simply, there are no jobs for university graduates in Burma. This is because there is almost no local industry, there is no research and development, and there is little priority given to graduates by the members of a military regime which is made up largely of uneducated people. In short, there is currently almost no role for a professional middle class in Burma.

Nonetheless, despite this vacuum, in *The New Light of Myanmar* graduates are nonetheless advised on the steps that they should take in order to obtain a position.

From: 'Enhancement of Calibre Perspective,' *The New Light of Myanmar*, 16 November 1997.

> In the many advertisements for job vacancies to be filled by local staff, there are stipulations for good calibre or high calibre qualifications.
> There is keen competition for any and all such vacancies, with degree holders with extra assets such as proficiency in more languages, being computer friendly and good public relations vying for good positions, pay and other prospects. It is not only academic qualifications that counts, for those seeking good jobs must possess good local as well as general knowledge.
> At this juncture it is necessary to point out that anyone going for any personal interview must be adequately prepared to face the interviewers. In addition to knowing one's own subject well, the interviewee must have read up a good deal on allied subjects and on national, regional and international affairs. It is therefore important that more of the new generation of academically or technologically qualified young men and women strive harder to enhance their calibre in order to fit into deserving positions.

❏ ❏ ❏ ❏ ❏

After breakfast Ko Lay Nyo lends me his bicycle which has been especially repaired on my behalf. His father-in-law, U Thaung Aye, has been doing the work. He is a tall, slender man in his 60s; fit looking, respectable, and a senior civilian official in Bhamo. The two both offer to show me around the town. 'Thank you but no thank you, I would like to explore by myself.'

On the bicycle, I take the first dirt track that heads south along the

Irrawaddy. I think, 'I would like to see the countryside and surely not every road out of town can be patrolled by officials.' The road soon becomes a footpath along the top of a grassed levy bank with occasional trees growing beside it.

As I cycle, the older people that I pass smile at me. I 'mingala baa' them which broadens their smiles even more. But the young children stare in bewildered awe. Apparently only four tourists have visited Bhamo in the last three months. Add to this the facts that the town has only been open to tourists since 1996 and that there has always been a two-mile restriction on movement and one can conclude that some of these children would have never seen such a strange apparition of a human before. One of them who is working in a vegetable garden drops his hoe and runs away when he sees me.

The countryside is beautiful. Open fields and small vegetable plots dotted with houses, ploughs, cows, water buffalo and carts. Labour is manual, simple and hard. And the people who I pass... I am loath to call them peasants because the word has derogatory connotations. However, if these connotations could be removed and replaced with gentler overtones then these are indeed peasants; workers from the fields, rural villagers, very simple folk. Ploughing and hoeing and digging and cutting and driving buffalo. Simplicity and beauty and serenity. There is a sense of balance, harmony, peace and order which a city can never have.

I pass people asleep on sheltered platforms which have been erected in the fields for this very reason, to offer shade when workers eat or rest. I pass people washing in the river. I pass more staring children. In a thicket of trees I stumble upon an overgrown graveyard with only a few tombstones. The sunlight through the branches casts a lost-world, light on the headstones. I pass a village but skirt around it thinking that every village has at least one official or informer who will report back to Bhamo immigration if a white person is seen out of bounds. Even innocent words of mouth, passed from one farmer or from one child to the next could lead to problems. I am the only white person in Bhamo so it's not as if there would be any trouble identifying me. In another village, one that I cannot avoid, pigs and dogs and chickens groink and bark and squawk at me. Even they recognize me as an alien.

Before completing my bicycle ride I stop to see Daw Htar Yi, the Kachin woman that I had met on the boat, and her brother who are living on the outskirts of Bhamo. As we talk and drink tea a nephew climbs the stairs into the house and enters. He is a young man in military uniform, a soldier from Bhamo. I am immediately wary but there is no problem. He bows politely, we shake hands, and Daw Htar Yi and her brother continue talking. Daw Htar Yi asks me what I have done in Bhamo and I tell her about my bicycle ride into the country. She warns me that the military and immigration will be checking up on my movements. 'You are a danger to the government,' she exclaims. 'They will find out about your ride.'

Despite this warning, I manage to complete my ride without apparent incident. I do not come across any military checkpoints and no one pulls me over except a soldier from the boat. 'Hello, how are you?' he asks before continuing to cycle on his way.

Returning to my hotel I look at the view from my hotel window. It is over the Irrawaddy, the trees that line it, the Bhamo market, the sunset and the big, red, bold-lettered sign 'People's Desire, Crush and Destroy Internal Stooges and External Influences'. Soothing. As I look, Mr U Cho Wen knocks on my door. Immigration again, I think. But no, I had left my jewellery in the bathroom this morning and he is returning it to me. Thank you very much. My mistrust of him dissolves immediately.

Later in the afternoon the elderly immigration man does indeed come to my hotel room. I am concerned that maybe he has found out about my trip this morning. He asks me where I have been. I am evasive. Around. He asks me from whom I got the bicycle. Friends, I reply. Who? Friends. But as he continues to ask questions it becomes clear that he doesn't know what I have been doing. A frail-looking man, he is not unfriendly in his questioning. He asks me where I am going tonight. To the festival, I answer. Then I change the topic and ask about going to the initiation ceremony of the monk. He tells me that I will have to go and speak to the head of Bhamo Immigration. I show him the note written by the monk. 'You write this?' asks a young sidekick of the official. 'No, a monk wrote it. Look, here is his name.' 'You write this?' he asks again. 'No, I can't write Burmese.' But the sidekick doesn't believe me.

❏ ❏ ❏ ❏ ❏

7.30 p.m. The main street of Bhamo is dark and almost deserted but for five cows parked in front of the hotel. Three-quarters of an hour later and they are still there, no owner in sight. He's probably at the festival. My hotel room light is flickering with the pulses of the generator as I write my notes. There is no electricity grid in Bhamo and it is the second largest town in Kachin State. But next year Bhamo hopes to be on a central power grid.

I go to the *paya* festival and within ten minutes a large, middle-aged Burmese man attaches himself to me. I tell him that I do not want his company. I do not trust him. He looks too old and fat to be a regular inquisitive tag-along. 'I will come with you,' he persists and I repeat, thank you but no. Nonetheless he does not leave me alone. Trying to get rid of him I go into one of the pagodas and kneel before the Buddha statue. Even in this he does not leave me alone but kneels beside me. I begin to meditate but I am thinking about this man who is following me. Why? What will I do about it? I am also thinking about the drunken young men that are standing at the doorway to the shrine and shouting out 'Hey you, mister, fuck you.' They are showing off their knowledge of English.

As I sit, I resolve to confront my tagger directly. However, when I go to talk to him he asks, 'You think that I am from military intelligence?' 'Yes,' I say but very soon after I realize that I have been wrong and that this is perhaps the worst insult that I could have levelled at him. He is deeply offended. I try to convey my apologies but end up feeling embarrassed at the lengths to which he goes to explain himself. 'I am a logging merchant from Mandalay,' he explains. 'I am in Bhamo on business. I am very sorry if you think that I am from the military. I am not. I am very sorry. Please can I buy you a drink.'

As we drink, the man is subdued, often thoughtful. He knows exactly why I didn't trust him, fear for my own personal security, fear of the military just as is experienced every day by the Burmese. This is the way in this country; in Burma it is hard to know whom to trust.

The man tells me about his brother who lives in Toowoomba, Queensland, Australia. He says that he would like to go but cannot. It is too expensive. He says that his brother will never come back to Burma. He looks sad, far away, when he says this. Poor man, I think.

There are two men in T-shirts, jeans, and black vinyl leather jackets sitting at the table beside us. They've obviously been watching too many police films but I think they like being so easily identified. It's a power thing. 'Military intelligence,' observes my host. 'They are following you. They are watching you. Tomorrow they will ask me about you. They will ask me what we were talking about.' 'Are you worried?' I ask. 'No,' he replies and then he nods to them in acknowledgment of their presence.

BY WORD OF MOUTH

For the second day in succession I venture beyond the two-mile limit. Today the journey is some twenty kilometres to the monastery at Namma Tu where Chin Nanda Malar will become a monk. Once again I make this journey by bicycle although this time Ko Lay Nyo and his father-in-law, U Thaung Aye, accompany me as guides. Upon asking them where the monastery was they had insisted on cycling with me so as to keep me out of trouble. 'Please, cycle eight furlongs behind us,' Ko Lay Nyo had asked when we departed.

Cycling north of Bhamo we pass two tree-lined lakes with mists rising off them. Houses on the water's edge lean over at precarious angles and one looks as if it is about to fall in. A small bridge spans the neck of water that joins the lakes, and villagers make their way across this and into town. On the bank a man is fishing with a net. On each cast he catches something; maybe one, two, or three small fish and an occasional hand-sized, freshwater prawn.

Near the lakes are the Bhamo military barracks and soldiers are evident everywhere. Not far on two prisoners are being marched along the side of the road by a soldier with a semi-automatic weapon. The prisoners are wearing white sack-cloth clothing and are chained together by leg-irons. They look like nineteenth century convicts, walking with small steps and a shuffling gait. The military presence concerns me, but later Ko Lay Nyo explains that by taking the route along the side of the military compound, checkpoints out of the town are avoided.

Further on we pass a young girl hopscotching with her sister strapped to her back. Meanwhile, a father teaches his son to walk by walking slowly backwards himself while dragging two parallel pieces of bamboo, one in each hand. The son stands between these and uses them as two moving rails as he totters forward. And in a nearby paya a man leads three horses through the compound, past the giant lion statues, past a pond full of flowers and lilies, and past the old teak part of the temple. Off in the distance children are playing in the fields and a kilometre away a little Chinese lawnmower tractor is chugging along. Every now and again there is a 'Ha!' as a farmer redirects his water buffalo.

We continue, twisting and turning our way along dirt tracks and through villages and after an hour we reach Namma Tu monastery. It is perched on a balding hill and boasts a number of quite unattractive buildings with wooden frames and flat, shiny, corrugated iron roofs. There is a lake to one side and in the background are the mountains and China.

Cycling up to the monastery I think that perhaps Chin Nanda Malar had extended his invitation to me without any real expectation that I would accept it. Perhaps arriving in Namma Tu will be a bit like arriving at a party where everyone knows that I am not part of 'the crowd' and they will all wonder why I am there. But such concerns are unfounded and Chin Nanda Malar comes straight up to me with a broad smile. He is a soft-eyed, polite, quietly-spoken young monk. Two nights ago at the festival he had been wearing jeans, a shirt and a baseball cap but today he is clad in the orange robes of a monk. 'I did not think that you would be here,' he exclaims. 'Thank you very much for coming,' and with that he takes Ko Lay Nyo, U Thaung Aye and myself to meet his teachers and the other senior monks of the monastery. These people then offer us breakfast, morning tea, lunch, and then more lunch. Green tealeaf salad, shredded cabbage salad, wobbly gelatinous pork fat curry. 'Please, don't be embarrassed to eat more,' the monks keep saying.

As we eat, arrangements for my departure in the afternoon are discussed. Entering in to these discussions are all of the senior people present at the monastery – monks, a former military officer who is now an official in Bhamo, a university graduate, a school teacher, and a dignitary from Mandalay who is present as a special guest. Some of these people do not know that it is illegal for me to be here. Once it is explained to them their concern is obvious. A monk offers to drive me back to Bhamo in a car but this will put him at too much risk. The Mandalay official offers to drive me back under a blanket but this idea is also dismissed. In the end it is decided that U Thaung Aye and Ko Lay Nyo will depart and return for me in the late afternoon with a motorbike. Then, says Ko Lay Nyo, we will return to Bhamo under the cover of darkness. 'My father-in-law is very worried for you,' he says.

As I sit and listen to these people I think about why the military places such restrictions on the movement of tourists through Burma. Over three-quarters of the country, after all, is officially out of bounds. The obvious reason for this is that outside Bhamo, Lashio, Putao, Myikyina, and Keng Tung there are things to which the military do not want tourists exposed. They do not want them to see evidence of the black market, the opium fields, or the oppression of the ethnic minorities. But here, now, in Namma Tu monastery another reason occurs to me. These people treat me with such a measure of generosity and hospitality but they do not know that I am not allowed to leave Bhamo township. Nor do they know that in Thailand or my own country I am allowed to travel freely. But as we share food and tea they ask me about these things and they ask me about the world from which I come. They want to hear about what I do, how I live, about my government. They are very interested in these things and when they hear about them I am sure that in their minds, without ever broaching the topics directly, they are comparing this information with what they know of their own country. The contrasts do not escape them and this, perhaps, is another reason why the military do not want travellers to go outside towns like Bhamo.

In Burma the military restricts all foreign press. In Burma the military censors all local press. In Burma, in May 2000, the military sentenced a man to three years imprisonment for listening to the Voice of America on short wave radio. And in places like Namma Tu, even contact between tourists and locals is banned by the military. The military says that this is for my protection. What rubbish. More likely is that it will go to every length to keep the general population in the dark.

Meanwhile, outside the quarters of the head monk, the day's festivities are in full swing. A procession of dancers, musicians, monks, families, and children dressed in crowned, bright, glittering ceremonial attire make their way from the forest, along the side of the lake, and into the monastery. It is a procession in honour of the children who are to become novices and it finishes in a long, open, iron-roofed shed under which families have set up camp. Musicians play clashing music and two drummers, perspiration pouring off them, flail their arms, thrash their drums, and laugh and shout over the din as they play continuously for the next four hours. The oboe player, by contrast, is an older, balding man who reclines in a chair and lulls himself to sleep as he plays.

Once settled, the young children, male and female, aged from four through to twelve, are fussed over by mothers like child actors being dressed, preened and pampered before they go on stage for their moment of glory in the annual Christmas nativity play. And like their European counterparts, the sense of the moment is completely lost on them. The pearls around the neck of one are too tight, and his hands idly pull at them as mother tries to paint fingernails and make last minute adjustments to make up. Lipstick is applied, hair is combed and clothes are straightened. The music ends.

Seven bowls of food are spread on a circular platter before each child. These are to be ignored despite the fact that it is now approaching midday and the children have been fasting since yesterday. A master of ceremonies takes a seat before each one and rolls seven balls of rice in his hands. Every few minutes a ball is taken and symbolically dipped into each of the seven bowls of food. It is then put next to the mouth of the soon-to-be novice. The food must be ignored. This is done seven times. When the last ball of rice is dipped, proffered, and ignored it is only then that the children are allowed to eat.

After eating, the munchkins (that's what they are in their make up and their oversized fairytale costumes) are walked or driven off to the houses of their friends and relatives to collect donations for the upkeep of Namma Tu monastery. This event coincides with a line of civilians forming in front of a shed from which chanting has been emanating for the last hour. Each person in the line has a bundle of kyat notes in his or her hand. More notes, tightly folded, are placed in large silver bowls. Then, when monks emerge from the shed at the completion of their ordination, they walk single file along the line and receive a donation from each guest. At the front of this procession two men carry the silver bowls and throw a mixture of rice, popcorn, and money into the air. As it comes to ground children scrabble frantically for it, strength and speed prevailing, the rice and popcorn acting as a confusing distraction from the notes. In the line of monks is

Chin Nanda Malar. Now that he is a monk his name has been changed to U Than Weh Toh, 'U' being a sign of respect in Burmese nomenclature. Literally it means uncle.

The final stage of the ceremony is the shaving of the heads, not of the monks but of the new novices. Submissive, bedraggled, miserable munchkins have their black mops shaved off, their faces scrunching up as the lather on their heads trickles down through their make-up and into their eyes. An old monk with a feverishly shaking hand wields a cutthroat razor and scrapes and scratches and nicks his way over the scalps.

Late in the afternoon Ko Lay Nyo and U Thaung Aye return to the monastery. I thank my hosts, especially U Than Weh Toh and I promise to see him in a few days' time. Then I leave Namma Tu on a motor scooter with Ko Lay Nyo. 'Now that it is dark no one can see that you are white,' he explains.

As we ride back to Bhamo, Ko Lay Nyo asks if we can stop at the house of a friend of his for a drink. I am due for dinner with Nyein Thu later in the evening but do not see this as presenting a problem. And so we pull up behind a house, still outside Bhamo town limits, and drink Kachin wine, an illicit brew which tastes like a fermented cross between beer, lemonade and wine. Although it is up to 20 per cent alcohol we knock it back like soft drink. As we do so, Ko Lay Nyo, his friend and I smile and laugh, becoming increasingly animated and understanding each other with greater ease, or so it seems. We laugh about my lunch with Nyein Thu and this becomes an ongoing joke. Burmese men jokes, not so different to men jokes from anywhere. After we finish the second bottle of wine Ko Lay Nyo asks, 'Shall we have one more?' And after we finish the third Ko Lay Nyo asks, 'Shall we have one more?' By the time we leave the three of us have laughed a great deal and finished off five bottles. This is too much for Ko Lay Nyo and, as he later explains, after dropping me off he returned home and had an argument with his wife. 'I flood,' he says. 'What?' 'I flood, I wom-it and my wife was very angry.'

Arriving at Nyein Thu's, I too am in trouble. 'I am very angry with you. You are late,' she says and indeed dinner has been finished but the spread is still out on the table waiting for me. 'I'm sorry,' I reply and accept the chair that is offered to me at the dining table. When I do so the father joins me, just the two of us at the table, son and father-in-law to be – 'Do you mind if I call you dad.' 'No, not at all, son.' He tells Nyein Thu to stop pestering me whilst I eat and so she departs. Then he serves me food including fat-bodied, angular-legged locusts. Not so bad, crunching away with their little legs snap, crackle and popping. Also crunching away are the freshwater prawns which the father eats whole; head, shell, legs and all.

After dinner Nyein Thu and Aye Thandar ask me about my life and my

family in Australia. I am an only son, I explain in response to their questions, and my mother and father are divorced. My family is small. This is
very bad they say. 'Do you live with your mother?' 'No.' 'Why not?' I try
to explain that in Australia it is different and that I like having my own
apartment and my own space. 'Who do you live with then?' they ask. 'By
myself', I reply. Aye Thandar concludes, 'I think you are very lonely then.'
'Yes, sometimes,' I admit, which is true. 'Who does your mother live with?'
'By herself.' Then Aye Thandar continues, 'I think this is very bad. I am
very scared to ever be living by myself. I think that your mother must be
very unhappy. What about your grandmother?' 'She lives by herself also.'
I do not tell her that sometimes we only see my grandmother once a
week, and sometimes I do not see her for two, three or four weeks. This
would add to her horror. Even so, she sums up, 'I think your family is very
poor.' I would like to argue that our culture is different in Australia but
although this may be true I am not convinced that it is a good excuse.
People are indeed poor if family is a lower priority than work or money or
friends or any one of many other things. So yes, I am poor and I do get
lonely.

'My advice to you is to marry soon,' says Aye Thandar.

Later in the evening Aye Thandar says that her father is saving money
to send her to live in Japan. He works in the travel industry, she explains,
but even so it will cost three million kyat to obtain the requisite passport,
visas, and air fare. It will take many years to save the money and get
through all of the bureaucracy. 'My father would like me to leave this
country but it is not easy for me to leave Burma.'

A point of comparison. Three million kyat is 208 years work for a high
school teacher. I tell Aye Thandar that in Australia it costs me the price of
an evening meal at a restaurant to buy my passport. To her, this is
unbelievable.

And for the second time today I realize that merely by conversing with
Burmese people they obtain a perspective on their own country from
which they are otherwise sheltered.

A STUDENT, A MONK AND THE IMMIGRATION MAN

One morning I visit Ko Thi Ha, the Engineering student whom I met
on the boat, as he works in his family's jewellery shop. His father
used to do most of the work but because of its fiddly nature his eyes are
now not very good. So when he is not studying English, Ko Thi Ha comes
to Bhamo and makes rings. 'To make one ring takes one and a half days

but I can make five in four days. The frames of the rings are solid gold,' he explains, 'but on top there is a gold leaf compound. This is six parts gold, one part silver and one part copper. This is why gold in Chinese jewellry shops is such a bright yellow colour. This is what Chinese people like, more than pure gold. The stones that are set into the rings are fakes. Everyone knows this. It is the size and the colour which people like. The best fakes are imported from Russia and I buy them in Rangoon.' When they are finished each ring sells for about 5,000 kyat.

As he works, Ko Thi Ha solders a friend's broken wristband. Another friend brings in a red stone the faces of which need to be filed to make them more prominent. These jobs for friends are completed free of charge and take precedence over other work.

As we talk, Ko Thi Ha says tells me that I am his first Western friend and he likes to talk with me because when he does he learns a lot. And today I tell him something about the Americas. 'North America and South America are not the same place,' I say. 'Brazil is a separate country in South America and Bill Clinton is not the President of Brazil or any other part of South America. South America and North America are the name of continents which are made up of many different countries, just like the continent of Africa is made up of many different countries. And Bill Clinton is not the President of all of the countries that make up the American continents, just part of North America.' Ko Thi Ha responds that he did not know this.

I go on to explain that the English language was based on Latin which was the language of the Romans. I draw a rough map of Europe and show him the countries which used to be part of the Roman Empire – Italy, Spain, France, Britain, northern Africa, Greece, Turkey, and into some of the Arab nations (although here my knowledge, as well as my map draw-ing skills, become very generalized). Again, Ko Thi Ha did not know about Latin or the Roman Empire. 'At school we are taught mathematics, sci-ence, English and about the history of our country.' 'What do they teach you about your country?' 'They only teach us the history of our country until Independence. They do not tell us anything about our country for the last forty years.' 'And what about overseas history?' 'For history one year we were taught about the histories of other countries. They did not teach us very much. I do not think that they want to teach us about these things.'

So now I talk with Ko Thi Ha about the world and history and politics. Much of what I say is so far beyond him that it feels like I am recounting fairytales or myths from an ancient culture. But Ko Thi Ha is not a child but an intelligent young man with English as good as any that I have encountered so far in Burma. Furthermore, he is a young man who, despite being from a provincial town in Burma, gained entrance into Burma's premier university, Rangoon University, to study Engineering. This, of course, was before it was closed down. Yet he does not know that Bill Clinton is not the President of the whole America landmass. This absence of knowledge is not a reflection on Ko Thi Ha's intelligence, it is an indictment upon the nature of the education that the military regime allows in Burma. Equally condemning are statistics concerning attendance at Burmese schools.

❑ ❑ ❑ ❑ ❑

According to United Nations and International Labour Organization statistics there are 16.24 million children in Burma aged fourteen or below. Of these an estimated 6.7 million children (41 per cent) attend primary level education. The other 9.5 million do not have access to educational facilities. Of the children that do attend primary school, only one in four complete their basic education. Over 50 per cent of the drop-out rate can be attributed to the costs of education. These costs include enrolment fees (typically 500 kyat per year), fees for text and exercise books, compulsory payments levied for school buildings and furniture, and even fees for test/exam papers. Combined, these costs total three, four, five thousand kyat a year, (US$10-17), more in secondary school. By Western standards it is a small total. In Burma it is often prohibitive.

The regime in Burma does little to alleviate this predicament, allotting 7.7 per cent of the national budget to education but 40.1 per cent of the budget to the military. Yet the only enemies of the Burmese military are the people within its own borders that oppose the current regime.

❑ ❑ ❑ ❑ ❑

'Students are the most dangerous for the SPDC,' says Ko Thi Ha. 'Burmese people in Rangoon and Mandalay think that maybe the future of democracy in our country is in the hands of the students. This is why the military is scared of students. Maybe if the students demonstrate again many of them will be killed. If people in Burma hear about this then many people will be angry. Maybe the SPDC will be finished,' he concludes.

I leave Ko Thi Ha knowing that in all likelihood the officials will come and question him soon after I leave. He has already explained that after we last met the military stopped him on the street and questioned him about our conversations. Who was I, what did we talk about, where was I going, where had I been, what was my work? Koh Thi Ha had responded that he did not know.

Ko Thi Ha is a student, I am a Westerner. It is not a liason that the Burmese military like to see.

❑ ❑ ❑ ❑ ❑

Having spent the morning talking with Ko Thi Ha, I spend the afternoon walking across Bhamo. I go to a temple in search of my friend U Than Weh Toh. When I find him he takes me into the main hall of a *paya* where we sit and talk with one of his former teachers, a senior monk in the temple. Just as it has been with other Burmese in Bhamo, so too do these people welcome the opportunity to talk to a foreigner.

Taking advantage of the fact that both of the gentlemen with whom I sit speak quite good English, I ask about my experiences with the candles and meditation on the side of Mandalay Hill. They smile and explain to me that in Burma there are five stages in the teaching of meditation. To begin with novices do not sit in the full lotus position. Instead they sit 'almost cross-legged' with their eyes closed and count 120 relaxed breaths. Later, their focus moves from the breath itself to the tip of the nose, the entry of air, and its circulation through the body. It is only at the final stage of learning meditation that monks sit in the full lotus position with their eyes open and do not break concentration from a single object. This is considered to represent the state of Buddha when he was seeking enlightenment through meditation under the Bodhi tree. The local villagers mocked and scorned him, threw rocks at him and beat him with sticks yet because of his concentration, *tah ma taah*, he was not disturbed by the distraction of pain. U Ti Law Kah in Mandalay was proficient at this level of meditation.

As we talk, U Than Weh Toh asks if he can travel with me around Burma. For me this would be a marvellous way to travel but at the same time I think it would be very dangerous for the young monk. I explain this and both he and the senior monk agree. 'It is hard to travel in Burma. It is hard because of the government. I think for the people in Burma, every country is a better country to live in. I think everyone would leave if they could but it is very difficult to leave Burma,' says U Than Weh Toh. As he talks, he is sitting cross-legged, wrapped in his orange monk's robe. He has the most gentle manner and the softest eyes. It seems incongruous to hear him speak so directly about the military.

'It is very difficult for people to live in Burma. Everything is expensive. Six years ago, in Bhamo, five planks of teak cost 1,500 kyat. Now one teak plank is 1,500 kyat. This price is too expensive. Ten years ago, everyone in Bhamo built their houses out of teak. Now people cannot afford it and the teak is sold to China. Three years ago the most important

military official of Bhamo was buying and selling many truck loads of black
market teak and selling it directly to the Chinese. Now he is in prison. He
has been replaced by the second lieutenant colonel. The new colonel is
like a king. He takes money from everyone in Bhamo.'

'If you work in a government job in a bank or as a clerk or as a policeman or a soldier, your pay is 1,000 kyat each month. If you have a family
and children then it is not easy to live for less than 10,000 kyat each
month. It is very difficult to live with so small an amount of money. This is
why government people must take more money. Everywhere people need
more money. This is why people are corrupt.'

U Than Weh Toh asks me, 'Do you think that the situation will change
in Burma?' I give the opinion that all oppressive dictatorships have a limited life expectancy before they inevitably capitulate. It is a truth of history.
'I do not think so,' he replies, 'I do not think that Burma will change. The
government controls everything. In our country the guns are turned in
upon ourselves.' Again I think, what a strange discussion to be having
with a monk whilst sitting on the floor eating bananas in front of a statue
of Buddha surrounded by the peace and quiet of a monastery.

Maybe U Than Weh Toh is right. This particular oppressive regime has
now been in power for thirty-eight years. It is good at doing the things it
takes to maintain control. But another theory suggests that the military
regime is destined for capitulation on economic grounds. The lengths to
which it goes in order to maintain its grip on power are unsustainable and
come at the expense of the people and the economy of the nation. Widespread change must occur if the country is to move forward. A workable
and non-corrupt infrastructure must be created and the imbalance between the expenditure of state funds on soldiers and weaponry as opposed to expenditure on education and other long-term development strat-
egies must be redressed. This will not happen as long as the military is in
power and as such the situation will continue to steadily deteriorate. Ultimately, the situation will reach a level intolerable to the Burmese people.
Then, like in 1988, popular sentiment will once again come to the fore. If
the future of Burma is to take this course, capitulation may take many,
many years.

There are factions within Burmese democracy activist communities which
say, 'Impose sanctions against our nation now and let the suffering be
quick and hard rather than long and slow. Do not further condemn us to
having a non-functional education system. Do not further allow our natural resources to be sold off. Do not further entrench the problems of this
country. Impose all of the hardship now, quickly, let it be done even if this
means that the people suffer more in the short term. But do not continue

to prop up a regime which is destroying its country. Beneath the band aids the wounds become more severe.'

❏ ❏ ❏ ❏ ❏

Scratch the surface, talk to someone who trusts you or who is not too scared to talk and all of a sudden you discover political consciousness in Burma. There is not a good word to be said about the current regime. Before I leave the monastery U Than Weh Toh says regretfully, 'I am very afraid of the government. Please, when you write, do not say what I say about politics.'

By the time that I return to the hotel it is 9.30 p.m.

❏ ❏ ❏ ❏ ❏

'You remember me?' asks the old man. He is jolly and effusive and he moves a lot when he talks. He is the man whom I have run into on a number of occasions, either waiting for me or watching me from the other side of the street. He is the man who was here three days ago asking for my passport. He is the man who was here two days ago asking what I had been doing. He is the man who was sitting outside the shop on the other side of the street from the hotel this morning. But tonight he reeks of alcohol and is so drunk that when he gesticulates he almost topples himself over. 'I am the immigration officer,' he declares. 'I know.' 'What did you do two days ago?' he asks. '*Nah mah leh ba boo*,' I reply, 'I don't understand.' He repeats himself but again I say *nah mah leh ba boo*. He doesn't want this answer and starts drawing circles on the table with his forefinger and then stabs a point outside the circle. 'Two days ago...' Then he starts tapping his top pocket with his hand. '*Nah ma leh ba boo, nah ma leh ba boo*,' I keep repeating which makes him more and more flustered, his fingers alternating between tapping his pocket and stabbing the table with increasing force as he tries to make me understand. He's drunk and knows it. His English is not particularly good even when he's sober and right now he would like to keep this as quick and simple as possible and walk away with some money in his pocket.

The immigration official tries a new approach and goes downstairs to get a note pad and pen. When he returns he instructs, 'You write...two days ago.' Okay, I write and I write not only about what I did two days ago but *every* useless, facile, immaterial detail about what I have done since I arrived in Bhamo. Three pages of barely-legible scribble outlining when I eat, where I eat, what I eat, when I shower, when and where I walk when it is legal, my time at the festival, when I go to bed, when I get up, when I have an afternoon nap. And hidden amongst these lines are the sentences, 'Went for a walk south along the Irrawaddy River,' and 'Spent time learning about Buddhism in a monastery.' I hope that maybe by giving him a written explanation of all of my actions I can perhaps pre-empt future questioning about my trip to Namma Tu.

The immigration man leaves with the papers, no money and no verbal explanation. As he does so, I think 'This man might not be too much of a threat. In fact, he still strikes me as a quite nice man. Drunk, old, and not unfriendly. But at the same time, it is likely that his superior will be neither drunk nor friendly and may well cause problems for me.'

Meanwhile, on the television there is an advertisement for a credit card, which shows images of bundles of American dollars on a table, a credit card going into an auto-teller machine and then a pile of American dollars being flicked back out of it. The first auto-tellers are only now being opened in Rangoon. Another advertisement is for Oasis bottled water. It is the technologically-advanced water. Bottles are shown on conveyor belts passing a shiny, stainless steel vat with a man in a lab coat overseeing progress. Then there is a picture of a bottle next to a computer with a cardiograph pattern scribbled across it. Then the water bottles are shown passing over rollers. Finally there is a shot of a forklift truck lifting pallets of the bottles in a spotless warehouse. Oasis, it is the water of progress, the water of innovation, the water of a modern nation.

Finally, before the end of the broadcast, the crush and destroy stooges and all external elements slogans are scrolled across the screen in both English and Burmese. Then there is footage of generals doing meritorious deeds around the country. This is so that you can go to sleep with a smile on your face. I do not.

A MAGNIFICENT MAN AND HIS FLYING MACHINE

I wake at five o'clock in the morning, rising to the tranquillity of Central Hotel. This morning the regular six o'clock hubbub is preceded by two dogs going the full fifteen rounds of wolf-like snarling, growling and scrapping on the street below my window. Their bout is finally declared a draw and rescheduled for four o'clock the following morning. Then the standard early morning din begins. The market's iron gates are clanked open and people literally run in scrambling and shouting to grab the prime stalls. A chugging, spluttering, revving diesel truck tests the decibel level of its horn whilst a trolley-pushing street vendor dongs his bell and shouts out his sales pitch to attract buyers. Soon the local temple administrators will start their drone-like chant asking for donations. And meanwhile, within Central, doors begin to open and slam shut shaking my flimsy, cheap, theatre-set walls. Voices shout, a child runs up and down the hall, and Mr U Cho Wen, the hotel owner, takes the resident prostitute giggling and squealing into one of the rooms for on-the-job training. A few variations but this is much the same as every other morning.

I have been in Bhamo for seven days now and it feels like time to move on to somewhere new. I cannot leave Bhamo overland and have decided against smuggling myself out of the town. Because of this there is little choice but to return to Mandalay and then go from there to my next destination.

At the boat ticket-booking office I inquire about departure times. A boat leaves in two days and I can buy a ticket tomorrow. The official then asks for my details and goes across to a hand-crank telephone, winds it up, dials a number, and reads out my name and passport number to someone whom I suspect is an official in Mandalay.

❑ ❑ ❑ ❑ ❑

What to do with my remaining time in Bhamo? I decide to wander through the streets, try to get lost, and see what adventure I can find. It does not take long for one to materialize.

I walk along a Bhamo backstreet and someone waves to me from the window of a house and shouts out for me to please come in. 'No I'm walking,' I shout back and begin to move on. I am in a hurry to find my next adventure. He calls out to me again and I change my mind thinking I'll stay for half an hour and then excuse myself. I go through the gate of the house, a big house, and the man meets me in the front garden. We walk down towards the front door and when I look through the window of the sitting room I see an ultra-light helicopter. Ah-ha, the Bhamo helicopter factory. Someone had asked me whether I would like to see the helicopter factory but I had declined thinking that it must be a military operation. Later inquiries had suggested that there was no such thing, not here, not in Bhamo, not in a town without central electricity, without computers, and in which military bureaucrats still use Morse code and hand-cranked field telephones to communicate between distant destinations. But here it is, in the sitting room of this house, the Bhamo helicopter factory, and this is the magnificent man with his flying machine.

We go through the front door and the sitting room is bare but for the helicopter. The man's name is U Sein Win, an original Burmese Wright brother. In very good English he says that he had heard that I was in town and was wondering when I would come to see him. We talk and soon he

brings out a monumental slab-like tome of an American/Burmese dictio-
nary to look up any words I might say which he does not understand.
Then he makes notes of them.

I ask him about flying. 'I was very interested to fly in the air since I was
thirteen,' he explains. 'I started studying the design of aeroplanes and
helicopters from magazines when I was twenty-four. Now I have been
studying design for thirty years.' He shows me his much-prized collection
of aeroplane, helicopter and assorted mechanical magazines dating back
to 1960. It is from these that he teaches himself aeronautic design. 'I have
not been to university but have taught myself practical engineering and
design. My first job was repairing car and motor bike engines. Then I
worked with my father in his oil mill and after that I used to sink water
pipes. When I was thirty I began working as a lathe operator and welder.
Now I could build a big helicopter or a plane if I had the materials.' He
goes on to tell me that his father was a World War II US Army truck driver
before running the oil mill. 'My father was more intelligent than me. He
learnt in a monastery. He did not go to school at all.'

U Sein Win has been working on the helicopter for ten years and it is
made up of an assortment of bits and pieces. The rotor assembly is made
partially from the barrel of a tank machine-gun and partially from the
hydraulic lift system of a dump truck. The latter part was too small, says U
Sein Win, so he had to cut it, insert another piece, reshape it, weld it, and
smooth it. To complete this rotor assembly has taken six years. A pulley
system connects the rotors to the engine by means of two fan belts, the
tension of which is adjusted by gear levers. The wheels of the pulleys are
aluminium and self-crafted. The frame of the helicopter is made from
water pipes, the wires attached to the rudders are telephone wires with a
steel interior and a copper exterior and the vertical and horizontal tail
rudders are made of cloth. There is no rear rotor which U Sein Win be-
lieves to be a technological first. Maybe, I don't know. The seat for the
helicopter is a bicycle seat and the rotors, 6.5 metres in length, are made
of teak. On the right of the cockpit is a hand control which adjusts the
rear horizontal rudder. A foot pedal adjusts the rear vertical rudder and
another pedal controls the engine revs. There is a centrally-positioned
joystick, and on the left hand side is a clutch which maintains tension on
each of the two fan belts that drive the rotor. All that U Sein Win now
needs is the money to buy a ten horsepower Japanese Honda engine to
drive his flying machine. The whole contraption is a masterpiece of im-
provisation and, despite the hotchpotch of materials, appears to an un-
trained eye to be an accomplished and well-finished feat of design.

As we sit and talk U Sein Win shows me letters that have been sent to
him by other travellers who have enjoyed his hospitality. One of the

letters says,

> To Mr Helicopter Man, I am sorry but I am from England and
> therefore it is impossible for me to find you and your son a job in
> Brunei. However if I come across a position for a welder and turner...

Now I understand. This is one of the things for which U Sein Win is
hoping – maybe one of the tourists that he invites into his house will be
able to help to get him and his son out of Burma.

'I cannot be happy in my own country,' says U Sein Win. 'The United
States or Australia or England would be very good for me. I think I could
work very well in these countries. I could become a citizen. I could help
them with my designs. I think that I can help those governments very
much. I cannot improve if I live in Burma. The military people came only
three times to visit me in the last nine years. They are not interested in my
work. They are only interested in money and to see if they can tax me for
what I build.'

U Sein Win, a silent, thoughtful, faraway-looking man, sitting in his
chair. 'If I can get to America or Australia or England...' What he does not
realize is that his style of design became redundant in the West decades ago.
Now it is computers and analysts, but he knows very little of the digital age.

U Sein Win gets up and goes to make coffee. When he returns he takes
me around his house and shows me more of his other designs. There is a
knife that he keeps under his pillow. It is a fine-looking knife with a steel
blade that has been machined from the fender of a car. The handle is
made of two curved pieces of aluminium with the steel blade sandwiched
between them. The whole piece has then been riveted together, shaped,
and has a wooden butt placed on the end. A professional piece of work.
He has also designed the hinges in his house because the ones available in
the market are too flimsy, he explains, and he has designed and built the
house itself including its kitchen, its cooking facilities, its sinks, and an
iron tool which he uses to lay the floorboards. He has made guns, both
rifles and pistols. One pistol, he tells me, had a three inch (seventy-five
millimetre) barrel and, firing a .22 calibre bullet, could shoot through ten
centimetres of wood at ten metres. He also designed a boat which could
seat forty people and featured an outboard propeller capable of rotating
through three hundred and sixty degrees so as to give complete
manoeuverability. He later sold this boat to people from Myikyina, the
capital of Kachin State. And of course, there is his helicopter.

'I can work very hard. I can help your country. When you return to your
country, please tell your government about me. I think they will help me
and my family come to your country. I can be good for your country.'

We leave the house and walk to U Sein Win's factory. It is a block of

land with two sheds on it. I meet his son, Maung Htoo Tin, who is working a lathe, first machining a part for a Willies jeep and then doing some
work for monks who come by. The machinery in the shop is old and
heavy. The lathe is a combination of World War II British and American
parts and more recent Burmese and Chinese parts. The British parts are
the best says U Sein Win. The generator for the lathe is the generator
from the landing gear of a Dakota aeroplane. A hand drill press was bought
by U Sein Win's father from the US army in 1940 for US$2 and the
whole lathe outfit is driven by a 12 HP diesel engine, hand cranked, which
chugs along at what seem to be 30 revs per minute. There are a confusing
array of knobs, levers, controls, measuring sticks, rulers and callipers, all
being manipulated with dexterity by Maung Htoo Tin to machine the requisite steel parts.

'This land used to belong to my father,' explains U Sein Win. 'He used
to process oil here. Now it is for sale. If I can sell it for five million kyat
then that is enough money for my son to leave. Please help my son. He is
intelligent. He can do any work.'

I have no doubt that he is very intelligent. Like his father.

❑   ❑   ❑   ❑   ❑

Flight is the ultimate embodiment of human freedom and here is a man
designing a flying machine but who has no freedom. People in Bhamo
make fun of him for his continuing endeavours and because he is happy
for tourists to come and talk with him. He is hoping that one of them will
be in a position to help him leave his country. 'If I come to your country,
I can help your country. I cannot help my country. My government is not
interested in my work. They are only interested in making money and
making pressure on the people.'

I'm sorry, I cannot help you U Sein Win.

UNTIL NEXT TIME...

After spending the best part of two days with U Sein Win, I bid my
farewells to my other friends in Bhamo. I visit Nyein Thu whose love
attraction seems to have shifted to a young Burmese man with a flashy
bicycle. 'Please send me presents from your country,' she requests
nonetheless. Then I have tea and pork buns with my friend Ko Thi Ha at
the Heaven Restaurant. I take out my camera for a photo but he warns,
'No, please, not here.' My mistake. Heaven, like the Friendship Hotel, is
run by wealthy Chinese who work hand in glove with the military. 'Too

many of the wrong people here,' he explains. Ko Thi Ha has already had many run-ins with the police and the military because of his friendship with me. They question him almost every day.

Finishing off my farewells, I sit in the candle-lit house of Ko Lay Nyo and U Thaung Aye. I have seen them every day since I met them and every day they have fed me either a snack or a meal. They have been courteous, generous, and hospitable hosts as well as good friends. Much of what I have seen or done in Bhamo has been thanks to them. Yesterday they facilitated my VIP entry into a stage performance held as part of a Bhamo Pagoda Festival. I had met the principal actor, sat in the musicians' pit, and was even invited to dance with some bandana-wearing Burmese Back Street Boys. Then, at the end of the performance, they had thanked me for coming.

Tonight, as we sit and eat in the dim light two gentlemen come to the house. U Thaung Aye, the father-in-law, excuses himself and takes a torch and a large registry from a cupboard. The men are from a nearby town and they will be staying in Bhamo for three days. In order to do this they must officially state their destination and sign out of the town from which they are leaving. Then they must sign in at their destination. U Thaung Aye, as a district official, is one of the people with whom they can register to declare that they have arrived in Bhamo. He will have to pass the details on to the military officials tomorrow.

After the men leave U Thaung Aye shows me a photo of himself serving in the Burmese army. It is a picture of a shirtless young man standing by a river in the jungle and it was taken whilst he was fighting against the Kuomintang on the Chinese border.

Soon afterwards Ko Lay Nyo takes an envelope from the shrine in his house. It contains the skeletal forms of three leaves from a sacred Bodhi tree in a temple in Nepal and he gives two of these to me, one for me and one for my girlfriend. U Thaung Aye takes a film canister down from the shrine. In it there is a Buddhist pendant. 'Our God,' he murmurs and gives it to me. 'I hope we meet again somewhere.'

'I would like to travel and see the world,' says Ko Lay Nyo. 'To see America, to see Australia, and to see England but this is not possible for me. It is not possible for Burmese people to leave this country.'

Bhamo – it hasn't turned out as I thought I wanted it to. Instead I have seen something of the beauty of Burmese people and the wishful, sad and impossible nature of their dreams. May I never forget the generosity and decency of these people. Good, good people.

U Thaung Aye walks me back to the hotel through the dark and quiet streets. What a fine, and dignified man. I too hope that we will meet again.

BACK DOWN THE RIVER

A man is walking across a plain and he sees a yellow flower. He looks at it, keeps walking and then sees another yellow flower. Hmm, he thinks, and continues walking. Soon he sees another yellow flower and then another yellow flower and it reaches the stage that he is actually looking for the yellow flowers along his path.

Later, when talking to his friends, he admits that it was strange but it was the yellow flowers that seemed to lead him across the plains. 'But why did you not follow the blue flowers or the purple flowers or the scrub bushes or the stringybark trees?' asked his friend. 'I don't know,' replied the man, 'I just followed the yellow flowers instead.'

I came to Bhamo looking for excitement, adventure, mountains, but instead it turned out very differently to that.

Bhamo, an insight into some of the realities of living under the SLORC/ SPDC regime. I have spent my time with Burmese people, I have dined with them, I have drunk with them, I have talked with them. I have come to know some of the university graduates who have no opportunity for employment; I have come to know the university students who have no opportunity for university. I have seen the holes in people's education and understanding of the world outside Burma; I have been the recipient of petitions to please get sons, daughters and nephews out of the country. I have seen the watchful eye of the military at work trying to keep tabs on everything and anything deemed to pose a potential threat. In Bhamo I was considered such a thing and so too were the people to whom I spoke, simply on the basis of their having talked with me. I have seen people who need to work two jobs in order to exist and I have seen and heard of the corruption of officials. I have also seen the signatures, dates and addresses that locals must fill in on registries when they move from town to town, and I have heard the daily phone calls from my hotel to immigration. Not because Mr U Cho Wen is an informer but merely because he must do so – report on my movements. These are the day-to-day machinations of Bhamo life under an oppressive military dictatorship. This is Burmese reality.

❏ ❏ ❏ ❏ ❏

Up early and a horse and trap takes me through the streets of Bhamo to the spot from which the boat leaves. Ko Thi Ha makes the journey down from town at 6.30 a.m. to see me off and we stand on the back of the boat and say our farewells before he goes back to work in his family's jewellery shop.

The boat departs and once again I have a spot on the deck, once again I experience the serene beauty of the Irrawaddy River, and once again I am surrounded by Burmese people.

The journey back to Mandalay should take two days but this stretches to three. The boat is overloaded with cargo and we run aground twice. On the first occasion it takes us an hour and a half to work our way back into the main current. A local farmer with a buffalo sits himself down on the bank and watches proceedings. Two other people join him but they depart after half an hour. The original man stays for the duration.

The second time we run aground is more of an ordeal. As soon as we touch the bottom the driver makes a beeline for deeper water. It doesn't work and we run aground completely. A number of men have to jump in to the river and hang on to a log that is dug into the sand and used as a pivot point around which the driver tries to swing the boat. After an hour the men in the water are shivering vigourously. The boat is lightened when other boats pull up and ferry away the people who are to disembark at the next stop. It takes us more than two hours before we begin moving again.

❏ ❏ ❏ ❏ ❏

Just as on the trip to Bhamo, there is a soldier on board who spends much of his time on the boat staring at me from behind his sunglasses. He has a kind face and one night when I get up to go to the toilet he reaches across, touches me on the ankle, and offers me his torch to find the way. The next morning I offer him some of my breakfast but he refuses. Then, at lunch-time, he asks me to join his family, which I do. As I eat, I can again see on this man's face the difficulty he has in fitting me in to the military preconceptions with which soldiers are bombarded concerning Westerners.

Also on board is the Northern Command Army Unit Track and Field Team. This one is the gymnast, that one the high jumper, another two are sprinters and then there are two very young middle-distance runners who come on shore with me when we make an unplanned night-time stop at a tiny riverside village. These soldiers are lively and cheerful and before going to sleep they offer me tea and grasshoppers as a pre-bed snack.

Bedtime. The deck lights of the boat are on and beneath them there are erratic typhoons of swirling, swarming, whirling insects. Midges, gnats, mosquitoes, moths, little flies and big flies. At ground level, beetles, crickets, and grasshoppers cannonade into the people preparing to bed down for the night. Then, when the deck lights are turned off, insect infestation. They land and bounce and crash and crawl all over the decks. I hear the 'bok' as they hit the walls and ceiling and nosedive onto sleeping mats. They crawl under blankets and onto bodies, arms, legs and stomachs. They crawl on faces and into ears, and all up and down the deck I hear the sounds of people swatting and sweeping insects away, and the sounds of people getting up and shaking out their bedclothes.

On another night, after eating at a restaurant in the town of Katha, I am walking through the streets when a scruffy man with good English walks up beside me and starts asking me questions about where I come from, where I have been, and whether I liked it. As he does so a second man comes up alongside him and says vehemently and in English, 'You are a bastard, you are a bastard,' and shakes his fist at him. It is a strange incident and I wonder why this second Burmese man has been so angry with the first for asking me questions. I also wonder why he has abused him in English. I disengage myself from the scruffy man with good English as quickly as I can. He follows me, however, and ten minutes later, when I am back on board the boat, he arrives next to my spot. It is disconcerting and in no uncertain terms I tell him to go away. Maybe I have affronted another innocent person, just as I did the logging merchant in the temple in Bhamo. But maybe not. That there is a web of informers who keeps tabs on me and any other tourist who wanders off the beaten track is patently obvious. Maybe this man is an informer, maybe he is not. I don't know but the whole incident is odd.

❏ ❏ ❏ ❏ ❏

After three days the boat arrives back in Mandalay. It is more than a world away from the whore-house and my friends in Bhamo. The journey back downstream, the Bhamo Army Track and Field Team, the locusts spread out to dry all over the stern of the boat, my space on the floor of the deck, everything that preceded my actually getting off the boat; all of this was still part of the Bhamo adventure. But in Mandalay, tourists are common and my hotel room has clean white sheets, a ceiling fan, a sit-down toilet, a hot shower and almost continual electricity except for the two, three, or maybe four times a day when the power grid goes down. On the return boat trip I was looking forward to these things but almost as soon as I arrive in Mandalay I am ready to leave again.

Within two days I am on my way to Hsipaw in Shan State.

IN
loving Memory
— of —
CHARLES WILLIAM LAMBERT
(MISSIONARY)
NATIVE OF BLACKHEATH KENT ENGLAND
WHO WAS MURDERED
IN THE A B MISSION HOUSE THIBAW
ON THE 23 OF MAY 1895
AGED 39 YEARS
FATHER FORGIVE THEM, THEY KNOW NOT WHAT THEY DO

chapter 5
Shan State

FLORES PARA LOS MUERTOS

From: 'Going too Far' by Sithu Nyein Aye, *The New Light of Myanmar*,
1 June 1996.

Myanmar Ngaing Ngan that is overwhelmed by the four cardinal
values of *Byamaso Taya* is so pleasant and tranquil. Blossoms of such
beauteous truths are blossoming in the countryside and all over the
country with nothing to vie and surpass them. An international
tourist who had been to many countries of the world, speaking in an
interview on a European television programme about the best scenery,
the best food, the best hotel etc. in the world, had said that the best
people were the Myanmar people.

□ □ □ □ □

It is two hundred kilometres from Mandalay to Hsipaw. Deducting a one-
hour food stop this journey takes eight hours, along what proves to be a
narrow, windy and very heavily potholed road. The rattle, clatter, rumble,
bump, bang-your-elbows, bang-your-knees bus ride into Shan State.

Not far out of Mandalay the bus passes a rock quarry on the left-hand
side of the road. Prisoners in dirty white uniforms and leg-irons are doing
their hard labour, manually breaking and moving rocks behind a barbed
wire fence with soldiers standing and guarding them with rifles. It looks
like a scene from an escape sequence in a prison film.

Beyond the quarry the road begins to twist and turn up and in to the
bald, bare hills; hills cleared of all their timber, logged and left. No cultiva-
tion, no agriculture, no nothing once their obvious income earner has
been taken. Abandoned land. In marked contrast is the roadside itself
which is lined with flowers – crimsons, violets, mauves, oranges, light
blues, reds, a diversity of blossoming colour with the most frequently seen
being the trees of large bright yellow flowers. Many have been planted
recently and are now two-metre-tall saplings.

The town of Maymyo is two hours from Mandalay and is located on a
plateau a thousand metres above sea level. The weather here is different
to that of the plains below and it is little wonder the British Colonials
found it to be such an attractive retreat. The air is cool and clean and there
has been persistent drizzle as we have been driving. People walk along the
road wearing jeans and woollen hats and jumpers and the surrounding
countryside is green. Vegetable plots abound and, as if to illustrate the
point, we drive past the thatched roof of a hut which doubles as a garden
of creepers and pumpkins.

At midday the bus descends into a deep gorge and briefly we are
surrounded by jungle. But once we emerge back on to the plateau the

vegetable plots return along with rice paddies, cornfields, small orchards, and fields of bright yellow flowers. But more abundant than any of these is the cleared land that bears only scraggly, stunted growths. An occasional buffalo is tethered and an occasional someone walks to somewhere, although no definite recollection of seeing anyone walking to anywhere springs to mind.

In the early afternoon the bus stops and is soon rocking backwards and forwards. We're on a jack, and the bus has broken down. Tapping from underneath. A ratchet at work. Hammering and rocking. The unloading of some of the spare parts that had been loaded on to the bus before we left Mandalay this morning. Half an hour later we continue our journey.

More drizzle as we continue to drive east through countryside very different to the Irrawaddy and its flood plains and its brown colours and its beating sun and its primitive, Spartan appearance.

❑ ❑ ❑ ❑ ❑

Shan State is south of Kachin State, directly east of Mandalay, and is the largest state in Burma with the largest ethnic minority population. It is also a state which for centuries enjoyed either independence or autonomy from the ethnic Burmans and their kings. From 1287 until 1604 the Shan ruled Upper Burma. Thereafter, although tributes were levied by the ethnic Burman kings, direct rule of Shan State was left to a series of princes and chiefs called *sawbwas*. Each of these presided over one of the principalities into which the State was divided.

When the British annexed Upper Burma in 1886 they recognized thirty-seven Shan princedoms. Whilst central and Lower Burma were directly administered as a British colony, Shan State was treated as a protectorate with the *sawbwas* maintaining significant autonomy, including responsibility for administering economic policy, law, order and justice. Perhaps it was because of this autonomy that the Shan people remained loyal to the British when the Japanese invaded Burma in World War II. Many ethnic Burmans, on the other hand, supported the Japanese.

At the end of the war, it was a tribute to the diplomatic skills of Bogyoke Aung San that he was able to broker an agreement between the Shan and Burman peoples. This agreement, the Panglong Agreement of February 1947, stipulated that the Shan people would join the Union of Burma on the condition that after ten years of Burmese independence they would be granted the right to determine their own future. This future could be that of an autonomous state within the Union or they could secede. This agreement was included in the first Constitution of Burma.

The Panglong Agreement never came into effect. Bogyoke Aung San and other ethnic leaders were assassinated in June 1947 and thereafter, although independence was gained in January 1948 and the Union of Burma was formed, the country slid progressively into a state of chaos. Ethnic minorities took up arms and demanded autonomy, Kuomintang troops from China carved out their own territory in northern Burma and the Burmese Communist Party tried to manoeuvre itself into power. Fighting even divided Rangoon. In a bid to restore stability to the country, Parliament handed power to General Ne Win's military in 1958. The Shan people's response came in April 1959 when thirty-four *sawbwas* revoked their positions as individual princes in Shan State and embraced the concept of one Shan State with its own elected government. Many of the princes took positions in the Shan State Council. Others gained positions in the Burmese National Government's Upper House when democracy was restored to Burma in the elections of 1960. Then, on the night of 2 March 1962, the military staged a *coup d'état*. Parliament was dissolved, ministers were imprisoned and General Ne Win formed his own seventeen-member Revolutionary Council. Shan leader Sao Shwe Thaike, the first president of the Union of Burma, was taken into detention and later executed. His son was shot dead on the night of the coup.

This is how the recent history of the Shan people in Burma began.

❑ ❑ ❑ ❑ ❑

Upon arriving in Hsipaw there is no more drizzle and the sky is a blue-grey which accentuates the green of the surrounding fields in the afternoon sun. Like Bhamo, the town is small and is only half an hour's walk from one end to the other. Unlike Bhamo, however, there is a square, walled cinema in the centre of town and power is provided by an electricity grid, albeit a temperamental one which is turned off at nine o'clock every evening. There is also an open-walled gaming parlour which faces the street. It boasts an array of Atari-style video games and television screens. The graphics are basic by current Western standards but nonetheless the parlour is a sign of development not evident in Bhamo.

Also evident in Hsipaw is a steady trickle of travellers, with perhaps fifteen to twenty-five here at any given time. Many stay at Mr Charles' guesthouse, a peaceful establishment in a residential street on the outskirts of town. It boasts bathrooms which are clean (not green) and an upstairs balcony with a table and bamboo chairs in which to relax. In the evening people sit and talk about their experiences of the day. Sometimes the talk is about what they have heard about the Burmese military in the region.

Hsipaw. Once it was the centre of a small Shan principality, then it became the heartland of the Shan State Army (North), and now it is in an area which the military government has opened up to tourism.

A question: why are the people of Hsipaw more willing to talk to travellers about the Burmese military regime? There are three answers. (1) People in Hsipaw have learnt that many of the tourists who make their way to this town like to hear about the military regime and the atrocities that it commits. By telling such stories hawkers and would-be guides hope to curry favour with travellers. (2) Although the Shan State Army (North) has officially signed a cease-fire agreement with the military regime, it have refused to put down its weapons and it still have an armed presence on the streets of Hsipaw. (3) The Shan people hate the Burmans and have endured persecution at the hands of the military for decades.

MR G AND THE INSURGENTS

From: 'A Lament' by Kyi Kyi Hla, *The New Light of Myanmar*, 13 May 1997.

It was the people in 'black areas', that is the areas where the insurgents had gained a foothold and where the government forces were in actual combat with the various armed insurgent groups, who lived in daily fear of their lives and the safety of their homes and villages. Then there were also the 'brown zones', the areas open to intermittent attacks by the insurgents. Most of the attacks were of the hit and run kind on the civilian population in the area. So the people in these black and brown zones were the ones who really had to face the dangers, especially the poor villagers who were at the mercy of the terrorists. Trains were mined, villagers got blown up or had their limbs torn off by earth mines if they ventured out to till their fields. They lost their homes, their children were denied schooling, they themselves remained ignorant, malnourished, unhealthy and without access to any kind of social services. Their mortality rate was indeed high. There was no hue and cry then from any quarter whatsoever about the plight of the villagers especially in the remote border areas. The only succour they received was from the government troops in the area who were aware of the actual situation and tried to alleviate their suffering. But the troops themselves had their hands full with their efforts to contain the insurgency. The Myanmar Armed Forces knew the true extent of the devastation caused by the insurgency.

The State Law and Order Restoration Council being composed of members of the armed forces (Tatmadaw) have first hand knowledge of the plight of the national races and other simple folk in the insurgent areas. Yet they also showed a deep understanding of the insurgents themselves by building up mutual trust and respect with those who had once been their sworn enemies. Thus the peace was achieved with most of the armed groups and with peace the trials and tribulations of the people of the remote border areas are now in the past. Each of the armed groups who made a pact for peace are at present working hand in hand with the Government for the development of their respective regions and their people, and the results of these efforts are there for all to see.

❑ ❑ ❑ ❑ ❑

Snapshots from a former brown zone: a bridge, a monastery, a liquor factory and a chance meeting with an insurgent leader.

Running along one side of Hsipaw township is the Dokhtawady River. A single-lane bridge spans it and trailing back from this bridge is a queue of lumbering, groaning trucks. The queue extends for hundreds of metres, almost back into Hsipaw township itself. This is the only bridge crossing the Dokhtawady for 160 kilometres, and to travel to any other bridge requires driving along bad roads through territory in which there is the threat of bandits or rebels seizing goods. Because of this, traffic travelling between Mandalay, Lashio, and the Chinese border passes through Hsipaw and must cross the river at this point.

The bridge, however, is currently under repair and cannot be crossed, or at least so the soldiers at the checkpoints say. Indeed, there is no regulation of the weight of the vehicles which cross the bridge and little maintenance work has been done since it was built by the British. Not surprisingly, therefore, the bridge has seen better days.

Abracadabra, if a driver of a truck is able to give a present to the soldiers on the bridge then it is no longer under repair and he will be allowed cross. It is only those who do not have the money who remain stuck in the queue. At the back is a truck driver who has parked his vehicle on a grassy bank under a tree. To cross the bridge he must pay the soldiers 20,000 kyat as a contribution towards its repair. Smaller vehicles pay smaller amounts but the driver does not have the money and he has been waiting in Hsipaw with his truck for ten days trying to raise some funds.

Bribery at the Hsipaw bridge, an informal levy, a necessary operating cost for companies transporting goods. It is all part of a pervasive, sophisticated, egalitarian Burmese wealth redistribution policy. It's called the Presentation of Presents to the Military Policy.

I love the fact that these bribes are called presents. Presents are also called presents which can be confusing.

As I walk across the bridge the driver of a car with black-tinted windows skips the queue, stops for a few perfunctory words at the levy point, and then continues straight onward over the bridge.

Beyond the bridge, on top of a hill, is a modest *paya*. It has a concrete forecourt, lodging for twenty monks and a small white washed *zedi*. I stop for tea and talk to the monks.

The *paya* used to be the residence of a venerable, 106-year-old monk called U Lah Bah Wun Tha. He had been the chief monk of Hsipaw and one of the most revered monks in Burma. Now deceased, his remains – teeth, bits of skeleton and tufts of hair that have been taken from either his corpse or pulled from the ashes of his cremation – are kept as relics beside a statue of the Buddha.

Before U Lah Bah Wun Tha died the military summoned him to Rangoon ostensibly to confer honours upon him. He took Mr Donald, a resident of Hsipaw and the nephew of the former Shan Prince as his aide and secretary. Upon arrival he was taken from one engagement to another to pose for media photographs with all of the SLORC heavies – Khin Nyunt, U Tin Oo, Than Shwe. Also at the behest of the generals, U Lah Bah Wun Tha was required to lunch with opium warlord Loh Hsing Han. *The New Light of Myanmar* photos show a smiling Loh Hsing both eating with and shaking the hand of the venerable monk. In the background stand an assortment of smiling generals. Once these public relations exercises were complete, U Lah Bah Wun Tah was returned to Hsipaw. It was an undignified affair, unsatisfactory and not appropriate for a man of his age or standing.

Leaving the monastery on top of the hill I walk on to the whisky factory of Mr Charles, the guesthouse owner. Inside, over a 'good-morning glass of whisky' Mr Charles explains that the liquor factory has thirty employees, some in Mandalay, some in the villages and some in Hsipaw. A variety of whisky-like spirits are produced and these vary in price from US$2-6 per bottle. Bottles themselves are purchased from China as there are no bottle factories in Upper Burma. The bottles are used and then repurchased from second-hand bottle dealers. Sugar comes from Mandalay, previously in its pure form but increased overheads on sugar have meant that this is no longer affordable. Instead, Mr Charles buys sweet water that is a waste product from another factory and then distills it for use in his whisky production.

Mr Charles then explains that the whisky factory was bought from the military government at an auction ten years ago, at a time when many state-run businesses were sold off to the private sector. Since then he pays both annual licensing fees and taxes on produce. His licence allows him to sell liquor from Mandalay to Hsipaw, but no further. The problem is that with the cost of military government fees, and the increasing cost of raw produce which is also subject to military government licensing fees and taxation, the cost of liquor is well beyond the means of all but the wealthiest of Burmese tipplers. Hence the proliferation of illicit distilleries and booze houses in Burma. Black market liquor costs a fraction of the price of even the cheapest of licensed liquor. This illicit alcohol is then sold in booze dens or peddled around the towns and villages. This poses a problem for Mr Charles, to tell or not to tell the government about these local distributors. On one hand they take away the business for which he is paying expensive fees but on the other, government crackdowns on black marketeers are severe – the SPDC do not take kindly to people who encroach upon its avenues for income earning.

Three weeks prior to my arrival in Hsipaw this was illustrated by a military crackdown, not on illicit alcohol but on black market timber cutters. Different industry, similar issues. Timber is an SPDC monopoly, with all cutting and processing coming under licensing agreements controlled by the Myanmar Timber Enterprise. The problem is that this timber is too expensive for townsfolk and villagers to buy and consequently black market produce is in demand. The mills are hidden in the jungle and are well protected, sometimes by members of armed ethnic minority groups. The SPDC recently took action against one such mill in the forests to the south-east of Hsipaw. Soldiers moved in, destroyed buildings, confiscated timber, and killed three of the workers. Market control by superior firepower, at least as far as the military are concerned.

'Shan people do not like the Burmans,' says Mr Charles. 'Do you know Nam Kan? It is a Shan town on the Chinese border. If you go there and speak Burmese or wear a *longii* they will fight you or kill you. In Nam Kan they hate the Burmans.'

Walking back into Hsipaw I pass three soldiers. They have semi-automatic weapons and one has a string of hand grenades on his belt. These are soldiers of the Shan State Army.

❑ ❑ ❑ ❑ ❑

Late in the afternoon I meet one of the tourist touts of Hsipaw. He is nearly two metres tall; a long-haired, shaggy-bearded, broad-shouldered and broad-faced fellow who looks like an Australian bushranger. His name is Sai and his distinctive looks are the result of his cultural heritage – a Shan national but also with Indian and Chinese blood. As I walk past his house he calls out to me and asks me to join him for a cup of tea. 'I like to be friends with tourists,' he explains. 'I want to help them. I want them to have a good time in my town and in my country. But I do not want their money. Some people, when they leave Hsipaw, they give me gifts. I have been given a camera, T-shirts, sun-glasses and money. One person gave me money and I said "No, no, I cannot take your money," but they gave it to me anyway and I gave it to the people in the hospital. I do not want your money. This is my hobby, helping tourists.' Some days later an Austrian traveller comments to me, 'Okay, if someone tells you once they don't want your money, maybe they don't want your money. If someone tells you twenty times that they don't want your money, then they DEFinitely want your money.'

This notwithstanding, the first time I meet Sai he is friendly and I have dinner with him, his wife and a restaurant owner. The food is pickled peanut paste and something which I take to be beef but which is in fact broiled pieces of wood. I know the type of stick it is because I have seen little bundles of them in the market. Little bundles for little fires I had always thought. But no, Shan food and it is good food. Earthy. Washed down with an orange-flavoured liqueur. Cointreau minus the subtlety.

The restaurant in which we eat is on the outskirts of Hsipaw and when we finish it is dark. Sai walks me back towards town and as he does so we are waved over by a group of men who are sitting at a table in front of a house and drinking. We join them and I am introduced to the owner of the house. He is a General of the Shan State Army (North), Mr G to me, on account of never quite having caught his name.

Mr G – you can see it in the way he sits, you can see it in the angles of his body. They announce, 'I am in charge.' Confidence and control. You see it in the way he looks and in the way he watches people – attentive, composed and comfortable. His eyes do not flit from one thing to another and rarely do they settle on inanimate objects. They always watch people. They watch and they take in. Eyes in command. But his welcome to me is warm, as are his handshake and smile.

Then I am introduced to his teenage son, Little G. He is in the process of learning the postures, the images, the look of ownership and strength of his father; learning to uphold the dignity and status of his position. But like his father he is friendly and smiles with me. I am a foreigner and a guest. One of the men at the table comments that he is learning to speak English and they coax him into saying a few words. Then he becomes shy.

❑ ❑ ❑ ❑ ❑

'The Shan are strong people and the Burmese government is scared of them. But we must be humble. If we are not, the government will kill us,' declares Mr G. 'The government wants to make peace with us, we make peace but we do not lay down our arms. The government gives rice and oil and money to us because we have made a cease-fire but what they want are the rubies from the mines and the teak from the forests. Before, if they want to go to the forest in Shan State they know that our soldiers will kill them. This is why the government makes peace with us, this is why they give us the rice. But the SPDC is a snake in the grass. It goes quietly and from side to side. It can never be trusted. Shan people smile on the

surface but deep down we do not smile. This is why we still have our
weapons.'
Smiles which hide darker feelings. It is not dissimilar to the rows of
flowers along the road from Mandalay to Maymyo.

❏ ❏ ❏ ❏ ❏

I stay drinking orange liqueur until late into the night and before I leave
Mrs G invites me to the wedding of their son which is to be held in two
days' time.
Returning to the hotel and the Hsipaw power grid is down. I sit on my
bed and write holding a cigarette lighter in one hand. Tonight I did not
intend to be sitting and drinking liquor with the general of an insurgent
army. I did not seek this out. It was a string of circumstances that led me
to this meeting – a left turn here, a right turn there, a decision to not go
into a temple but to keep walking, a decision to take a cup of tea with Sai
which I had initially resisted. Then, four hours later...
My lighter goes out. The steel of the lighting mechanism is now very
hot and I burn myself trying to re-light it.

MR DONALD

It is 9.30 a.m. and I am at the front gate of the estate of Mr Donald,
guardian of the Shan Palace. He is the nephew of the last Shan Prince
of Hsipaw, who was killed by Ne Win's military junta when taken into
custody in 1962. It feels strange to walk in uninvited and unintroduced.
Many people do and all are admitted but nonetheless it feels awkward. So
I wait at the front gate for someone to come by.
Peering into the estate I can see a driveway that leads down and around
to a large, double-storey English-style manor house. The grass is long, too
long, and off to the right of the driveway a cyclone wire fence and net
posts, evidence what was once a grass tennis court. The house itself has
seen better days. I find out later that most of the land beyond the walls has
been claimed by the army, most recently a fourteen-hectare orchard. In
addition to this, last year the traditional timber Shan Palace was bull-
dozed. This was done as part of the continuing bid by the SPDC to de-
moralize the Shan People.
Once, not too long ago, this surely must have been a beautiful estate.
After twenty minutes a car arrives and the people in it ask me what I am
doing. I explain that I would like to see Mr Donald. Come in they reply.
We go through the gate and they show me to the front door of the house.

There I meet Fern, Mr Donald's wife, and she takes me to meet Mr Donald who is working in a vegetable patch beside an old swimming pool, empty now but for some shallow, stagnant green water which is used for the garden. Mr Donald, a stocky man, is wearing a large-brimmed bamboo hat, fawn trousers and a clean white T-shirt. He has an immediately recognizable air of dignity about him.

'Primitive people light a candle not with a match or lighter but with a flint. They strike it and hold the candle close so that it can catch alight. After many attempts, finally the wick catches. Then the flame is protected because it is weak. The candle is raised slowly and a hand is used to shield it from drafts and the wind. People hardly dare breathe lest their breath extinguishes the flame. Then, as it is raised, so slowly, it lights a cave, but not the whole of the cave because the flame is weak. And the first thing that is illuminated is the glitter and the sparkle of jewels, but not only jewels, the treasure of Solomon's caves. To see the treasure first, this is human nature; to see the crowns and the sceptres and the gems and the money that glitters in the faint candlelight. So people reach out to take the most beautiful of all of the jewels, an ornamented crown. But what is not seen is the snake that is beneath the crown and the scorpion. These are the ones that are hiding beneath the jewels, these are the ones that will bite and kill.'

Whilst telling this story Mr Donald is expressive, almost theatrical, as he acts out the lighting, protecting, and raising of the candle, the seeing of the gems and the seeing of the snake. He has a powerful, modulated voice, good for story telling. And although he does not explain his stories, there is always a specific purpose behind his telling them.

'I was told that you would be coming to see me,' continues Mr Donald. 'I wondered why you did not come yesterday.' I ask how he had known. 'Ahh,' he replies. 'Your reputation precedes you like the wind that carries the scent of a flower.' Later in the afternoon I realize that many of our conversations are coloured by this wind of foreknowledge.

Mr Donald excuses himself and attends to his other guests. Fern meanwhile takes me into the sitting room and explains to me something of the history of the family. Like Mr Donald, she too is exceptionally well spoken.

❑ ❑ ❑ ❑ ❑

Sao Ong Kya was the Shan Prince of Hsipaw from 1927 until his death in 1938. He had attained both his Batchelor of History and his Masters in History at Oxford University and upon returning to Burma he had designed the Shan Palace in which Mr Donald now resides. When he died he was succeeded by Mr Donald's grandfather who was Prince of Hsipaw until the takeover of Burma by the Japanese in 1942. In 1948, after Independence, Mr Donald's father was called to Taunggyi, the capital of Shan State, to fill the government position of Shan Secretary of State. Thus it fell to his younger brother, Mr Donald's uncle, to fill the position of Prince of the Shan State.

Mr Donald's uncle had been an Engineering student at Oxford. Whilst there he met an Austrian, Inge Eberhard whom he was to marry. As in all of the fairy stories, when she was a student Inge did not realize that she was dating an oriental prince. Upon their arrival in Rangoon they received a splendid reception before travelling to Hsipaw.

In January 1962 the Shan State Council was drafting a resolution requesting the federation of the Burmese States and the bloodless gaining of ethnic autonomy. At this time Mr Donald's uncle was the Shan Member of Parliament for Hsipaw.

General Ne Win, however, pre-empted this initiative and Mr Donald's uncle was seized by the military. On the 3 February 1962 he penned a letter from prison which was smuggled to his wife:

> Liebling,
> I am writing this secretly. I am being locked up at the army lock up at Ba Htao Myo at Iron Bark. Please ask Khin Mg Chin to request Tommy Clift to use his influence to get me out....

The last communication of the Shan Prince. In response to the family's questions as to his whereabouts, the Burmese military denied having taken him into custody. Although he has not been seen or heard of since, in the time that I am to know them neither Mr Donald nor Fern say that he was killed by the military. That this was the case is obvious.

On the living room wall of the Donald household there is a chronologically sequential set of photographs of family members. As Fern tells me about the family history she points out the photos of relevant members of the family. At one point there is a border in the oak panelling on the left-hand side of which is the older family history and on the right-hand side of which are photos of the late Shan Prince. On the 29 February 1996 a delegation of twenty-two foreign diplomats and ambassadors came to the Shan Palace accompanied by members of the SLORC military staff. Mr Donald talked them through the family history following the photographs along the wall. When he reached the border in the oak panelling the SLORC representative, U Thura Hung That from the General Protocol Department, Ministry of Foreign Affairs, interrupted and announced that that was the end of the story. None of the photos of the late Shan Prince were discussed.

Arbitrary arrest, arbitrary execution, arbitrary seizure of goods and property, widespread rape, forced labour, forced portering for the army, forced relocation, use as human mine sweepers, use as human defence shields, these are the hardships that have confronted the Shan people since the military took power in 1962. And these gross abuses of the rights of Shan people continue to this day.

In 1995 there were an estimated 100,000 Tatmadaw soldiers enforcing military policy in Shan State. The particular policy employed is known as the Four Cuts Policy and is designed to cut off food, funds, intelligence, and recruits provided by local villagers to resistance fighters. What this amounts to is the Burmese military mounting an offensive against the Shan people in a particular region. Troops are sent in and inhabitants of villages are relocated to areas under control by the Burmese army. In 1996 an estimated 100,000 Shan people from 600 villages were relocated by the military to 45 main sites. Between 1997 and 2000 a further 200,000 Shan people were relocated. Often the sites to which the villagers are moved are barren land where people must find their own food and build their own shelters. The only work is forced labour on SLORC/SPDC projects. Villagers found returning to their homes or to farm their land are shot on sight.

After an area has been cleared of Shan people, the army moves in and builds barracks and access roads with Shan slave labour. Then, sometimes, Shan people are allowed to move back into the areas considered safely under military control. Upon returning, the Shan are further exploited as slave labour.

If there is any retaliation or resistance, villages are destroyed and villagers, including village elders, are executed arbitrarily as a deterrent. As an example, on 8-9 May 2000 the Shan State Army (South) ambushed a Burmese army convoy travelling between Kunhing and Takaw, southern Shan State. Some Burmese soldiers and officers were killed in this raid. On the 23 May 2000 one hundred Burmese troops under the command of Captain Than Aung, Infantry Battalion 246 based in Kunhing surprised farmers who were working in the rice and sesame fields near the deserted Shan village of Huaypu. The farmers were from a relocation settlement near Kunhing town. Sixty-four were shot in cold blood. Such is life in a military-designated 'brown zone'.

❑ ❑ ❑ ❑ ❑

In the late afternoon a small procession passes by the Donald residence. It has been assembled and paid for courtesy of donations and labour from one of the high schools in Hsipaw. Two cars have loudspeakers mounted

on them and behind come traditional Shan *Ozi* drums. When beaten,
these are used to sound out invitations to ceremonies as well as for the
calling of people to war. In the latter instance, whilst the drums were
beating Shan soldiers were reputed to be invincible.

The procession ends at a small wooden temple. Crowds mill around as
people banging gongs and drums walk around the compound. A circle
forms and a dancer dressed as a deer emerges with his head ducking and
weaving and twitching and then jolting upright. Then there is another
dance in which the young dancer wears a costume which sprouts out
colourfully from behind him like a peacock displaying its plumage.

As we watch Mr Donald explains that many of the traditional musical
instruments, costumes, and masks of the Shan people have been bought
up by overseas traders. Many are sold in Thailand. 'This is the selling of
our culture,' says Mr Donald.

As night comes food is served. I sit with Mr Donald and an old man
from one of the nearby villages in the hills. This gentleman has tattoos
scribbled and scratched all the way up and down his forearms. 'These
were part of his initiation into manhood,' explains Mr Donald. 'The tattoo
is made with bamboo needles and the soot from kerosene and when it has
been completed an ointment is applied. The recipient is then pushed from
a platform and should twist mid air, like a cat, and land upright. This is
because once a man has been tattooed he is meant to be invincible. Weapons will not be able to hit or wound him.' Mr Donald then goes on to say
that the traditional Shan tattoo of a warrior is the boar's head, either on
the back or the chest. People with this tattoo are often the most fearsome
of the Shan resistance fighters and when the Burmese army capture them
they are usually killed immediately.

A new dance begins, this time inside a hall in the *paya*. Performed by
two lines of school children, it is a welcoming dance in which the word
'Welcome' is spelt out in English. Mr Donald takes the opportunity to
manoeuvre me into a position where I can speak to one of the teachers
from the school. 'If you went to her school, she would not be able to talk
to you,' says Mr Donald, 'but here there are no problems.' Mr Donald
then explains that she teaches in one of the villages near Hsipaw and her
students are up to twelve years old. Each class that she teaches has more
than fifty students although sometimes she must teach up to three classes
simultaneously. Out of her annual wage she saves one dollar each month
to contribute towards the costs of this ceremony. Then Mr Donald explains that in Buddhism the magnitude of any donation is immaterial so as
not to discriminate between rich and poor. All merit is given equally and
the important aspect is not to waver before or during giving and after

having presented a gift to be happy that you have done so.

When I leave the *paya* I am warned that the Hsipaw police and military will know that I have been to the Shan Palace. They will have been watching me. And I am warned to be careful with whom I talk in Hsipaw. Some people will make trouble. Be careful.

❑ ❑ ❑ ❑ ❑

'There must be a complete change in our country,' an old Shan gentleman tells me. 'When you kill a snake, you must really kill a snake. A snake is poisonous so you must kill it properly because otherwise it will come back and bite you.'

TWO WEDDINGS AND AN M-16

From: 'On Sunday Under Azure Sky' by Byatti, *The New Light of Myanmar*, 23 June 1996.

The wedding reception had already begun at Inya Lake Hotel when I arrived there. The bride, the groom and parents of both sides seemed unhappy. I was overwhelmed by the thought of what made things difficult for them.

Usually, wedding receptions would be lively with the blare of music. Now the vocalists looked awkward. The musicians were fidgety with restless eyes. The bride's father walked up to a man in the band with whom he talked arms akimbo. Their voices could not be heard but his attitude showed discontent over something. The man in the band seemed to plead with him. The vocalists also walked up to them and joined the man and helped him plead with the bride's father.

"Not like that, Uncle. It has never happened so to our band leader," explained the man. The bride's father seemed not to accept it. Mopping the sweat on his brow with a handkerchief which he pulled out of his Myanmar jacket pocket, he replied, "That it has never happened is not my concern. What concerns me is your band's stark lack of care at this reception of my daughter."

The man in the band kept his head down. Meanwhile, the groom's mother came by. She said, "We've lost our dignity only when we chose Inya Lake for the reception. I don't want to say anything more..." I had come to realize the situation. The problem was none other than the band leader who had not appeared. I went back to my seat.

It was certain more or less that the bride, the groom and parents of both sides, who were frustrated by the entertainment program, had to brace themselves for possible criticism and blame from the guests. The more guests arrived, the more shameful the hosts felt. Some guests who could not spare their time went back. Meanwhile, there was a stir.

"Here he comes."

A voice from the guests made me, as well as all others, look in the direction of the entrance. I saw the band leader whom I knew at once though he was not an acquaintance of mine. Immediately, he asked the hosts for forgiveness. I did not know how he had done but the hosts seemed to have been contented.

Soon afterwards, the reception became enlivened with music. Parents of both sides explained to the guests nearby why the band leader was late. When I asked the groom's father, close by, about the band leader, he replied, "Yes, he was right with his excuse. The car he was in was caught in a traffic jam on University Avenue."

Only then could I conclude, "Oh ...after all... that's because of them, the NLD. They are a nuisance to everyone."

"Yes, that's right. Do not think of passing through the avenue on Saturdays and Sundays. You'll be in trouble. They encroach upon the road. If you honk the horn lest they might get hurt, they will glower or hurl abuse at you as if it were their own road."

University Avenue is a main road in Yangon. Most people choose Saturdays and Sundays, the weekend holidays, for social and charitable occasions. The NLD are busy moving about on these days. Using both sides of the road they are causing a public nuisance. It is not for any cause of democracy. One way or another, they organize from behind the fence a group of inexperienced, unemployed, and hilarious persons and their attempt for political gain is pestering the public mentally and physically. If this goes on like this there will be a problem one day.

The cause to write this article about a wedding reception which could not be free from the pester of the hilarious gangsters came up when I learned of grievances through letters to the editor and bursting out from the residents of neighbouring wards and bus drivers earning their livelihood about the trouble caused by the hilarious gangsters on the pavements on Saturdays and Sundays.

❑ ❑ ❑ ❑ ❑

Meanwhile, in Hsipaw, a very different type of wedding is taking place, the wedding of the son of Mr G. It is like the wedding at the beginning of the film 'The Godfather' except that this is not the wedding of an Italian Mafia family in New York but that of a Shan family in eastern Burma. Mr G senior spends most of his time in a dark, smoky room on the ground floor of his house. Shades of Marlon Brando. I enter and pay my respects. There is a round table at which elderly men sit puffing on cheroots, engaging in quiet conversation, and looking very serious. As the wedding progresses I see these and other older men come and go from this room but Mr G spends most of the day here, leaving the wedding fuss and festivities to other family members.

Outside this room and in front of the house is a concrete forecourt upon which tables for family members and special guests have been set up. There are six of them, each table seating fifteen guests, and it is here that I am invited to sit. Lavish amounts of food are served. Yesterday three fully-grown pigs (of the huge variety) were slaughtered and today trays so large that it takes two people to carry them ferry pork from the kitchens to the tables. They are emptied and then returned to the kitchens for reloading. And the food... fatty pork cube soup, deep-fried pig stomach lining, deep-fried crackling, roast thinly-sliced prime cut meat, roast black innards of some description, deep-fried frilly intestinal items, and, accompanying this feast, broiled noodles with peanuts, rice, and heaped platters of bean sprout salad. This is all washed down with Chinese tea and the orange flavoured liqueur. As soon as one plate of food is empty it is replaced by another. As soon as my bowl is empty, someone fills it with more food and more food and more food until in the end I turn it upside down to stop it from being filled once again.

At the back of the house temporary kitchens have been set up. There are canvas awnings overhead, trellis tables beneath, simmering cauldrons, and woks like small satellite dishes that spit and crackle as the cooks toss the pig parts around. Altogether there are eleven people working in the kitchens, some slicing and dicing, some tossing and stirring, others keeping wood on the fires and washing the steady stream of plates as they come in. Then there are the three pairs of tray bearers. Altogether they will be feeding a thousand guests during the course of the day, maybe two thousand. It is a transient guest list with people coming, paying their respects, eating, staying for a while and then leaving.

Returning to the front of the house, past the tables for families and special guests, out through the front gates. There is a broad strip of grass between the front fence and the road and it is here that a marquee tent and awning have been set up. Under this are another eight tables for guests. There is also a stage for a band. At the front of the stage is a row of seats where the son and his bride sit, both dressed in traditional Shan costume, both looking out over the assembled guests. When I approach, Little G smiles, shakes my hand, and is pleased that I have come to his wedding.

Around the periphery of the house, around the tables, the marquee, the kitchen and the toilets are soldiers from the Shan State Army. At the back of the house four sit in the sun and look out over the rice paddies, semi-automatic rifles resting idly on laps or propped up against a wall. At the front of the house a soldier has a grenade launcher on his back, grenades on his belt, a walkie-talkie, and a holstered handgun. One officer has a handgun, a large bowie knife, and a walkie-talkie. Others bear more automatic rifles. Down the road and closer to town is a truck where four soldiers loiter. It is an advance guard.

Trying to take advantage of my special guest status, I ask the bearer of the grenade launcher if I may take a photo. Not possible, which is a pity because he looks like something out of a Hollywood action film.

So this is peace without laying down weapons, a co-existence of opposing military forces. And in Hsipaw the soldiers who seem to have the bigger and more prominent hardware are the members of the Shan State Army.

At the wedding a concert bash of unrhythmic instrument clatterers begins. I realize that the middle of an insurgent state barely on the power grid is unlikely to the home of a Burmese Fab Four, but even so this is not a good band. One particular song is stopped and restarted on a number of occasions because the singer misses her cue. Eventually the musicians decide not to stop and the singer races through the opening lyrics in order to catch up. Then she pauses because she has gone too far too fast. Little G, now dressed in a suit and silk shirt, comes across to me and asks if I would sing. I politely decline.

By four o'clock guests still come and go as they have done since the morning. Food is still being served and I am offered more by everyone I meet. And on the presents table, the array of gifts has now overflowed on to the grass beside and below. The party will go on into the night, just as it did the night before but I take the opportunity to wish people good luck, say my farewells and depart.

THANK YOU MR BOOK

Take a poor country, take a town which has a small but steady flow of tourist dollars coming into it, see what happens.

Mr Book is a balding, beaming Muslim bookshop owner who directed me to the guesthouse of Mr Charles when I first arrived in Hsipaw. Mr Charles is a guesthouse and liquor factory owner. Sai is the owner of a teashop, a cow, and works as a cabinet-maker. Mr Donald is the nephew of the last Shan Prince. These are four of the main characters that have a part in the game played to attract the dollars that come into Hsipaw. Relations are not cordial.

Sai tells travellers coming into Hsipaw that they should visit 'Mr Dollars Donald', a man whom he describes as a Shan Prince with a lot of money but who does nothing for his people. Mr Donald claims that Sai openly courts tourists but then pressures them into giving him money or gifts. Furthermore, he used to bring tourists to the gates of the Shan Estate and then ask them for money for having done so. This angered Mr Donald and this has been a cause of ongoing animosity between the two.

Even greater animosity exists between Sai and Mr Book. When Hsipaw was first opened to tourists at the end of 1996 the two used to work together. They soon fell out and today, if one asks Sai about Mr Book, he will tell derogatory stories about bald people and Muslims with their crude habits. It is thinly veiled abuse. Ask Mr Book about Sai, however, and there is little by way of response. Instead, he produces a letter addressed to the police and written by a traveller complaining about Sai. Mr Book's possession and occasional display of this letter have contributed to running Sai out of the competition for tourist dollars in Hsipaw.

One might ask how Mr Book came to obtain a copy of this letter from the police.

Like Sai, Mr Charles feels the pressure exerted by Mr Book. Again, when Hsipaw first opened to tourists Mr Book used to charge a ten-kyat commission for every tourist that he would take from the centre of town to Mr Charles' guesthouse. As more tourists came and Mr Charles extended his guesthouse, Mr Book upped his commission to twenty kyat and asked it of every tourist who stayed with Mr Charles, irrespective of whether or not they had been brought by him. Mr Charles refused to pay the commission and as a result Mr Book stopped directing travellers to the guesthouse. Furthermore a rumour began to circulate, do not talk to Mr Charles about politics in Burma because he is a police informer. A note to this effect even made it into the travellers' book in the US Café in Rangoon.

At the end of 1997 Mr Charles increased the price of his guesthouse from 300 kyat per night to 320 kyat. The twenty kyat extra was to pay Mr Book's commission and thereafter the beaming, balding, bookshop owner once again began to direct people to Mr Charles' guesthouse.

Mr Book has run Sai out of town, has re-established relations with Mr Charles, and now does everything he can to help tourists in Hsipaw and everything that he does earns him a commission. Trishaw drivers pay him commissions, tailors pay him commissions, grocers pay him commissions, even a local doctor pays him commissions. Ten kyat here, fifty kyat there. What it really adds up to is a web of commissions and in the middle sits the beaming, balding Mr Book.

And concerning the rumours about police informants? In Hsipaw, it is said that Mr Book's own preparedness to discuss politics may help local authorities to assess which tourists are serious in their pursuit of local knowledge.

And now, without knowing any better, it is Mr Book to whom I have turned to advise me about a walk out of Hsipaw. Certainly he is helpful and he provides me with advice, a small hand-drawn map, and a note in Burmese to give to a local teacher with whom I will stay overnight in the village of Nam Kam. But at the same time he collects his commissions from everyone with whom he recommends I have any dealings.

❏ ❏ ❏ ❏ ❏

Walking out of Hsipaw, hidden behind a row of houses, is the Christian Cemetery. It is small and unkempt and a number of the graves are unnamed, bearing no more than a wooden cross, the message 'Rest in Peace', and candles on mounds of dirt. Some of the graves are not unnamed but have had the names painted out in white. On one such grave someone has rewritten a name on top of a painted out name, 'Mark, aged 16, died 27/11/1996.' On another grave, one with a more permanent headstone, the epitaph reads 'In Loving memory of Charles William Lambert (Missionary). Native of Blackheath, Kent, England, who was murdered in the Mission House, Thibaw, on the 23 May 1895, age 39 years. Father Forgive Them, They Know Not What They Do.'

What happened to this gentleman from Blackheath, Kent? What sort of life did he live in Hsipaw one hundred years ago? It would have been a primitive outpost then, surrounded by jungle and animals and monkeys. Did he do wrong to meet his premature end or was he the victim of primitive brutality?

Beyond the cemetery is a house with a large water-wheel and beyond this, the Chinese and Muslim cemeteries. A gurgling brook runs beside them and a deciduous tree hangs over a crook in its course. All around are rice paddies, bright green, terraced and watered by tributaries and bamboo aqueducts from the river. And then there are the flowers. From where I sit and write, close to the entrance of the first village along my way, I am surrounded by little yellow cups on tiny wooden trees, by pale blue scruffy flowers on straggly plants, by starburst flowers with mauve protrusions extending in every direction from a red centre. Each protrusion has a white dot on the end. There are large, yellow, trumpet flowers with red centres and red stalks and there are the green berry flowers which, as they mature, open up into tiny red flowers, and then as they mature further grow into tightly-packed clusters of orange and red. There are six-pointed white star flowers and more yellow flowers and purple-petalled flowers. And somewhere in the distance there is a pig groinking and oinking and a lizard scuttling off into the grasses. A big-hatted little man with a yellow Shan shoulder-bag passes by on the back of a water buffalo. There is a calf following behind. In the stream there is a woman beating clothes against a washboard. An older lady walks past with a wicker basket on her head and a musket in her hands and a working gang of four comes in from the fields for lunch.

As I continue to walk, a bullock-drawn wagon clatters down the track and I squash myself into the vegetation so as to avoid its passage. Walking on I think about poverty and what it means. In Burma the list of sufferances endured by the population may well be as great as that endured by any other nation in the world. And it is a list that touches on all facets of life: education, health, employment, income, standard of living, absence of basic human rights. Yet walking through the country, looking at the people from the villages, it strikes me that although they have so little, they smile more. They are not as stressed and they seem to have a better time than do their counterparts in the Western world; this despite their sufferings. And so I wonder, who is poorer?

I pass huts built on stilts beside rice paddies. They have thatched roofs, bamboo slat floors, and bamboo woven mat walls. Inside, the living areas are divided into two, a cooking area with a fire in the centre and a second area for sleeping. Beneath the house livestock are tethered so that they are hard to steal. Sometimes there is a buffalo, maybe one or two pigs, and always some chickens. Many houses have small vegetable plots.

There is no doubt that these houses are the houses of the poor in Burma but even so they adequately fulfil the functions which a house must fulfil. So how poor are these people?

Then, as I walk further, I see a mother standing outside one of these houses with her son who is perhaps five years old. He has scabies or eczema or some sort of skin disorder on the back of his head and behind his ear. It has become an open wound and red raw. I think, in this image there is a key to the nature of the poverty of the Burmese. It is a poverty in which there is neither the money nor the facilities to have this affliction treated. Perhaps this is what poverty is. Not being able to avoid suffering.

Absence of freedom and pervasive fear of the military, these are further factors which should somehow be worked into equations concerning Burmese poverty.

Interrupting my thoughts, someone shouts to me, 'Hellloooo, hellloooo.' Looking around, I see, on the top of a distant hill, a silhouetted figure waving at me. I wave back. 'Thaaank youuuuuu,' he shouts, 'thaaaaank youuuuuu.' '*Maaaaa soooon kaaaaaah*,' I shout back. 'Thaaaank youuuuuuu,' he continues to cry as he walks across the hill tops.

It is four o'clock in the afternoon when I finally walk over the shoulder of a hill and between the vertical planks and horizontal crossbeam that signify the entrance to Pankan, a village of perhaps two hundred houses cradled in between three hills. Beyond the entrance are two massive trees with sprawling intertwined root systems. They flank a wooden Buddhist monastery but one which has strong animist overtones. Like in any other monastery or *paya*, there is a large statue of the Buddha which has had gold leaf rubbed on it. Surrounding this are smaller statues, candles, sticks of incense, and photographs of some of the famous temples of Pagan, Rangoon, and Mandalay. But up on the walls around the temple are pictures of animals, mainly buffalo and deer. A thousand years ago animism and the worship of *Nats* and Spirits was the predominant belief in Burma. In more remote regions, the remnants of these beliefs can still be seen coexisting with Buddhism.

Beyond the *paya* and the monastery is a cobblestone road which leads down and into the village. A system of bamboo pipes feeds two troughs beside which villagers queue with tin pails to collect water for the evening. Horses are being led back to the village for the night, pigs and buffalo are tethered under huts, gardens boast brightly-coloured flowers, and chickens scratch where they will. Along one track, five scruffy children fire rubber bands at a hand-sized spider which has made its web in the upper boughs of a tree. And nearby, on the top of one of the surrounding hills is the local school. It is here that I go to meet the teacher with whom I am to stay for the night.

The Pankan school is a rectangular barn which boasts a roof and three walls. When I arrive there is a teacher at each end of the barn pointing to a blackboard attached to the wall. Half the barn is full of students facing one teacher and the other half is full of students facing the other. Between the respective back rows is a dirt walkway a metre wide and this is all that separates the two classes. Each class is made up of approximately forty to fifty students of assorted ages from six to twelve. When I enter a general disorganized hubbub ensues as both classes turn to look at the white person.

Pankan. No electricity, no cars, no roads, only a single rustic cobblestone track through the centre. As I walk back to the teacher's house people want me to come and drink with them. When I do not, they follow me to the teacher's house and we eat and drink there instead. Dinner is a staple meal of bean paste, broiled spinach and rice. Breakfast the following morning is the same. 'Meat is too expensive,' explains the teacher. 'On special occasions we kill a chicken.'

I go to sleep early, next to the cooking fire, and likewise get up early after a night in which my body tries to accustom itself to sleeping on a mat on a bamboo floor.

❑ ❑ ❑ ❑ ❑

Early morning, looking out from the hills around Pankan. A sea of mists covers Hsipaw and the Shan plateau. Island-like hills rise out of this sea and the sun rises above the scene. And from the village come the sounds of bells clanking as horses and water buffalo are led out to the fields for the day.

When I leave Pankan I diverge from the path that I followed yesterday as soon as I can, making my way along a river and then through the fields and rice paddies. A brick-maker has fallen asleep in a deck-chair beside a roaring kiln and two young boys are in the river washing the buffalo which have been entrusted to their care. And in the rice paddies, farm workers scythe and stack and pick and plant.

❑ ❑ ❑ ❑ ❑

Burma used to be the largest exporter of rice in South-East Asia. Now rice production is largely controlled by the military and the life of the farmers suffers accordingly. There is a law in Burma which says that any rice farmer who owns more than five acres (two hectares) of paddies is subject to having extra paddy land confiscated by the military for redistribution. In addition to this, rice farmers must sell a quota of their harvest to the military government at predetermined prices. Sometimes these can be as low as half of the market value. If farmers cannot make the quota, short-falls must be paid for with money or the provision of labour. Rice farmers further have to contend with corruption at weigh-in stations where under-paid employees set aside rice for themselves to supplement their own meagre incomes. Finally, to add to a farmer's woes, there is always the possibility of soldiers demanding rice for personal use or provisions.

In the depression years prior to World War II the peasants of Burma revolted against the British in the Saya San Peasants' Revolt. Then, for thirty-five years of military rule, the peasants did not dare to oppose the junta. In March 1997, however, in the town of Depayiun some 500 kilometres north of Rangoon, 3,000 peasants marched against the local SLORC. They demanded an end to the forced selling of their rice paddies to the military junta at ridiculously low prices. The military suppressed their demonstrations and there was no change to local policies.

Rice farmer. It is not a good career choice in Burma.

RUMOURS OF HSIPAW

Walk through Hsipaw, eat kidney beans in a monastery, drink lime-juice in a garage, have dinner with two Burmese gentlemen who have just finished singing in an open-fronted karaoke bar beside the res-taurant, do these things and hear the stories that circulate about the mili-tary. Sometimes there are almost too many of these to keep track.

'We cannot afford to buy the apples that are grown in Burma. There are levies on the growing of apples that make the prices more expensive than the apples that come through from China. Black market apples are cheap but the penalties for growing without a licence are harsh.'

'A bridge collapsed across a river in the district. Wait and I will show you a photo that I have kept from the newspaper. On page one the story says that the government has rebuilt the bridge. What it does not say is that soldiers from Hsipaw rounded up villagers to rebuild the bridge.'

'See that helicopter in the sky? It was funded by the United Nations to try to combat the drug problem in Burma. Now it is used to fly Chinese businessmen in and out of this country.'

'And in 1996 a large Chinese delegation came to Burma and wanted to look into the possibility of building a highway from Yunnan Province, through Lashio and then on to Hsipaw. The delegation flew into Rangoon but then wanted to travel between Hsipaw and Lashio by road to survey the terrain. Before this trip took place, the Burmese military forced local villagers to work on the road.'

'When they do not force us to work, they take our money. At any time the army can knock on the door and say that we must give fifty kyat to sponsor the planting of a tree. Sometimes they ask for two thousand kyat for reforestation programs. And this can happen any time.'

'Everybody in Hsipaw uses charcoal to cook. In the last six months the price of charcoal has increased from 100 to 180 kyat. This is difficult for the people.'

'In our country inflation is corruption. If they can't take our money they take our labour,' says U Lit Leh Du.

These are the stories of simple folk. Sometimes I hear so many I wonder if they are being fabricated or exaggerated. They cannot all be true.

On 2 July 1998 the International Labour Organization (ILO) considered a report from a Commission of Inquiry into the observance by the Burmese Military Government of the Forced Labour Convention, 1930 (No.29). This was a convention ratified by a civilian Burmese Government in 1957. The following are some of the conclusions of the Commission.

> *528. There is abundant evidence before the Commission showing the pervasive use of forced labour imposed on the civilian population throughout Myanmar by the authorities and the military for portering, the construction, maintenance and servicing of military camps, other work in support of the military, work on agriculture, logging and other production projects undertaken by the authorities or the military, sometimes for the profit of private individuals,*

the construction and maintenance of roads, railways and bridges, other infrastructure work and a range of other tasks, none of which comes under any of the exceptions listed in Article 2(2) of the Forced Labour Convention.

529. The call-up of labour is provided for in very wide terms under...the Village Act and...the Towns Act, which are incompatible with the Forced Labour Convention. The procedure used in practice often follows the pattern of those provisions, in relying on the village head or ward authorities for requisitioning the labour that any military or government officer may order them to supply; but the provisions of the Village Act and the Towns Act were never actually referred to in those orders for the call-up of forced labourers that were submitted to the Commission; it thus appears that unfettered powers of military and government officers to exact forced labour from the civilian population are taken for granted, without coordination among different demands made on the same population, and people are also frequently rounded up directly by the military for forced labour, bypassing the local authorities.

530. Failure to comply with a call-up for labour is punishable under the Village Act with a fine or imprisonment for a term not exceeding one month, or both, and under the Towns Act, with a fine. In actual practice, the manifold exactions of forced labour often give rise to the extortion of money in exchange for a temporary alleviation of the burden, but also to threats to life and security and extrajudicial punishment of those unwilling, slow or unable to comply with a demand for forced labour; such punishment or reprisals range from money demands to physical abuse, beatings, torture, rape and murder.

531. Forced labour in Myanmar is widely performed by women, children and elderly persons as well as persons otherwise unfit for work.

532. Forced labour in Myanmar is almost never remunerated nor compensated, secret directives notwithstanding, but on the contrary often goes hand in hand with the exaction of money, food and other supplies as well from the civilian population.

533. Forced labour is a heavy burden on the general population in Myanmar, preventing farmers from tending to the needs of their holdings and children from attending school; it falls most heavily on landless labourers and the poorer sections of the population, which depend on hiring out their labour for subsistence and generally have no means to comply with various money demands made by the authorities in lieu of, or over and above, the exaction of forced labour. The impossibility of making a living because of the amount of forced labour exacted is a frequent reason for fleeing the country.

*534. The burden of forced labour also appears to be particularly
great for non-Burman ethnic groups, especially in areas where there
is a strong military presence...*

*535. All the information and evidence before the Commission shows
utter disregard by the authorities for the safety and health as well
as the basic needs of the people performing forced or compulsory
labour. Porters, including women, are often sent ahead in particularly dangerous situations as in suspected minefields, and many
are killed or injured this way. Porters are rarely given medical treatment of any kind; injuries to shoulders, backs and feet are frequent, but medical treatment is minimal or non-existent and some
sick or injured are left behind in the jungle. Similarly, on road
building projects, injuries are in most cases not treated, and deaths
from sickness and work accidents are frequent on some projects.
Forced labourers, including those sick or injured, are frequently
beaten or otherwise physically abused by soldiers, resulting in serious injuries; some are killed, and women performing compulsory
labour are raped or otherwise sexually abused by soldiers. Forced
labourers are, in most cases, not supplied with food – they sometimes even have to bring food, water, bamboo and wood to the
military; porters may receive minimal rations of rotten rice, but be
prevented from drinking water. No clothing or adequate footwear
is provided to porters, including those rounded up without prior
warning. At night, porters are kept in bunkers or have to sleep in
the open, without shelter or blankets provided, even in cold or wet
situations, often tied together in groups. Forced labourers on road
and railway construction have to make their own arrangements
for shelter as well as all other basic needs.*

Two follow-up reports were presented to the ILO concerning the use of
forced labour in Burma. Both of these acknowledged that there was no
evidence that the military regime were taking measures to prevent the
practice. As a result, in June 2000 the ILO took the unprecedented step
of voting 257 to 41 to impose sanctions against a member country, Burma,
in order to punish the regime for its abuse of these particular human rights.

Today the International Confederation of Free Trades Unions estimates
that in Burma, at any given time, there are 800,000 people being forced
to work by the military, against their will and without pay.

❑ ❑ ❑ ❑ ❑

Meanwhile in Hsipaw I sit back in an easy chair and talk to Frankie, but
not about the current situation in Burma, or at least not directly.

Frankie is a coffee-coloured, curly black-haired garage owner who lives on the outskirts of Hsipaw and whose grandfather was a Briton who married a Shan. He has a degree in History and his English is excellent. When we talk he tells me about the good old days when there were soirées and tennis competitions at the Shan Palace. 'My father was Shan State Tennis champion,' Frankie tells me, 'and our favourite tennis player was Rod Laver. The Shan Palace was so beautiful with its gardens and orchards and rolling lawns and its swimming pool. Yes, the good old days.' Then we talk about films, about Doctor Zhivago, Gone with the Wind, and Lawrence of Arabia. He asks whether his favourite actors are still alive. Burt Lancaster? Anthony Quinn? Tony Curtis? Rock Hudson and Yul Brynner, such a pity. It is a strange and unexpected conversation.

The good old days of Hsipaw. Even the villagers talk about them; the days of British rule and the years after independence. Inflation was lower, there was no seizure of goods and property by the military, there was no forced labour, and Shan State enjoyed a degree of autonomy. Yes, the good old days.

MILITARY INTELLIGENCE

Always look for the guavas with the worms in them,' says Mr Donald, 'because the worms know which of the guavas are the best.' With two days left in Hsipaw I spend much of my time with Mr Donald. On my final visit he is in the back corner of the garden planting guava trees. 'Let me tell you a story about a fisherman,' he says.

'There is a fisherman on the Irrawaddy River and every day he catches three or four fish, although sometimes he is lucky and catches six fish and sometimes he is unlucky and only catches two. But sometimes he catches a particularly large catfish which weighs ten pounds [4.5 kilograms] or more and when he catches such a fish, then his family is very happy, their stomachs are full and they share the fish with their neighbours who may not have caught so many fish. If the fisherman only catches two fish then the stomachs of his family are not so full.'

'One day a wealthy man sees the fisherman fishing. He comes over to him, looks at the twine and the bent wire hook which the fisherman is using and says, "Look here, Mr Fisherman, why don't you use nylon fishing line and a stainless steel hook that you can buy for not so much money and then you will be able to catch more fish?"

"Thank you for the advice," says the fisherman, "but what will I do with more fish?"

"Well," says the rich man, "when you catch more fish you will be able to sell them at the market and buy things for yourself."

"What things?" asks the fisherman.

"Well," says the rich man, "you can buy a net."

"And what will I do with a net?" asks the fisherman.

"You will be able to go fishing and catch even more fish."

"And what will I do with even more fish?" asks the fisherman.

"Well, when you catch even more fish you will be able to sell more fish and then you will be able to buy a boat," replies the rich man.

"And what will I do with a boat?" asks the fisherman.

"Well," says the rich man, "when you have a boat you will be able to catch even more fish and then you will be able to buy a bigger boat and more nets."

"And what will I do then?" asks the fisherman.

"Then you will be able to have enough money to be able build a processing plant," explains the rich man.

"And what will I do then?" asks the fisherman.

"Then you will become a millionaire and you will be so rich that you won't have to work very much any more," says the rich man.

"And what will I do then?" asks the fisherman.

"Well, then you will have plenty of spare time, just like me," says the rich man.

"And what do you do with your spare time?" asks the fisherman.

"I go fishing," says the rich man.'

In the context of my own thoughts about poverty, it is a strange coincidence that Mr Donald should tell me this story about the fisherman and the rich man. Could the family of the fisherman ever be as happy as on the days when the fisherman catches a ten-pound catfish?

Mr Donald's dignity and intelligence are striking.

After digging and planting the guava trees ('For the next generation,' says Mr Donald), Fern sets up a table and chairs in the garden and we sit and drink guava juice and eat bread with guava jam. Mr Donald talks about his tertiary education. He explains that after he finished his university studies, two alternatives were made available to him: to join the military academy or to go to a trade school run by the military. He chose the latter. In front of the school there were a pond and a bridge and within the compound there was a parade ground, dormitories, halls for teaching and many people in military uniform. On the first morning the new students, all university graduates, were lined up in the parade-ground and greeted by the Lieutenant Colonel in charge. They remained there for four hours under the hot sun. Some fainted and were dragged away but no one dared to complain as soldiers were overseeing the exercise. This was the first class at the new school. Mr Donald was part of the agricultural section of the trade school and thereafter his post-university education included tasks such as feeding pigs and cleaning out their sties, cleaning out the school pond, and learning to fire a .303 military rifle. Mr Donald counts, 'Of the 600 students, only 250 were granted leave and this was granted on the basis of proficiency with the .303. On the firing range, our results would often depend on whether the rifle that we were given was Chinese or British. We all wanted the British ones, older but more reliable and accurate. You have to understand that 90 per cent of our teachers were not educated. Many had no schooling above primary level. They were soldiers who had risen to be officers. These were our teachers and the basis of this school was to break down our idea that we were university graduates. "University," we were told by our teachers, "was somewhere where painted teachers in high-heels brainwashed people." This was the main lesson at agricultural school.'

❑ ❑ ❑ ❑ ❑

I hear what I hear and see what I see but in my everyday existence in Hsipaw I am surrounded by pleasant greenery and peacefulness; I go for leisurely morning walks and I feel the security of having other travellers around me. By doing these things, I lose my sense of the immediacy of the way things are in Burma. Yes, I take on board the things that I hear and see. Yes, I listen when I am told that I am being watched, monitored, and that the military will be keeping tabs on me. But the thing is that when there are other tourists around it all seems much more remote. There is not the sense of the physical proximity that was so inescapable in Bhamo.

Six hours ago I was having afternoon tea at a table set up in the gardens of a prince's manor house. I was invited to dinner and stayed, chatting to my hosts until 10 p.m. Then I left because I had to go back to my guesthouse and pack.

Mr Donald had walked me to the front gate of his house and then beyond, along a small dirt road. 'Seek teachers,' he had advised. 'There may be an ocean between you and the sage but then you must cross the ocean. And fear the man who smiles but will do you harm.' Then, when we reached the first of the partially-lit tracks heading back towards town, we had parted company. There was no one around, it was late, and the outskirts of Hsipaw were about a kilometre away.

Smack! Reality comes crashing back in the most immediate sense imaginable.

Five minutes after Mr Donald and I part, two members of Military Intelligence emerge from the trees beside the path. They have been lying in wait for me, hiding in the darkness until I come past. Now, seeing me, they stop me on the path. As if from a cheap film, they both pull back their black, fake leather jackets to show me that they have holsters and guns. Then, in good English, they begin to question me. It is dark, there is no one else around, no houses, no nothing. 'What are you doing? What is your name? What nationality? Why are you here? Where are you staying? How long have you been here? When are you leaving? Where is your passport? Why do you not have it? Who do you work for? What is your job? How old are you? What were you doing? Who were you talking to? What were you talking about? Which embassy do you come from?' I give them evasive answers but am not thinking clearly. My heart races and the only thoughts that seem to come to my mind are the strings of profanities that I would like to shout at them. How dare they accost me here in this fashion. How dare they be so arrogantly confident. How dare they make sure that their guns are so visible throughout proceedings?

After ten minutes the two men go back into the darkness, pick up their bikes, and cycle off down the road. They are so happy with their efforts that they sing as they leave and laugh and talk loudly. Then they turn into the main road and I see them cycle down the hill, across the bridge, and on towards town. They stop at the turn-off to the guesthouse in which I stay. Two more figures step out of the shadows where they had been hiding, lying in wait just as these two had. A brief conversation ensues and then the two new figures leave their post and walk off towards the centre of town. The two on bikes cycle back up the hill, towards me. I hide in the darkness and watch them as they cycle past. They cycle further up the road to a military compound, stay outside for a few minutes whilst they look back down the road towards town, and then go inside.

The reality of life in Burma comes crashing back. I have been told that what I do is being watched, monitored and checked. I hear the words and I believe them but, 'seeing is believing' and now, in Hsipaw, like in Bhamo, I see and I believe.

Returning to the hotel, everyone is asleep and I make my way to my room. By the time I finish packing it is past midnight and I lie in bed and wait for the morning to come. I'm glad that I'm leaving Hsipaw. I don't want to be here any more.

chapter 6
Human Wr☹ngs

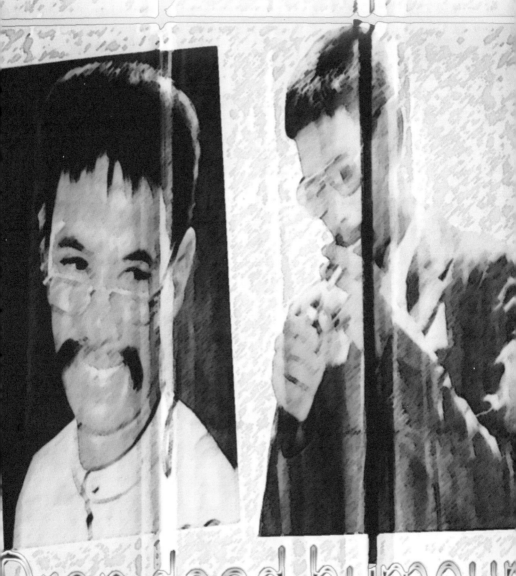

Drop-dead humour

I leave Hsipaw early, miss the bus that I am meant to be on, and as a result end up sitting squashed in the baggage compartment of a second bus. I share this with twelve Burmese, as well as sacks of rice, spare wheels, baskets of food, bags of clothes and crates of bottles. It is a particularly uncomfortable journey and we bounce along, heads all swaying in one direction before being jerked back in another.

Arriving in Mandalay, I return to the hotel in which I have previously stayed and lie down on my bed with a book. Yesterday morning I was walking along the Dokhtawady River in Hsipaw. Yesterday afternoon was spent with Mr Donald and Fern. Then there was last night. Now, as I lie here, a loudspeaker next to the hotel is blaring out Buddhist incantations. But here I am, on my bed reading a book in a hotel full of backpackers. It is a very strange feeling. Surreal, almost disorientating.

In my imagination two jigsaws are being pieced together. One is a jigsaw which concerns my perception of Burma. But the other is one about which I know very little. It is the jigsaw that the military, immigration, and the police may be putting together about me. Photographing the street children, going to University Avenue, going out of bounds in Bhamo, attending the wedding of Little G, speaking to people about life in Burma; these are the pieces that they may have. But how much of a picture they have assembled, this I do not know.

Yes, strange feelings. Sitting on a beach in Thailand ten weeks ago I wouldn't have been able to guess that travelling to Burma would turn out to be anything like this. But here I am and now that I am back in Mandalay my aim is to speak to the family of a gentleman who is currently serving time as a political prisoner.

PAR PAR LAY

From: 'Let's Tell the Truth' by Myo Chit, *The New Light of Myanmar*, 2 July 1996.

There was a ceremony held under the pretext of Independence Day Anniversary to make political capital. After the so called chairman of the party U Aung Shwe's opening address, the General Secretary (the Bogadaw) spoke with cunning tricks to ignite riot. Later, without playing her part in the plot on the stage as usual, for a change in tactics on public relations the puppet showed off by clinging to her consort and young son, enjoying the show as an audience member on the lawn in front of the stage.

It was Myodaw Win Mar Anyient on the stage entertaining the audience. After the comedians had invited the orchestra and the dancer to start entertainment, Myodaw Win Mar performed. The

V.I.P. family was enjoying the dance delightfully. Then came the turn of comedians Par Par Lay and Lu Zaw. The two in synchronicity satirized and mischievously attacked any undertakings of the Na Wa Ta government of Myanmar, disparaging its dignity, making it a laughing stock and inciting riot and instability. The puppeteer profoundly enjoyed the malicious jokes of the two comedians satirizing and making a laughing stock of their own race and the Myanmar government.

When I first meet Mr Moustache he is sitting outside his house in a backstreet of Mandalay drinking tea and reading from tome-like dictionaries of English and American slang. He is instantly recognizable because of the long, black, handlebar moustache which gives him his nick-name. 'Welcome,' he responds when I introduce myself. 'This is my house of Vaudeville, my masque burlesque, my thespian troupe, my ensemble. This is a rendezvous for tourists. I am the clown, the buffoon, the jester, the harlequin. I am top banana.' And then he introduces himself. He is Lu Maw, one of the two Moustache Brother comedians. The other is his elder brother, Moustache Par Par Lay. And they are just two of a family with a tradition of performance. Their grandfather had been the singer in a marionette show and their father was also a stage comedian. Ko Shwe Bo, the third and youngest Moustache brother (the one without a moustache) is a marionette maker and their sister, Ma Teik Chi, is a dancer in the family troupe. The wives of all three brothers, Ma Wein Ma, Ni Ni Lin, and Ma Cho Tu, are also dancers.

It is the eldest Moustache, Par Par Lay, who is currently serving a seven-year prison sentence because of a comic performance which he gave at the National League for Democracy Independence Day Celebration.

Says Moustache Lu Maw, 'I used to have two jobs. I was a comedian one day, performing at weddings and festivals, and then the next day I would be a doctor.' Mr Moustache changes postures in order to play the part of what would normally be his comic partner.

'You used to be a doctor, Mr Moustache?'

'Yes,' he replies as he changes back. 'I was a doctor and I would treat the villagers. One day comedian and then one day doctor. But now I cannot be a doctor any more.'

'But why not Mr Moustache?'

'I have lost my doctor's licence.'

'But why Mr Moustache?'

'Well, one day a patient came to see me and he said that he had a headache. I did not know that he was a military official. "Doctor, I have such a bad headache," the patient said. "I cannot sleep, I cannot eat, I cannot think, I cannot work, I have such a pain in my head." "Okay, I will fix it for you," I said. So I lay him down on a bed and hooked him to a computer so that I could see what the problem was in his head. "I see what the problem is," I said, "There is nothing in your head, there is no brain, no brain at all. Oh it is really, really empty. It is the most empty it could be."'

'This is why I lost my licence to be a doctor. I should have realized that he was a from military intelligence.'

In a different time the Moustache Brothers used to tour northern and central Burma and perform at a variety of ceremonies and events – funerals, weddings, Buddhist ceremonies, house-warmings, and town *paya*, and village festivals. Indeed, they were one of the most popular troupes in Upper Burma. But this is no longer possible. To perform at public or private events, troupes must present a list of performers to the local SPDC office. The list must then be approved by the military, the local police, the town council and the hospital. 'Why the hospital?' I ask Mr Moustache. 'That is to make sure that the entertainment will be healthy for the audience to watch. To obtain permission always needs a little grease in palm.' Since the imprisonment of Par Par Lay, however, the Moustaches have been blacklisted and cannot gain permission to perform. People probably would not invite them anyway, says Mr Moustache, because of the risks involved in being associated with the family of a political prisoner. So now the Moustaches perform only in Mandalay for the few backpackers who come to see them at their house. Package and guided tours do not come. 'Package tours are the tours of the military,' explains Mr Moustache.

On the walls of the main room of the Moustache house are many pictures of the family. There are also pictures of Daw Aung San Suu Kyi, some of which show her with Moustache Par Par Lay. It is the only house in Burma where I have seen her picture displayed. 'It does not matter,' says Mr Moustache, 'The military know all of this already. They have been here many times. And they know that not many tourists come here any more.'

We sit downstairs and Mr Moustache offers me tea. He is an energetic, bubbling, effusive man who talks continuously and very quickly. 'I have so much to say,' he exclaims. 'I talk too much, I have too much to say, I talk too quickly. And if you write anything about our family, don't forget to write down that the three wives are all dancers.' Okay, I'll remember.

In the lead-up to the 1990 general elections the parties which were running had different symbols – the oboe, the umbrella, the bridge. The trade mark of the National League for Democracy was the farmer's hat. In the performances made by the Moustache family's dance and theatre troupe, Par Par Lay would say that the farmer's hat of the NLD was big enough to protect the whole of Burma. For this he was arrested and served one year in prison in 1990. After his release he continued to perform.

On the 4 January 1996, at the National League of Democracy Independence Day Performance, Par Par Lay performed in Rangoon at the house of Daw Aung San Suu Kyi. Also performing were Par Par Lay's wife, a second dancer, four musicians, and fellow comedian Lu Zaw (a cousin). Mr Moustache tells me one of his brother's jokes from that performance.

'Have you ever seen the hands of a Chinese Dancer?' Par Par Lay had asked. 'No I have not Mr Moustache,' the second comedian replied. With that Par Par Lay danced as a Chinese dancer would, an almost perfect mimic, paying special attention to the fluttering, fanning movements of the hands.

Mr Moustache says that Par Par Lay is an excellent dancer.

'Have you ever seen the hands of an Indian dancer?' 'No I have not Mr Moustache.' And so Par Par Lay mimicked the dancing of an Indian dancer, with special emphasis on the circular, wristy movements of the hands.

Mr Moustache is a pretty good dancer himself.

'Have you ever seen the hands of a Shan dancer?' 'No, I have not Mr Moustache.' And so Par Par Lay mimicked the dancing of a Shan dancer, with special emphasis on the still, sweeping movements of the hands.

'Have you ever seen the hands of the SLORC Government dancers?' 'No, I have not Mr Moustache.' Par Par Lay then performed the dance of the SLORC, slinking around with his hand behind his back, rubbing his fingers together in knaiving, Scrooge-like, money-grabbing gestures.

The performance was well received and it is with pride that Mr Moustache tells me that in the video-tape of the performance, Daw Aung San Suu Kyi herself can be seen laughing at the jokes of the comedians. SLORC spies at the performance did not find it so funny.

Mr Moustache says that his brother knew of the risks involved in performing but decided to do so anyway.

Par Par Lay came back to Mandalay on the morning of 7 January 1996. That night he was seized from his home by members of the Number Sixteen Military Intelligence Unit. In another raid in Mandalay cousin Lu Zaw, the second comedian at the performance, was also seized and in Rangoon, twelve National League for Democracy members were taken to Insein Prison, notorious headquarters of SLORC/SPDC Military Intelligence, torture, and detention.

The Mandalay comedians were detained by military intelligence in an interrogation centre for two weeks before being taken to jail. After two months they were tried. Satire is a serious crime in Burma. Daw Aung San Suu Kyi volunteered to act as a witness on their behalf but even as she made the train journey from Rangoon to Mandalay, there was purportedly a mechanical fault that led to the military detaching the carriage in which she was travelling. Many say the train was derailed deliberately. Also prevented from testifying at the brief and summary trial of Lu Zaw and Par Par Lay were U Kyi Maung, Win Thein, and U Tin Oo, all senior members of the National League for Democracy.

Although confined to Rangoon, Daw Aung San Suu Kyi condemned the trial in her weekend speeches in University Avenue and also spoke to the BBC about the case. All to no avail. Par Par Lay and Lu Zaw were sentenced to seven years imprisonment with hard labour.

Par Par Lay was kept in Mandalay until the official verdict was announced. After this his wife had gone to see him but was told that he was no longer there. 'Where is he then?' she had asked. They did not know but by a little magic, a little grease in palm, they knew that he had been sent to Myikyina. 'But,' says Mr Moustache, 'we still did not know where. We paid more money but in the end had to travel to Myikyina and pay people there to tell us. Then we knew his location. He was being kept in a prison outside of Myikyina, maybe twenty-five miles [forty kilometres] north, near a village called Kyien Kran Kha. He was in the Yebet hard labour camp, a prison used for the detention of political prisoners. He was being put to work on a government water project.'

On the 4 August 1996, Bangkok's *The Nation* newspaper ran a feature article on the imprisonment of Par Par Lay in Burma. At the beginning of 1997 ten American comedians including Rob Reiner and Ted Danson drafted and signed a letter demanding the release from prison of fellow comedian Par Par Lay. A copy of this letter was forwarded to each of Chairman 1 and Chairman 2 of the State Law and Order Restoration Council. A third letter was sent to a United Nations Human Rights Conference in Geneva. In previous years the Burmese representative at this conference had denied allegations of human rights abuses in Burma. In 1997 he was questioned about Par Par Lay.

In 1998 Lu Maw had hoped that the SPDC would grant his brother clemency. But today he is still in prison. 'The SLORCs want my brother to die in prison,' says Mr Moustache. 'This would end their problems with him.'

From: 'Myanmar Policy Respected by the World' by Takkatho Myat
Thu, *The New Light of Myanmar*, 20 July 1996, and from 'The Truth
that People Have Seen' by Tekkatho Myat Thu, *The New Light of
Myanmar*, 31 May 1996.

The foreign policy of the West bloc that is interfering in internal affairs
of countries of the world with profuse and suffocating use of such
terms as human rights and democracy is but a weapon of its bullying
and domination and a tactic of neo colonialism.

Today the West Bloc, muttering the words "human rights,"
disregards the national people's right in deference to the right of a
particular group of NLD persons to enable them to do what they like
and to grab power. With this attitude the West Bloc is attempting to
cause disintegration of nations which they do not desire. Keeping a
blind eye to the majority of people who do not wish to be influenced
by any other nation, they are engaged in a policy of interference to
bring power to a person or group whom they can control and ma-
nipulate.

The West assisted so called human rights groups are turning a
blind eye to the nation's true situation and are shouting false accusations on Myanmar in accord with the wishes of the West, internal axe-
handles and traitors.

❑ ❑ ❑ ❑ ❑

In the first year of his imprisonment Maw Win Ma, wife of Par Par Lay,
was able to see her husband on three occasions. The first time was in
Kyein Kran Kha labour camp in April 1996. She then saw him again after
he was transferred back to Myikyina prison and the last time that she was
allowed to see him in person was in September 1996. Now Ma Win Ma is
allowed to visit Par Par Lay every two months, all visitors being allocated
different days upon which to attend. This is done in order to make it
harder for members of families to communicate between themselves about
the detention of their relatives.

On 3 November 1997, both Ko Shwe Bo, the youngest brother, and
Ma Win Ma travelled to Myikyina by train. The trip took four days and
included two twenty-four-hour train rides. The pair left on a Friday, arrived on Saturday, went to the prison on Sunday (their assigned day), left
for Mandalay on Monday and arrived back on Tuesday. The SPDC deliberately locates prisoners a long way from their families.

On the Sunday morning Ma Win Ma and Ko Shwe Bo caught a rick-
shaw from the guesthouse in which they were staying to the jail. Ko Shwe
Bo waited in a teashop outside the prison while Ma Win Ma went in. She
remained inside for thirty minutes. Upon entering she was asked to write
a list of everything that was in a package which she had brought to give to

her husband. It contained essentials including coffee mix, canned pork, canned beef, deep-fried fish, soap, toothpaste, and some plastic bags. A member of Number Eight Military Intelligence Unit came and checked through the package. Ma Win Ma then signed a list of the items and the MI Officer took both it and the package to Par Par Lay. Ma Win Ma, meanwhile, stayed in the waiting-room. When the MI Officer returned the list was countersigned by Par Par Lay in acknowledgment of the fact that he had received the package. The MI Officer showed the signature to Ma Win Ma and told her that he was in good health, which she did not believe, and then asked her for one thousand kyat because there were things which needed to be bought, such as new clothes and shoes. She paid, received a receipt for the payment, and then left the prison.

Seeing the signature on the list was the only contact that Ma Win Ma was allowed to have with her husband. It was the only evidence that she was given of his continuing existence.

Meanwhile, outside the jail, Ko Shwe Bo was able to discover by word of mouth that Par Par Lay's health had deteriorated but was stable.

'We are not the only family who suffers in Burma. We are not the only family who have been broken up,' says Ko Shwe Bo. He is a gentle-looking man, talkative but soft-spoken.

'If you write, please mention my brother's stories,' asks Mr Moustache. 'Many tourists come here and the more that come the better. Maybe you can write a story of his seven years in jail and his jokes at the Daw Aung San Suu Kyi Performance. See, here in the Italian guidebook it mentions the performance at the house of Daw Aung San Suu Kyi. For the family it is "no sweat" if it is mentioned, we will not get in trouble. See, it is in the French guidebook also. No sweat for our family. The government knows already. See the *Routard Guidebook*. So please, tell Mr Joe Cummings that it is now okay to mention Par Par Lay by name in the updated *Lonely Planet* guides on Burma. And the farmer's hat joke, now everybody knows that it was this joke that put Par Par Lay in prison for the first time, so there is no trouble for us. And the hands of the SLORC dancer joke, it is alright to publish that also. There is a video of that joke which the government and Daw Aung San Suu Kyi have seen. The military have written articles about Par Par Lay and his jokes and there are articles in English and other foreign languages about him. So now it is alright to use his name. And please, say thank you to Mr Joe Cummings for us and say that we remember him well. Please get him to publish the new information about Par Par Lay.'

As we talk Lu Maw gets some puppets and lays them on a small table in front of me. 'So that if people are watching it will look like we are talking about the puppets.' Then he goes on. 'The more tourists that know about

my brother, the more foreigners, the more help it is to us. The letter from
the ten comedians, that was good also, very good for us. The world sees
Par Par Lay and the world sees our country. The more people that know
about my brother, the safer he is. The SLORCs hate Par Par Lay because
of the attention that he is attracting. The military want him to die. But if
people know about him, then it is harder for the SLORCs to kill him.'

By the time that I leave the Moustache household it is late in the evening.
I twist and turn my way back to the hotel and do not take any of the
obvious routes via the centre of town.

It is late when I arrive, and sitting in my room I worry about my security.
I now have photos of Daw Aung San Suu Kyi and Par Par Lay as well as
newspaper articles about the case. These are items that are immediately
recognizable as political. Then there are my own notes on Burma, some
two hundred pages of them, most of which are highly critical of the military regime. At the moment these are hidden, screwed in behind a mirror
on the bathroom wall. But tonight I sit and unpick the stitching of my
backpack. As I do so I almost expect the military authorities to come
knocking on my door. I can almost hear the sound of them marching up
the hall to come and question me.

Being pulled over in Hsipaw, there was no coincidence in that. I was
not just unlucky. And now I don't know if the military in Hsipaw have con-
tacted the authorities in Mandalay. I don't know if they know that I am spending time with the Moustaches. I do not want to be caught with my notes.

I feel tired and drained. Very tired. Talking, writing, being scared.

Now, where are my scissors and my needle and thread? I remove my
notes and photos from behind the mirror and sew everything, including
my diary, which is now ripped up, into the lining and padding of my bag.

The last words before the rip-up-and-sew job....

DIRTY JOKES AND POLITICS

In *The New Light of Myanmar* the winners of the Surpay Beikman
Manuscript Award are announced. Prizes for essays in History, Geogra-
phy, Literature, Culture and Science. The article notes, however, that
'There was no winner in political literature.'

❑ ❑ ❑ ❑ ❑

I return to the house of with the Moustaches but this time with two other
travellers. The three of us, as far as the family is concerned, constitute an
audience and they ask if we would like to see them perform. The answer

is yes and so, even as the family packs to catch a three o'clock bus to Pagan to sell Ko Shwe Bo's puppets, preparations are made. People put on costumes and make-up, a stage is laid, and a tape recorder and microphone are produced, the latter despite the fact that there are only three of us and we are sitting only a metre away. The show is led by a smiling and animated Mr Moustache who is dressed in the traditional pink jacket and wraparound hat of a Burmese comedian. As he talks it is abundantly clear that this is what he likes to do best. Perform.

Mr Moustache explains that in Burma there are two types of dance troupe: *Zat* and *Anyient*. *Zat* involves large troupes of seventy people or more. These form an orchestra and perform plays, dance and opera. *Anyient* troupes are smaller with maybe eight dancers, fourteen musicians, three or four stage helpers, and up to four comedians. The latter perform between dances, giving the dancers the opportunity to change costumes. Comedians in an *Anyient* troupe are, therefore, important from a functional perspective as well as for the entertainment which they provide. Says Mr Moustache, 'Burmese people in history have always liked to hear satire. Politics is the tradition of the Burmese comedian and for two hundred years we have made jokes about the government. This is what the comedian in *Anyient* does; comic but serious at the same time. This is traditional. And Burmese people also like jokes about sex. Usually it is the young men and the monks who laugh the most at these jokes. So now we take the dirty jokes and use words from politics because politics are in the minds of the Burmese people. Like the embargo and sanction joke.'

'Embargo and Sanction: I used to have two jobs,' Mr Moustache commences, and continues 'I was a doctor but then I lost my licence.'

'Why did you lose your licence, Mr Moustache?'

'Well, one day I had to treat the wife of a SLORC general but I did not know that this was who her husband was. She was pregnant but could not give birth so I had to perform a Caesarean section. After two weeks her husband came in to see me and he said, "Mr Moustache, you are under arrest." "Under what number?" I said. "What code number, what crime number?" "You are charged under Crime Number 45, Embargo and Sanction," he said. "But how can this be?" I said. He replied, "I have not been able to make love to my wife since she gave birth. You have sewn too far. Embargo and Sanction."'

'This is a dirty joke,' Mr Moustache tells us. 'Everyone used to laugh when we would tell this joke.'

Mr Moustache continues, 'Tradition and superstition also used to play a large part in the troupes. For example, when puppets were made the puppet maker would look for one tree out of which he could carve all of the puppets that he required, maybe twenty-eight or thirty. To use different trees was bad luck. And once the tree had been cut into pieces each one would be tossed into a stream. If it floated bark side up it would be made into a woman. If it floated bark side down, then it would be made into a man. To do otherwise was bad luck. And a woman could never be a puppeteer. Also bad luck.'

'But the worst luck was for male and female members of the troupe to have relationships. If they did and anything went wrong, a flat tyre on a bus, a problem on stage, any personal bad luck of the performers, then it was the fault of these two.'

'I am guilty of this,' admits Mr Moustache. 'My wife joined the troupe in 1976, soon after she had finished dance training school. We could not be together although we liked each other. Then we were caught red-handed. We had to go to the head of the troupe and make an offering of two bananas and a coconut. He accepted this and gave us his permission to have our relationship. So after that we were allowed to sit next to each other on the bus and we could hold hands in public.'

In between the jokes and explanations the dancers come on and perform both Burman dances and dances of the ethnic minorities. 'Many traditional dances are from Thailand,' says Mr Moustache. 'The dance of Ayuthaya is the most famous dance and has 112 episodes. It was originally performed by Thai dancers and musicians who were captured in Thailand when the Burmese sacked the Thai capital, Ayuthaya, in the eighteenth century. The dance pays homage to the Burmese captors and also shows remembrance for the city which had been left behind. When the dancer makes the gesture of looking back over her shoulder, this symbolizes looking back to Ayuthaya.'

The final dance is 'The Moustache Strip Tease'. During this dance the audience is introduced to the characters of ethnic Burman folk tradition – the alchemist, the monkey, the ogre, and the court page. There is also the diplomat who waddles on with pillows layered under his tunic so as to look as fat as possible. He is a foolish character and it is he who represents the military.

❑ ❑ ❑ ❑ ❑

'The SPDC, they cannot continue, it is not possible. They change people's attention so that they are not thinking about politics but about personal things. They cut the power so that people have to struggle to find lights and sit in the dark. Then people are worried about light not about politics. This is what they do. You see, when the military comes to a particular part of the city there is never any problem with power. It is only a problem for us. They put on festivals and make it legal to gamble at the festivals. They run competitions. Then people think about festivals and competitions and not about politics. They are very clever doing this.'

'The SPDC are saying all the time, every day, that Daw Aung San Suu Kyi is bad, that she is a stool for America, that she works for the CIA, that she is a Bogadaw because she was married to an Englishman. But people still believe in what she does and they know that she stays here for her country. The Burmese people love her very much. She is our First Lady.'

'Now SPDC will be driven into a corner by ASEAN and Europe. ASEAN will go to Europe for a summit but Burma is not allowed to go. They will talk about Burma. The President of the Philippines came to Burma and he said that it was on business but that was not true. He came to see what the situation is like in Burma. The week after he left, his foreign minister came to Burma and had dinner with Daw Aung San Suu Kyi. SPDC denied this and the President denied that his foreign minister was doing anything behind SPDC's back but it is true that he met Daw Suu. And why are there so many other foreign ministers visiting Burma? It is so that they will know the situation in Burma when they speak to the European Union. Now the jury will be ASEAN and Europe. The SPDC, they want to show off a good situation to Europe and to ASEAN but they cannot hide that their greed is killing the country. I have much hope for these meetings.'

'We have also heard that maybe next year the SPDC will release political prisoners. Maybe next year my brother will be free. Maybe we will be able to perform together again.'

❏ ❏ ❏ ❏ ❏

Mr Moustache, part of what was formerly one of Burma's most prominent theatre, dance and comic troupes. Now, like the Bhamo helicopter builder whose natural talent as an engineer will never be fulfilled, like Mr Donald and his decaying Shan Estate, like U Thaung Aye and Ko Lay Nyo who know that they will never be able to see the world outside their country, like Daw Htar Yi who is trying to get her children out of Burma, like the university students who work as trishaw drivers or touts or help in shops, like Frankie who talks of Dr Zhivago and Gone With the Wind and Lawrence of Arabia; like all of these people, Mr Moustache often has a look of wistfulness in his eyes. It is the look of someone who is not only suffering under SPDC military rule but, despite a determination not to show it, may well be losing hope.

I am sorry Mr Moustache, I know that you would be offended to hear me say this but the look in your eyes... eyes are windows to the soul. Mr Moustache, your eyes are very sad when you talk of your country.

When I say goodbye to Mr Moustache he says to me, 'Please try to help my brother. Please help my country.'

chapter 7

The Heart of Burma

TRAVELLING AGAIN

Two weeks left in Burma and Kalaw and Pagan are the last destinations to which I will travel. I do so with a softly-softly approach. Things in Burma have escalated to a level where I feel neither safe nor entirely in control.

On my way to Kalaw a strange thing happens and the strange thing is this. The bus in which I ride drives over the flat central plains of Burma for about an hour and then pulls into a compound which consists of a few buildings surrounded by a barbed wire fence. Clearly it belongs to immigration, the military, or the police. Uniformed men can be seen sitting in the shade and six of them approach the bus. The driver stands up and looks as if he is going to ask everyone to disembark, but he exchanges words with an officer and sits down again. Two officials stand at the back of the bus and look at me through the window. I don't know why. Similarly, two officials at the front of the bus are looking at me, or at least at the seat which I am occupying. It is as if they are looking for someone who they expect to be with me, or sitting beside me, or something like that. Then two more officials board the bus and they too look towards my seat. Six other tourists, all of whom are sitting in the front rows of the bus, are completely ignored. Thoughts of being searched pass through my mind. Then, after further conversations between the driver and the officer, we drive back out of the compound. It is a very strange incident.

The episode brings to mind a backpacker anecdote, which is possibly apocryphal. A group of backpackers are on a bus driving to Pagan. At a military checkpoint, four Burmese men claiming to be from immigration board the bus and ask the backpackers for their passports. Perhaps buoyed by their numbers, perhaps not wanting to unpack their bags, perhaps wanting to take some sort of stand against Burmese military authority, the backpackers refuse to comply. In response to this the four Burmese men walk down the aisle to the front of the bus and talk briefly to the driver. The driver then gets up from his seat and leaves the bus with the four men. The bus does not move for two hours. For the duration of this time the driver can be seen standing by himself by the side of the road in the sun. He is being punished for the tourists' misdemeanours.

❏ ❏ ❏ ❏ ❏

Soon after the 'compound' incident the road winds upwards into the hills through trees and small roadside towns. Unlike the road to Hsipaw, the land has not all been cleared and this raises my expectations as to what Kalaw will be like. *Lonely Planet* describes it as being a pretty, former

British hill station surrounded by pine trees and bamboo forests.

Upon arrival, however, the bus stops on the main road through town and this is lined with a row of four, square, concrete hotels of the newly-made, no-atmosphere-but-many-rooms variety. They are largely devoid of guests and the one in which I stay is echoing, cavernous and empty, like a dank vault. It smells of brand-new gym shoes which have just been pulled out of their box.

I wonder about these hotels. So few guests.

MEETING THE MILITARY

Kalaw. Soon after sunrise. There is thick dew on the ground and the town is shrouded in early morning mists. Spiders' webs glisten and in the sky a ghostly shadow of a sun can be seen. To the east is a hill covered in pine trees with a road winding round like a European hillside drive. Beside this are a number of turn-of-the-century English estates with impressive gateways and long driveways that sweep down to the residences. These were formerly the houses of the British officers stationed in Kalaw. Now many of them belong to the Burmese military and under their current ownership they have fallen into a dishevelled state of disrepair. Nonetheless, they have character and in their gardens there are small orchards, brightly coloured flowers, eucalyptus trees, and more glistening spiders' webs. On the road in front of one of the houses four children practise their putting with a golf ball and stick. They have dug a small hole and compete to sink their ball in the least number of shots. Other children are on their way to school.

At the end of the hillside drive is a locked gateway which leads into a military installation.

Nearby, I try to take a photo, not of the gate but of a row of huts with a boy walking along a path to school. A man shouts at me so I put my camera away. I suspect that the huts were soldiers' residences and this is why this particular shot is prohibited.

At the railway station there is a sign in English which says 'Kalaw' and the altitude, 4,297 feet [1,310 metres] above sea level. Nearby is an eighty-four-year-old man sitting and drinking tea in the front of his daughter's house. He tells me that he worked for his whole life on the Kalaw railways. 'When I started, I worked for the British and all of this was jungle,' he says. Then he asks me what I think of the military but I change the topic.

Along the railway tracks leading out of Kalaw is where some of the very poor people of the town live. As I walk little children dressed in tatters and with sniffly noses are introduced to me by parents.

Returning back towards Kalaw a lady stops me and indicates that I should not continue on the track upon which I am walking. I wait for her to pass and then proceed nonetheless. The track leads in to the back of the Kalaw military barracks. There are semicircular World War II corrugated iron drum-like Nissen huts which are used as halls and schools for the children of the soldiers. They are empty today and I peep through the windows. Inside, at the end of many of the halls is a large painted sign depicting a white helmet and crossed swords on a red background. It is the symbol of the Tatmadaw and it can be seen through doors, on placards, and on gateposts. Likewise it can be seen on the sheds in which rows of military vehicles are parked.

Nearby there are houses. Women are at work but very few soldiers are to be seen so I continue walking. Then, after fifteen minutes, I reach what is one of the main roads through the barracks. It is lined with white painted boulders and pretty flowers. Ahead is a gateway leading back towards town. There is a boom gate and a guard box with guards in it. I wave to them as I pass by and they wave back as if nothing untoward has occurred.

As I walk away from the barracks a truck full of soldiers passes by.

❏ ❏ ❏ ❏ ❏

If socialist governments spend more money on social welfare programs and liberal governments are more inclined towards business incentive schemes, then it stands to reason that a military regime will spend more money on the military. So it is in Burma. In 1987 the army comprised 120,000 troops. After the 1988 democracy demonstrations, however, the SLORC rapidly expanded its military capacity. An arms cache seized by the Israelis from the PLO was sold to the Burmese military; patrol boats and helicopters were bought from Yugoslavia, Poland and Russia. A single US$1.4 billion arms deal was negotiated with China which included the provision of three squadrons of F7 fighter aircraft, 145 battle tanks, 250 armoured personnel carriers, as well as anti-aircraft guns, howitzers and mobile rocket launchers. Training and technology have been provided by Pakistan and Singapore. One 1997 contract with the latter was for the development of a multi-million-dollar high-tech spy centre for domestic surveillance.

Today the Burmese army, navy, and airforce – the Tatmadaw – boast 400,000 standing personnel. An estimated 40 per cent of Burma's gross annual budget is spent on equipping and maintaining this army. According to United Nations statistics, the funds spent on the military are 222 per cent more than those spent on health and education combined. Only three countries in the world have a worse ratio – Iraq, Syria, and Oman.

Yet the only enemies of the Burmese military are its own people.

❑ ❑ ❑ ❑ ❑

Near the army barracks is a reminder of Kalaw's colonial heritage. It is an overgrown graveyard on the top of a bald hill with a Wild West gateway. It is here that the British of the region were buried.

'In Loving Memory of My Darling Daddy, Dr Chas S Lawrie, Born the 3rd April 1874, Shylet, Assam, Died 13 October 1943 Kalaw.'

'John Ross Brown, Son and Grandson of Browns who took part in the relief of Lucknow 1857 and Battle of Waterloo 1815, Born Deshawar 7 January 1875, Died Kalaw 24 February 1930.'

'Eva Constance Mary Brown, Born at Nani Talz Nov 1867, Died at Kalaw 19 October 1927, "She did the best that she could".'

John, Eva, Chas, Britons the remains of whom now lie in a run-down graveyard where the graves are cracked, broken, and overgrown. Forgotten people with no one laying flowers in a decaying cemetery on top of a bald hill in outer Kalaw. Bleak.

As I look at the tombstones, trying to decipher the names and details, it begins to rain and I take refuge in a shelter set up beside the ninth hole of the Kalaw golf course. Four soldiers have the same idea and we sit together. Three are young and smile when I talk in Burmese. The lieutenant, on the other hand, does not quite know how to handle a Westerner in his presence. Should he smile or should he scowl? In the end he adopts a middle path and offers me a cigarette.

The Kalaw golf course winds around the edge of the military base, up and down through the hills, and is surrounded by pine trees, flowering trees, and beds of flowers. The greens are very green and the fairways, the greens, and the decorative foliage are all well maintained. It is hardly surprising for there are literally hundreds of soldiers working on the upkeep of the course: cutting, hoeing, mowing, pruning and planting, all labour being done manually. On one particular hole the entire side of a hill is covered by soldiers scything away, slashing back grass. Many of the soldiers stare at me but most do so with smiles on their faces.

Perhaps this is why I did not see any soldiers in the barracks. They are all at work out on the golf course.

I follow a group of golfers and watch them play. They are good players and are clearly rich people, boasting an entourage of caddies, wives, girlfriends, military officials, and umbrella bearers, maybe thirty people all together. Golf in Burma is a game for the élite, a sign of prestige, often played by military officials who always seem to have to have an audience.

I watch the golfing party for a few holes but then depart, 'mingala baa-

ing' soldiers right, left and centre. They smile and laugh and '*mingala baa*' me back. One soldier approaches me with a smile on his face but then grabs my wrist more firmly than I would like. He leads me off telling me that I should come into the barracks. As we approach an entrance he points out someone and says, 'My major,' and at the same time releases his grip on my arm. Taking advantage of this, I hastily excuse myself and walk off in a different direction.

In the evening, as if to further emphasize the presence of the military in Kalaw, I ask the staff of my hotel to recommend a restaurant at which to eat. There is one nearby but when I arrive I see a host of Toyota Corollas with tinted windows and long aerials lined up outside. Inside there are nine military officials eating dinner. They are middle-aged, have arrived in cars with their partners, and are drinking Johnnie Walker Red Label whisky, a drink that is a prohibitively expensive by local standards. Five of them are wearing black leather jackets, two are in uniform, and two are in civvies. Like the golfers, in the context of other Burmese people, they are clearly wealthy.

Sitting at the table beside me are more officers. One is the Chief Commander of Kalaw Division. He is brazen in his confidence or maybe it is the whisky. He does not pour shots for himself but half glasses topped up with ice and water. We talk briefly and laugh about women and bachelorhood. He is a single man and in overstated jest he jokes about the absence of women in his life. Nudge-nudge, wink-wink.

Later in the evening I talk to a local student who studies at a private college in Taunggyi. He tells me that the people who had been dining in the restaurant were high-ranking military officers. Many have come from Rangoon and Mandalay. This is because the Kalaw military barracks also has an officer training school where many young Burmese officers come to study.

Sitting at the same table as both the student and I is a Swiss photographer. He asks, 'How do military officials come to be very rich in Burma? When are soldiers the richest people in a country? How do they have so much time to play golf?'

'Military officials have many jobs in Burma. There are many ways that they make money,' replies the Burmese student.

GOVERNMENT TRICKS

From: 'The Truth that People have Seen' by Tekkatho Myat Thu, *The New Light of Myanmar*, 31 May 1996.

During the Cold War between left and right, cunning propaganda methods were used for disintegration of their main rival group and to win the Cold War. Rumours and whispering campaigns were used to gain the upper hand at the time. The Western Capitalist Block applying various means could monopolize the mass media such as newspapers and radio and television. They have appointed in their mass media machinery persons who will do as they wish for them; especially opposition members of many nations and expatriates. They won over many journalists with money and by brainwashing, using them for their propaganda network. This way, news of Western media became dominated by lies.

The Western mass media totally blacked out information which they never want to disclose and made fabrications for propaganda, making the nonexistent exist, fakes as genuine and lies as truth.

At present Myanmar is gaining all round progress and many new roads, bridges, power stations, irrigation facilities, railroads, schools and institutions of higher learning are emerging. However, the Western media ignores the nation's developments and never reports them. They are only concocting lies to propagandize for persons who would be useful for them and who would become their minions and leaders of democracy and human rights.

❏ ❏ ❏ ❏ ❏

Kalaw is the Anglicization of the Shan word, 'Kalar' which means 'surrounded by hills'. In its original form it is an appropriate name for the town to which the military would like tourists to come if they want to go trekking. Indeed, walking through the streets of Kalaw every tout comes up to you and asks, 'Have you been trekking yet?' Trekking, however, is little more than a euphemism for walks into the hills to visit villages censored of anything that might create a negative impression about the situation in Burma.

Following one of the more frequently-used trekking tracks out of Kalaw, a group of children lie in wait for the morning's trekkers. 'Sweeties, sweeties,' they cry out as they come running out with their hands outstretched.

Further on, the track winds up and into the hills. From below, the sounds of the valley and its chickens and children and wood chopping float up on the same wind which rustles the leaves and sways the grasses.

Further still along the path is a *paya* which sits on top of a hill overlooking Kalaw and the surrounding countryside. It is a *paya* built by the army primarily for trekking tourists and has been named the World Peace Pagoda. And it is the task of the World Peace Pagoda to help convince tourists that the Burmese military are committed to peace, love and harmony. That's why the name has been painted in English at the entrance.

When I visit, there is not a monk to be seen. Instead there are Burmese civilians who offer me food and tea. They are friendly enough and I accept these offerings but at the same time I recognize that this is the work of these people, to give food to the tourists who arrive. It is all part of the picture that the World Peace Pagoda tries to paint.

Beyond the temple, walking down the hills and through the fields, an old man waves for me to follow him. I do so and as I walk behind I look at the gumboots which he wears. The backs of them are split from the heel to the top of the boot. I think of how little it would cost to buy a new pair.

The old man leads me back to his village. It is a Pa'O village, the Pa'O being another of the ethnic minorities of Burma. There are only six huts and one is his. Inside there is a single room that is split into two levels, a cooking level and a level for sitting and sleeping. One end of the hut is used for drying corn, garlic and the old man's cheroot leaf crop, cheroots being the cigars that are smoked throughout Burma. Like the other people in the village, the old man grows the leaves in which the cheroots are rolled. He also grows the herbs which are rolled into the cheroots, but the tobacco is bought from the market in Kalaw. This is the most expensive ingredient and consequently little is used, making the cheroots quite mild. Once rolled, the cheroots are sold in Kalaw.

Also in the hut is the old man's wife. She is lying under a blanket on the floor beside the cooking fire. She moves slowly, coughs a lot, and is obviously ill. Meanwhile the old man cuts a stalk of sugar cane, skins it with his knife, slices it into segments, and offers it to me along with Chinese tea, palm sugar cubes and, not surprisingly, a cheroot that is broader than my thumb and about twice as long.

These two people are kind people. They do not speak any English and my Burmese is not extensive. Despite this, we sit together for over an hour.

To say that I feel sorry for my hosts is patronizing and not right. To say that I love them is excessive and not right. To say that I am thankful to them for their hospitality to me as a stranger and that this thankfulness is something that I find quite moving, that is what I feel.

Burma. It is beautiful and it is sad. Much of its sadness lies in its beauty.

Back at the hotel and on the television there is a Burmese music video playing. I sit down to watch and ask the Burmese man next to me, a man who I know to have good English, to translate the singing on my behalf. A great deal of the message is self-evident.

The video begins with coverage of the 1988 demonstrations and then traces the last ten years of Burmese history. On the screen are pictures of skulls and riots and marches and more skulls and civil dissent and images symbolizing the destruction of the Union. The skulls look like something from Pol Pot's regime in Cambodia. 'They are saying that the people who rebelled against the military in 1988 were anarchists who wanted the destruction of Burma. They are also saying that the anarchists killed many people,' explains my translator. As well as the skulls, images of trees being felled are used to symbolize the destruction. It is a clever ploy by the SPDC, as indiscriminate slashing through teak forests and the sale of timber to international ventures is a contentious issue in Burma. But here, by visual association if nothing else, the students and the NLD are linked to the tree-felling problem.

The music clip goes on to show pictures of regrowth and consolidation. There are pictures of grand military parades, pictures of weaponry, pictures of the generals, pictures of fit-looking young soldiers jogging around a village, pictures of soldiers and villagers working side by side piling up sandbags to stem flood waters, pictures of soldiers rebuilding roads, laying tar and driving heavy rollers, pictures of soldiers handing out rice, pictures of soldiers working knee-deep in the rice paddies, still more pictures of energetic soldiers stripped to the waist and jogging through villages.

The next stage of the video is about growth and development. It is the military that is responsible for the maintenance of Shwedagon *Paya* in Rangoon. The military built the Yangon bridge, across which the singers walk, sing and dance. Then there are images of a modern industrial plant and a rice-cutting tractor and of smiling generals snipping tapes to mark the opening of new facilities.

Then there is more. A dance in a field with lines of people wearing traditional ethnic costumes, all holding hands, smiles on their faces, dancing along with the singers. More? The world loves us too. There are photographs of generals shaking hands with various heads of state and foreign ministers from around the world. Finally, the *pièce de résistance*, confirmation of the acceptance by the world community of the SLORC/SPDC regime, Burma's acceptance into ASEAN, on 24 July 1997. The greatest diplomatic success that the SLORC/SPDC has achieved and still one of the most-used propaganda items.

The song lasts for fifteen minutes and my interpreter tells me that it plays twice a day. It is more sophisticated than other propaganda, which usually consists of rolling title boards of SPDC slogans accompanied by a voice-over that reads what is seen on the screen.

Students were anarchists responsible for the destruction of Burmese unity and the killing of hundreds of people. Who could ever believe this? But then again, there have been forty years of such radio, television, newspapers, and billboards. This means that Burma is now entering its third generation of people who have never experienced any other type of media.

At the end of the video one of the two Burmese watching the television observes, 'The government does not speak the truth. Government tricks.' The other, my translator, shakes his head and says only one word, 'Propaganda.'

HE THAT SHOUTS THE LOUDEST

There is an adage that goes, 'He that shouteth the loudest...' and I think it continues, 'has the least to say.' There is also the Shakespearean line, 'Thou protesteth too much,' the implication being that thou protesteth too much to be believed. If one were to come to Burma knowing nothing else, the crass repetitiveness of the media would surely indicate that there is something terribly rotten in the State of Myanmar.

Unfortunately, there is another adage: if you throw enough mud eventually some of it will stick. It is upon this saying that the Burmese military relies.

❑ ❑ ❑ ❑ ❑

'Say no to heroin,' proclaims an advertisement on television. It is a precursor to the airing of a programme which documents the efforts undertaken by the military to combat the drug trade. Although I do not ask for a translation, it is unlikely that the programme says anything about Burma's producing an estimated 40 per cent of the world's heroin. Likewise, it probably doesn't refer to estimates from the Thai narcotics and securities agencies that in 1999 over six hundred million methamphetamine tablets were smuggled out of Burma and this is expected to increase to two billion by the year 2001. Instead, the commentary might go something like this:

From: 'Destruction of Seized Narcotics at Kentung' by Taungdwin Bo Thein, *The New Light of Myanmar*, 2 November 1997.

> I got a chance to observe and take news photos of proceedings of the ceremony which marked the destruction of seized narcotic drugs held at international standard garrison sports ground in Kentung.
> I do not want to repeat the details about the ceremony however I got an idea to reveal the omissions and false news broadcasts by the western radio stations especially BBC and Voice of America. It has been ten years since Myanmar observed International Anti Drug Abuse and Trafficking Day on a nationwide scale. The drug abuse problem is concerned with not only an individual, family, or a nation but also with the entire of mankind. Anti drug abuse control measures have

been taken by Myanmar as a national cause applying various methods. It is universally known that she annually set up landmarks in that connection.

It serves the interest of the entire mankind when more and more opium free zones emerge. To meet that end the State worked for socio economic development during the last eight years spending over 4957 million kyats (2 million US dollars). In that respect credit must go to the leadership of the nations leaders and conscientious participation of the regional people. I really got angry on hearing the broadcast by some western broadcasting stations to the effect that the US Administration is accusing Myanmar of producing 2500 tons of opium. They did so after ignoring the anti - narcotic drugs measures of Myanmar.

Our ancient Myanmar people did not accept the taking of intoxicants. Abuse of narcotic drugs was denounced. Hence the US accusations against Myanmar who opposes narcotic drug taking through out the history are far from the truth as they have been based on false reports.

Although there is no evidence of direct, centralized involvement of the Burmese military in the drug trade, complicity has been inferred. The military regime does not enforce laws that could be used to curb the laundering of drug money into legitimate national enterprises. Lieutenant General Khin Nyunt is said to have connections with Burma's largest drug producers, the United Wa State Army. Corruption amongst regional military leaders in drug-producing areas is said to be widespread. And, perhaps most importantly, the Burmese military turns a blind eye to the drug dealings of some of the most powerful ethnic insurgent armies in order to maintain cease-fire agreements.

In Burma it is the ethnic minorities who control drug production. Over the last four decades opium has been one of the primary resources relied upon for income to sustain armies who fight the Burmese military. In the late 1980s the most powerful of these was the United Wa State Army, also known as the Red Wa. The Red Wa was originally made up of remnants of the Burma Communist Party and enjoyed the legacy of training and armaments provided by Beijing. In 1989 the Red Wa and the Burmese military signed an ongoing cease fire. Under the provisions the Red Wa people were given significant autonomy, the right to maintain their own army, the right to develop their towns and villages and, most significantly, the Burmese military did not interfere with their involvement in the drug trade. In fact, the Burmese military may be seen to have directly benefited from this involvement. Not only have drugs brought large amounts of capital into the Burmese economy, but so too have the Red Wa helped the Burmese military in combating ethnic groups opposed to the regime. In expanding its control of the drug trade, the Red Wa army has come into direct conflict with groups still fighting for independence against the

Burmese military. In recent years the most notable of these has been the Shan State Army (South). The consequence has been that such armies have not only had to contend with the Burmese military but also the much feared Red Wa.

Today the Red Wa boast a fully-trained and well-equipped army of between 10,000 and 15,000 soldiers. In May 2000 the Wa were permitted to settle tracts of land that the Burmese military had cleared of Shan residents. Wa development and investment has increased and whole towns as well as hotels and dams have been built with profits from the drug trade. In September 2000 the Shan State Army (South) formed an alliance with their former rival, the Red Wa. Thai authorities believe that this alliance has further consolidated Red Wa control of the Burmese drug industry and will lead to increased production in the future. Meanwhile, the interference from the Burmese military has been marginal.

Publicly, the military regime has said that it cannot directly tackle the United Wa State Army. It also says that it would like to introduce crop substitution and drug eradication programmes which will wipe out drug production in Burma within fifteen years. According to military estimates, such a programme would cost US\$ 5.6 billion. The military regime has asked the international community to contribute to these costs.

But as president of the Karen National Union, Saw Ba Thin, has said, 'I don't understand how Burmese Foreign Minister Win Aung could tell ASEAN that the military junta was unable to crack down on the Wa drug business even though it could suppress the National League for Democracy, which was elected by more than 80 per cent of the people in the 1990 general election.'

These, however, are not the issues discussed on the television. Instead, echoing the dogma of *The New Light of Myanmar*, the documentary depicts coverage of bags of opium being burnt by the military in front of an audience of invited guests from the media. Drugs are seized every day, it says, and every day the culprits are punished. The military is tackling the problem.

DICTATORS AND TOUR GUIDES

Kalaw. I walk, I sit in temples, and I visit the Kalaw Hotel – an impressive structure built at the turn of the twentieth century as a resort for senior members of the British army. I do these things, but my mind is on two issues: staying out of trouble and preparing to leave Burma. These are the concerns that loom largest in my mind.

At lunch one day in a small restaurant there are two men in fake black leather jackets who come in, sit at a table, order tea and keep glancing at me. Maybe they are only looking at me because I am a Westerner but nonetheless it is disconcerting. It is ridiculous that they wear these black jackets. They are like badges which the military, especially military intelligence, seem compelled to wear when dressed in civvies.

❑ ❑ ❑ ❑ ❑

In every Burmese town or city that I have visited there has been at least one festival taking place. Kalaw is no exception, and my last day in this town is the first day of the most important Shan festival of the year. The hotel owners urge me to stay an extra night in order to witness the spectacle and although I am tempted, this is not possible. My time in Burma is running short and to come to this country and not see Pagan is like travelling to Egypt and not seeing the pyramids.

For a number of days now the people of Kalaw have been building floats for the festival. Many are two or even three-metre-high wire frames adorned with gifts of a utilitarian nature. They are put together by both civilians and monks and in one monastery I help as one such structure is assembled. It is the shape of a man and one arm is a sweeper, the other a broom. His eyes are stainless steel pans and on his feet he wears slippers. The rest of his body is given form with fans, ladles, aprons, buckets, candles, exercise books, a thermos flask, handkerchiefs, blankets, a torch, a soup container, a knife, soap, small forks, bowls, a water filter, tea towels, pencils, toothpaste, pillows, a toothbrush, chopsticks, drinking glasses, and Buddhist posters. Also on the float is a monk's robe. This, say the people in the monastery, is the key to what the festival is about. Traditionally, a monk is not supposed to buy his own robes. Instead, they must be donated to him by the people and if he does not have robes donated then he should collect scraps of thrown-away material and make his robes from these. In accordance with this tradition, the floor of the main *paya* in Kalaw is strewn with small, ragged pieces of material for the duration of the festival.

On the first morning of the festival, in a gala parade, the floats are carried for three circuits around the centre of town. All of Kalaw lines the streets to see them and banana pancakes, rice cakes, bread cakes, sliced fruits, tea and other assorted snacks are all sold from makeshift stalls. A float displaying a four-metre-high swan with feathers of thousands of one kyat notes passes by. Musicians and dancers accompany it as it staggers along on the shoulders of thirty people. Also evident are Shan people, Pa

O, Pa Lau and ethnic Burmans all in traditional costumes. Vivid red, yellow, green, white and black. A cacophony of colour.

Once the floats have done the rounds of the town they are carried to the main monastery in Kalaw. Novice monks line the walls and watch as they go by. Tomorrow they will be raffled off and the largest and most ostentatious float is just as likely to be won by the newest of novices as by the most senior of monks.

In the evening of the first day of the festival there is a second procession; a procession of giant, fire-blasting, gunpowder-filled, homemade, pine shingle logs. Again, as part of the main festivities they will be exploded tomorrow and the one creating the most spectacular explosion will be the winner. But tonight they are paraded around the streets by flaming torch light to the beating of drums. People jump around and the logs are rocked from side to side and then twirled around, almost collecting unwary roadside observers. There are rows of dancing men and women between each log. One group of dancers is dressed in traditional black clothing and wears sunglasses. Flares go off, fireworks go up, and from a temple on a nearby hill small hot-air balloons trailing tails of lights are released, the fire beneath them clearly visible in the night sky. As they rise, fireworks shoot out of them in all directions. One balloon goes up, a firework explodes in the balloon, the casket plummets earthward and crashes into the ground, shooting fireworks at houses, shops, and bystanders much to the delight of all.

Fire, noise, banging, beating and hundreds of drunken revellers in the street. Who needs safety regulations? They would only temper the excitement.

Tomorrow will be even more spectacular, I am told.

❑ ❑ ❑ ❑ ❑

Back in the restaurant which had been full of military personnel a few evenings before, I sit at dinner and listen in on a conversation which is taking place at the table next to me. It is a conversation between two licensed tour guides and three middle-aged Western tourists dressed in button-up shirts, shorts, and boots with their socks pulled up. The topic of discussion is the Shan people and the tourists pay keen attention, sitting and nodding their heads at all the appropriate times. The group arrived twenty minutes ago in a tinted-windowed 4WD Mitsubishi Pajero with tour company logos on its doors.

To be a licensed tour guide in Burma is to have one of the most sought-after jobs in the country. It is a favourite of sons, daughters, relatives, friends and cronies of senior military officials. Why? Because it guarantees direct access to hard-currency tourist dollars. In addition to this, tour guides, as a matter of course, take tourists to the gift shops, restaurants, and hotels that pay them the highest commissions to channel trade in their particular direction. As a result, the wage of a tour guide in Burma, relative to that of a teacher, is proportionately the same as the wage of a teacher in Australia compared to that of a businessman who earns $15 million per annum. This is ludicrous even by Burmese standards.

But it is not only because of the money involved that tour guide licences are hard to obtain. The military must also be confident that the potential guide will further the 'Isn't Myanmar a beautiful country' propaganda. Such confidence, naturally, is best gained by having good connections with senior members of the military, in particular Brigadier General Aye Myint Kyu of Myanmar Tours and Travel who dispenses the licences.

Once a licence is obtained, a tour guide is permitted to take tourists to towns like Putao, Keng Tung, and Mogok; towns otherwise off limits to tourists. The licensed tour guide then acts on behalf of the military, keeping tabs on the tourists and ensuring that they only see what the military is prepared to let them see. This is how closely tour guides and the military can be linked.

And so, in this restaurant in Kalaw, the tour guide explains to the nodding tourists, 'The Shan People, they do not like the Burmese. They make war with us for many years. All the time we are defending the Burmese people and Burmese unity. Now we have peace with the Shan armies. Our government has made peace. But still there are problems. It is very dangerous for tourists to travel in Shan State. There are many bandits that make trouble for tourists and they make trouble for our country. You know Khun Sa, you know the opium warlords, they are Shan people. Shan people make many problems for us. It is very hard for our government.'

Yes, there are problems in Shan State but to infer that the military regime is a responsible, peace-seeking government, this is when the diatribe of the tour guides begins to sound like a memorized transcript from the The New Light of Myanmar's SPDC guide to propaganda. It is not a pleasing scenario to see these tourists sitting and nodding as they literally hand hundreds of dollars over to the military. And then these same tourists return to their countries and explain what a lovely country Burma is and how it is full of smiling, happy people. One should ask, did they take the opportunity to look any further than the picture which was placed before them by some of the richest government-appointed licensees in a country where the government is a dictatorship?

Beggars and the disabled being removed from the streets of major cities. Houses on streets likely to be frequented by tourists being repainted by military decree at the owners' expense. Tourist infrastructure projects built by slave labour. The planting of trees and the beautification of the road between Mandalay and Maymyo. Is it any coincidence that this is a road well-travelled by tourists? Is it any wonder that the military did not miss this opportunity for more 'Isn't Myanmar a beautiful and contented country,' propaganda?

'Aaawww, geee honey, isn't it purty. Look at all them there flowers. Couldn't be no problems in this country, no sir-ee,' exclaims Mr Tourist to Mrs Tourist as they take their overnight adventure trip up and into the hills of Burma.

On one of the occasions that I had seen Mr Donald he had asked me why I, as a tourist, had come to Burma. I had tried to explain but had then asked whether or not he would have travellers in his country. Mr Donald had not answered directly. Instead his response had been, 'It is an easy question to ask but hard to answer. It is not enough for you to see because when you see you must taste. Burma is a forbidden fruit for you so you must come here.' Then, as was his want, he had told me a story. 'There was one man who came here from England and he bought an antique wooden statue of a Buddha. He brought it to show me because he was very pleased with his purchase. Then he had to decide how to take it out of the country. He could not fit it in his bag so he cut the base off the statue. When he did this he found that inside the Buddha was a small hole with gemstones in it. This is our tradition in Burma, to put gems in statues of Buddha. He was so happy when he left Burma because of this fortunate purchase. But what about Burma? Why did you come to Burma?'

As if to illustrate Mr Donald's underlying concerns, four tourists had then arrived at the Shan Estate. In the ensuing discussions it very quickly became apparent that two of them did not know that Burma has a military government, this despite having been in the country for two weeks. They had not seen a copy of The New Light of Myanmar, they did not question the discriminatory price systems, they had not noticed any of the propaganda signs, and they did not know who Daw Aung San Suu Kyi was. In essence, they were oblivious of the predicament of the country in which they were travelling. Mr Donald challenged them with regard to this and they replied 'But some people do not come here for politics, some just come here to have a good time.' There are many Burmese people who do not appreciate such ignorance or its ramifications.

There are many issues in Burma. Drugs, democracy, detention, education, ethnic minorities, health, human rights, propaganda, suppression, oppression, restriction, refugees, foreign affairs, forced relocation, international aid, sanctions. Many issues, each of grave concern. But my issue, the one of which I am a part, is this. I have been a tourist to Burma and coming to Burma is a contentious issue.

In *The Observer*, 1 June 2000, author Ms Dea Birkett, in response to articles criticizing tourists for travelling to Burma, wrote,

> But aren't holidays supposed to be carefree times, for suntans and self-indulgence? Is it really such a crime to seek out somewhere where you can simply enjoy yourself? Is spreading on factor 10, rather than reading up on the local medieval history and contemporary political systems, the sign of a lesser moral soul? Does every annual leave have to be an educational experience or a payback for the harm we westerners have done?

This represents one perspective on tourism in Burma.

A second perspective is that my own awareness regarding the situation in Burma has only come about because of the time I have spent travelling through the country. As a result of my travels I now work towards increasing awareness about Burma and its political and human rights situation.

In 1999 an estimated 120,000 tourists came to Burma. In the first two months of 2000 a further 60,000 tourists arrived. If one in ten of these tourists decided, upon leaving, to take pro-active steps towards helping this country, then perhaps tourism would be a good thing. The fear is that too many tourists come to Burma, hand over their money, and nod their heads when tour guides tell them about how hard the 'government' is working for the good of the people. And then, like the tourists in Hsipaw who so frustrated Mr Donald, they say, 'But some people do not come here for politics, some just come here to have a good time.'

A third perspective is this. Whilst in Burma I have spent my US$, I have paid the military-imposed fees to catch boats, for visa extensions, and to enter Shweddagon, Pagan, and the National Museum. It is a simple equation. In Burma infrastructure projects required for tourists are built by forced labour. In addition to this, half of all national revenue is spent on the army. I paid my US$300 at the airport. One half of this US$150 is the wage of a soldier for three years. US$9, half of the price that it costs to cross the border into Burma from Thailand for a day, is the wage of a soldier for two months. In Burma soldiers are used to keep a military regime in power. In Burma soldiers are used to kill Burmese people.

The message from Nobel Peace Prize winner Daw Aung San Suu Kyi to tourists is unequivocal. Please do not come to Burma at all. Your presence gives funds and legitimacy to a military dictatorship.

PAGAN

On the road to Pagan. Palms with prickly leaves that form a sphere on top of a stick-like trunk. Prickly lollipop palms. Dry ground. Sandy river beds. Erosion. Then there are fenced-off patches of new-growth vegetation. In front of each one, in English, is a sign proclaiming that the reforestation area was kindly donated by such and such a township or such and such an industry. The largest signpost clearly states the ongoing commitment of the State Peace and Development Council to a green future in Burma.

A Burmese gentleman tells me that in the first weeks of Visit Myanmar Year schools close to the road to Pagan were told to take their students to the roadside in the afternoons. Here they were required to smile and wave hands and flags at the coach loads of tourists which drove past. Today children still run out and wave at the buses. This does not happen elsewhere in Burma. Nor are there signs in English about reforestation programmes elsewhere in Burma.

But this is the road to Pagan, the road most travelled by tourists in Burma. Every tourist to this country comes to Pagan and it is here that many will form their impressions of Burma.

'Aw gee honey, aint that so neat, these villages helping to grow them there trees. Couldn't be no problems here, could there hon.'

As we drive, archaeological digs by the side of the road suggest that Pagan is close. I look through the palm trees for pagodas on the plains. I anticipate something impressive. Then I see a pagoda in the distance, then two, then three, then twenty, then a hundred. This is Pagan, the heart of Burma.

Pagan is one of the most spectacular tourist destinations in South-East Asia. But more than this, it is a site revered by the Burmese. As I have travelled, many of the people with whom I have talked asked me whether I had seen Pagan yet. When I had said no they insisted that I make sure that I do. It is clear that many Burmese are proud of Pagan. It represents the highest point in Burmese history.

Pagan was the capital of Burma during the eleventh, twelveth and thirteenth centuries. As a city it rose to eminence under the powerful King Anawrahta in AD 1044. This king unified much of what is modern Burma and ruled it from his court in Pagan. This was the first time that Burma had experienced a centralized government.

Of even more significance was King Anawrahta's desire to see Theravada Buddhism, to which he was a convert, become the accepted philosophy of his kingdom. Theravada Buddhism had traditionally been the religion of the Mon people in southern central Burma. The rest of Burma had practised a combination of Mahayana Buddism, Hinduism and Animism. Upon his ascent to the throne, however, King Anawarhta defeated the Mons in battle with the intention of bringing Theravada Buddhist relics, scriptures, statues, as well as monks and teachers back to Pagan to make this the centre of Theravada Buddhism.

What ensued was a building boom of unprecedented magnificence. Between 1044 and the takeover by the Mongols at the end of the thirteenth century, literally thousands of *payas* were built in and around Pagan. Today many of these are in ruins. They have succumbed to centuries of neglect and looting, as well as natural disasters such as the earthquake of 1975. Despite this, some structures still stand and even those which are only partially intact add to the magnificence of the spectacle.

When I was in Bhamo, the young monk U Than Weh Toh had told me, 'Pagan is a very special place for the Burmese.'

❏ ❏ ❏ ❏ ❏

Before we arrive the bus stops and all tourists are asked to disembark at a tourist checkpoint. We are required to show our passports, sign a register, and pay our US$10 fee for entry into Pagan.

TO SEE OR NOT TO SEE

In Burma, things pertaining to Buddhism seem to be significantly more evident than in neighbouring Buddhist countries. *Payas* dot the countryside and there are over 5,000 monasteries. These are populated by an estimated 250,000 monks. Of these, some remain monks for life but so too is there a transient population of many male children and teenagers who spend some time in a monastery as part of their education. Every morning from dawn monks walk the streets of towns and villages and receive alms from households and small businesses.

Nationally, it has been observed that Burma has preserved Theravada Buddhism in its historically purest form. Ironically, this preservation may be partly attributed to the isolationist policies imposed by General Ne Win after his military coup in 1962. Other Buddhist nations in South-East Asia have either been wracked by internal trouble and wars or, as is the case in Thailand, have simply been influenced by decades of Western culture. Burma, however, has been cut off from the rest of the world for the best part of thirty years and during this time its faith has remained intact.

Today, in Burma, the fear of harsh and violent reprisals may well outweigh popular motivation to actively pursue democracy, civil rights and civil liberties. But a stronger allegiance is that of the Burmese population to Buddhism. As a result of this the SPDC commits itself to a very public campaign of ingratiation and alignment with the national faith. The military restored Shwedagon *Paya* in Rangoon. The military is rebuilding Pagan. The military is building schools to promote Buddhism. Read the headlines of any *The New Light of Myanmar* and one's attention is draw to the donations made by military leaders and their families to temples and monasteries. Look at the photos and one sees generals shaking hands with revered and venerable monks.

The reality, however, is that SPDC policies represent the antithesis of Buddhist philosophy.

In 1988 monks joined students and democracy activists in calling for an end to military rule. Like the students and democracy activists, the military imprisoned, tortured and shot monks who chose to oppose it.

In 1990 Buddhist monks across Burma staged a boycott protesting against the SLORC regime. As part of the protest they refused to perform religious functions for military officials and their families. They also refused to receive alms from people related to the SLORC regime. On 9 September 1998, amid a wave of arrests of National League of Democracy members, monks from the Tennasserim Division called for a similar boycott.

In March 1996 soldiers shot a monk and wounded two others in Mandalay. The SLORC explained the incident as follows: a Buddhist girl had been killed by Muslims, which had led to riots between Buddhists and Muslims. The army was called in to keep the peace; the death and injuries of the monks had occurred when bullets ricocheted from buildings after being fired into the air as warning shots. The All Burma Young Monks' Union, however, said that the demonstration was political in nature and was a protest against the defrocking, imprisonment, maltreatment, torture, and killing of sixteen monks in captivity. They also said that when the soldiers arrived they aimed their guns directly at the monks. After this event, the Burmese military regime disrobed a further 150 monks.

❏   ❏   ❏   ❏   ❏

Pagan. The ruins and remains of a thousand temples which are almost a thousand years old all on a single desert plain. I hire a Chinese ricketycycle bicycle and spend my time pedalling off to see what I can see.

The first *paya* I come to is small, ruined, and attracts little popular attention. The second is Htilominlo Guphaya Gyi built in AD 1218 and 150 metres high. Temple number three is the one which was built on the site where a king found a small ruby, Sulamani Guphaya (AD 1183), the name of which means 'site where a king found a small ruby'.

Temple four is Ananda *Paya*, one of the premier sites for tourists and pilgrims alike. At the entrance there is a notice to all visitors: 'The following are not allowed in this shrine. Bringing shoes and footwears, spraying perfumes and offering incenses to the Buddha statues, paying obeisance in shorts or miniskirts.' I leave my footwears and miniskirt at the front door.

Ananda temple is an ancient white temple with towering ceilings, solid, fortress-like brick walls, and enormous teak doors. The stone inside is cool. Each of four Buddhas are over seven metres high and covered in layer after layer of gold leaf, applied by devotees. Even the rooms housing the Buddhas, taller than they are wide or long, are covered in gold leaf. And along the corridors leading to these rooms there are hundreds of niches cut into the walls and in each niche is another statue of Buddha.

Another grand temple is Dhammayan Gyi (AD 1163–1165). I take off my shoes and walk along the corridors. The cobblestones underfoot are worn smooth by thousands of feet having walked on them for hundreds of years. So smooth are they, in fact, that when I walk I deliberately drag my feet a bit so that I can enjoy just how smooth and worn they are. But not for very much longer. They are being cemented over as part of the restoration process that is taking place in Pagan. And the walls; a new cement render is being put over them and they are getting a fresh whitewashing. It is the same in Byinnyu *Paya* (AD 1144) where the walls have already been whitewashed except where the writing from centuries ago is sufficiently clear for the authorities to have decided to leave it.

This is the restoration of Pagan. Temples of with only half a *zedi*, now boast bamboo scaffolding and red brick reconstruction.

❑ ❑ ❑ ❑ ❑

On the outskirts of the other temples are the remains of an imposing but now ruined *paya*. It is some distance away and I cross ploughed fields and ride along bumpy, dusty tracks to reach it. It is deserted with no attempt made at renovation, no tourists, no road leading to it, only a dirt path along which a flock of goats is being cajoled. It would have been impressive once but now all of the upper tiers are gone, grass grows on its debris-covered roof, and only the square, solid base with its four entrances is left. One high-roofed corridor runs around the inside of its walls, all side corridors have been bricked up and there are no remaining Buddha statues in the building.

As I approach the entrance, a snake slithers off into the brickwork of the walls. Once inside, the corridor which runs around the central shrine is deserted but for the buzz of flies and the whisper of the wind. There are dry, dead grasses and animal droppings all over the floor; droppings from goats and cows and birds where people once knelt in worship. There is a lizard carcass on the ground, upright and prostrate on its four legs as if it had been frozen whilst straining to look at something on the ceiling. Nearby is a snake's skin that has been shed. And still there is the buzzing of the flies and the whisper of the wind. Around a corner there is a translucent embryonic lizard lying dead on its back. Its four legs and its tail are all waving this way and that in ghoulish animation as almost invisible ants pull them one way and then another. It is a macabre and grotesque sight in the half-light of the corridor.

After the Mongols came to Burma, Pagan went into decline. People moved away and over hundreds of years the temples were looted and vandalized. Superstition had it that Pagan was the home of evil spirits and the temples became a refuge for bandits and robbers. It was a dangerous area to be. During World War II, locals took shelter in the temples, hiding from advancing troops. Some of them would have hidden in this temple.

Silence but for the buzzing of flies and the whispering wind which curls through the deserted corridors of the temple. No sign of life, only death. An eight-hundred-year-old temple, hollow, empty, cavernous. Maybe once they started to rebuild it but then stopped. Or maybe there were sections which they wanted bricked up.

More snake skins that have been shed; three of them, small ones. Then another and another much larger one, well over a metre long. There is a strange feeling in this temple, almost as if it is haunted, almost as if around the next corner there will be something shocking, maybe something larger and dead and rotting.

More snake skins, and then more and then more again. It is unreal. It is as if all of the snakes from the plains come to this deserted temple on the outskirts of Pagan to shed their skins. And then there are the dead lizards and the droppings and the weeds and the dead grasses and the buzzing and the whispering.

Flies buzz louder. Something smells foul. More flies. In front of the last altar is the bloodied afterbirth of a cow. Flies crawling all over it. It's horrid. I leave the temple and go to my bike. The temple has spooked me.

❏   ❏   ❏   ❏   ❏

Sandy, dusky plains, dry rivers, red brick pagodas, goat herds, tourist herds; tourists herded into buses, herded into temples, herded back into buses and herded off. 'Been to Pagan. It was so spectacular. See, here are the photos.'

Pagan, the most developed tourist spot in Burma. It is the only place I have been where touts and hawkers constantly pester tourists.

'Where you come from? You want special ruby?'
'Where you come from? You want special antique?'
'Where you come from? You want special post card?'
'Where you come from? You want special antique postcard?'

And the little children...

'Where you come from? You give me pen?'
'Where you come from? You give me twenty kyat?'

A renowned spot for sunset watching in Pagan are the terraces of Shwesandaw *Paya*. Five-thirty and my camera has a front row spot amongst the tourists. Minoltas, Nikons, Canons, cameras on tripods, cameras in hands, Hi 8s, Super Hi 8s, Sony Digitals, 28mm lenses, 50mm lenses, 400mm lenses, wide angles, zooms, telephotos, instamatics and flash bulbs. Is there anyone here without a camera or three? Not me. Could stock a trans-Atlantic chain of camera stores with all of this equipment. And between the temples and behind a hill in the distance the sun sets in spectacular fashion.

The tourists descend the stairs, pile back into their buses, their pony carts, their taxis or onto their bicycles and within ten minutes of the sun's passing behind the hill the terraces are almost completely empty.

In New Pagan at night, stall after stall sells souvenirs to tourists. Marionette puppets, pictures, sculptures, teak elephants, opium weights, tapestries, Buddhist icons, and gems. The roads are lined with the stalls, fluorescent lights and meandering tourists.

WHEN SILENCE SPEAKS A THOUSAND WORDS

There is an affliction that catches up with you in Burma. It is the non-mentioning of 'those' names. Almost no one says them, certainly not in public, not anyone, never, and it is infectious. In a restaurant you find yourself, even when talking with tourists, saying her name quietly if at all. Yes, they love her; yes they call her the First Lady; yes, 82 per cent of the population voted for her party. But now, in Burma, fear for one's personal security is a more significant issue. Even the mention of 'those' names, if overheard, is enough to have a citizen interrogated or earmarked as a subversive.

In the time I have spent in Burma only a handful of people have dared to say the name Daw Aung San Suu Kyi. This is perhaps the best indicator of the pervasiveness of the culture of fear that has settled over Burma.

On my final day in Pagan I have lunch at a restaurant near my hotel. No one else is present and after eating I sit with the owner and his brother. One is reading a paper and the other is holding a guitar. They cut up a grapefruit and a banana for me and give me a cheroot. As we talk they ask me what I think about politics in Burma. 'Not good,' I reply. 'Many tourists say that,' the owner admits. 'What are politics in Thailand like? What are politics in Australia like?' Then I tell him about democracy in Australia and conclude by saying, 'Very different to Burma.' 'I know,' he agrees. Then he asks me which country I like to travel in most. I say that Burma is very beautiful and that the people are very friendly but that it is difficult to travel because of the military. 'I know,' he responds. 'Will it change here?' he asks. 'I don't know.'

And for the duration of the time that we talk about Burma he has 'that' look on his face. It is the same look as Daw Htar Yi had had and U Thaung Aye and U Than Weh Toh and Ko Lay Nyo and Mr Moustache and Mr Donald and the helicopter man and any one of the Burmese people who dared to talk about their country with me. Faraway, wistful, perhaps even desolate at the mention of democracy or freedom or anything to do with a life not full of restriction and fear. And this is the look which is on the faces of people who have no greater political agenda than the fact that they exist now, at this time, in Burma. It is this face, this look, which as much as anything condemns the current political regime.

It is sad that this restaurant owner has brought up a topic that has made him so unhappy.

❑ ❑ ❑ ❑ ❑

My bus back to Rangoon is an overnighter with no sleep. The aisles are full of boxes and crates. The Popadagon Express. Now it is time to leave.

LEAVING BURMA

In a bid to add credibility to its calumnies and slanders, one of the devices employed by the national press in Burma is to attribute articles to foreign newspapers or dignitaries. The following is an extract from an article purportedly written by the chairman of Merryl Lynch. According to *The New Light of Myanmar* in which it was reproduced, the article appeared in the *Japan Times* on 3 July 1996.

From: 'Japan Grow Up' *The New Light of Myanmar*, 5 July 1996.

For everyone in the US, Myanmar is a soft, risk free, human rights target which, irrespective of the facts, people from all walks of life, from politicians to students, can abuse with a great sense of both righteousness and that they are making a positive contribution. Nothing could be further from the truth. Their ignorant meddling is based primarily on misinformation provided by the opposition – activist groups (often students with little knowledge, experience and maturity) and the Daw Aung San Suu Kyi obsessed international media. These misguided, misinformed and malicious activists remind me of the late 17th, early 18th Century "Witch" trials in Salem, Massachusetts. The West and Japan have a general obsession that Suu Kyi is the elected saviour of the Myanmar people from the evil military government. What a nonsense! Most of the Japanese media makes little effort to get the facts but instead portrays Suu Kyi as a sort of modern Joan of Arc. They fail completely to appreciate that she was the daughter of General Aung San, the original leader of Burma's independence movement in 1947 before he was assassinated. She spent 28 years out of Myanmar, is married to an English academic, and only returned to Yangon because her mother was gravely ill. While a remarkable woman in many respects, she certainly has no relevant qualifications to lead her country. In fact it is widely alleged that many of her supporters complain that she is arrogant, stubborn, opinionated and often irrational because she is woefully ignorant to the facts relating to the issues.

Needless to say, this article was not written by a Chairman of Merryl Lynch, nor was it published in the *Japan Times*. At some point one must stop and ask, is there anything about which the State Peace and Development Council does not lie?

❑ ❑ ❑ ❑ ❑

Rangoon, my last night. Dark streets, deserted streets, dark nights, not too many road lights. The cars of the rich pull up at the kerb with over-weight drivers whose podgy hands sport fat, glittering rings. Sitting on the pavement side by side, one old Indian, one old Burman; white beard on the Indian, white hair on the Burman; black skin, coffee skin, sitting and talking on some steps beside the main street at ten o'clock. They are talking tonight just as they will tomorrow morning except that tomorrow morning there will be hundreds of people on these pavements, not tens. Not me. My last night.

I sit and write my final notes. I am going to stop soon. As much as I would like to postpone the finality of it, I am going to finish packing, hide my last notes and then go to bed. When I wake up it will be time to go, time to leave Burma.

As I write I think, 'Is there some sort of reform happening in Burma, is there some sort of change occurring, is there movement towards some sort of democracy?' If not, it all seems too unreal, too bizarre. How can a nation's 'leaders' lie so blatantly?

Then I tell myself, Daw Aung San Suu Kyi lives in a house the road to which is blocked by military barricades. She has no freedom of speech, movement, or association. She is stopped every time she tries to leave Rangoon. This is a benchmark for the state of affairs in Burma. Par Par lay is still in prison for telling jokes and in 1998 he was joined by over 1,000 members of the National League for Democracy. These too are benchmarks for the state of affairs in Burma. And there are the universities, closed across the nation in December 1996. In June 2000 they re-opened but the campuses have been relocated out of city centres, away from the public eye and close to military installations. In addition to this, before admission, students and parents must sign a guarantee declaring that they will support the military regime. Is this a sign of reform or is it yet another benchmark evidencing a regime that has no intention of relinquishing its grip on power?

I leave Burma. Departure had been a cause of concern for some time but as it transpires the gods of good fortune shine on me. As I stand in the departure queue the two young women who had found me a taxi when I first arrived in Burma see me, recognize me, and come over and ask me about my travels. Then they usher me from the queue in which I am standing and take me to the diplomatic counter. Customs takes a minute and my baggage is not searched. What an unexpected turn of events.

On the plane there are people who are leaving Burma for the first time. They are the ones who are waving to people on the observation deck as we taxi down the runway, imagining themselves to be visible. They are the ones who ignore the signs in the aeroplane saying 'fasten your seat belts' and instead try to walk across the aisle even as we begin to take off. They are told to sit down by cabin crew, friends and other Burmese. They are the ones whose faces are glued to the small oval windows for the duration of the flight. Some are visibly apprehensive and I wonder what they are thinking. I wonder also about the circumstances that have allowed them to be on this plane. In one hour, they, I, will touch down in the South-East Asian megatropolis of Bangkok.

A FAREWELL TO MR LIEUTENANT GENERAL
KHIN NYUNT

So, Mr Lieutenant General Khin Nyunt, Secretary One of the State Peace and Development Council, Head of Burmese Military Intelligence, Chairman of the Board of Education, and, as I have most recently heard, head of the Burmese Olympic Team in Sydney 2000, I leave your country. In your address of November 1996 you had said that the main purpose of Visit Myanmar Year was to enable tourists to visit Myanmar and see the facts. On their return to their own countries they would then be able to explain the true situation that they experienced and all the fabrications would be rebutted.

Mr Khin Nyunt, I have taken the opportunity to report the situation that I have experienced as fairly and as honestly as I have been able. I have seen beautiful sights, I have enjoyed the hospitality of Burmese people, and I have also seen the workings of a military dictatorship. The United Nations has ranked Burma alongside China and Afghanistan as having the worst human rights record in the world. Mr Khin Nyunt, in travelling through your country I have been able to see something of what this actually means.

Appendix

APPENDIX

Significant events in Burma. November 1996 to February 2001

November 1996. Visit Myanmar Year is officially launched. The Burmese military hope that it will attract upward of 500,000 tourists and that this will bring much needed foreign currency into Burma.

6 December 1996. In the largest student demonstrations since 1988/89, an estimated 4,000 students demonstrate in Rangoon. Riot police end the demonstrations detaining hundreds of students near Shwedagon Paya. Lt. Gen. Tin Oo, Secretary Two of the State Law and Order Restoration Council (SLORC), publicly states that he will annihilate anyone who opposes the military's work. Meanwhile, forty-seven members of the National League for Democracy (NLD) are arrested and the home of democracy leader Daw Aung San Suu Kyi is blockaded. She and twenty associates are prevented from leaving for two days and journalists are banned from approaching the house. All Universities across Burma are closed down.

24 December 1996. SLORC General and second in command of the army, Lt. Gen. Tin Oo, is targeted in a bomb attack in a temple. Five people are killed and 17 wounded. Authorities blame ethnic groups and student protestors. However, it is suggested that the assassination attempt could have been the result of factional fighting within the military. There are widespread rumours of rivalry between the head of Military Intelligence, Lt. Gen. Khin Nyunt and the commander in chief of the army, Gen. Maung Aye. Lt. Gen. Tin Oo, the target of the bomb attack, is a supporter of Gen. Maung Aye.

31 December 1996. Lt. Gen. Khin Nyunt declares that the Burmese Communist Party is responsible for the student demonstrations that occurred in Rangoon on 6 December. His intention is to portray students as Communist insurgents rather than pro-democracy protestors. Live ammunition is distributed to military battalions stationed throughout Rangoon and around University campuses.

January 1997. SLORC moves five tanks in front of the City Hall in Rangoon, fearing that the bombing which occurred over Christmas may be connected to demonstrations in December 1996.

January 1997. China and Burma sign a pact to strengthen military co-operation including China providing military training, weapons, and shared intelligence.

28 January 1997. Burmese soldiers enter Thailand, looting and setting ablaze three refugee camps in the Mae Sot district. One thousand buildings are razed by the troops and 10,000 refugees are left homeless. The refugees in the camps are ethnic Karens who have fled persecution at the hands of the Burmese military. Further Burmese military raids on refugee camps in Thailand occur on 2 February 1997 and in March 1997.

January/February 1997. The Burmese military launches its annual dry season offensive against the Karen and Shan ethnic minorities.

February 1997. American lawmakers send a delegation to Rangoon in an attempt to persuade military leaders to make concessions with the NLD and enter into dialogue with Daw Aung San Suu Kyi. The military refuses to do so.

February 1997. The Burmese Army burns hundreds of homes in a military offensive opposite Tak Province, sending Karens fleeing into Thailand. In March the Burmese offensive against the Karen National Union eases after an estimated 90,000 refugees have fled to Thailand for safety.

4 March 1997. Chinese officials and Burmese military leaders reach an agreement which will allow China to develop a 'road and river' transport route connecting Yunnan Province in China, through Burma, to the Bay of Bengal. The route is 5,800 km shorter than the currently-used route from Kunming in Yunnan Province to Shanghai.

April 1997. Because of its ongoing human rights violations, US President Bill Clinton imposes a ban on all new US investment in Burma.

6 April 1997. A bomb explodes at the house of the second secretary of the SLORC, Lt. Gen. Tin Oo. The bomb blast kills his thirty-four-year-old daughter. The military blame the Karen National Union and the All Burma Students Democratic Front. Both of these organizations deny involvement and instead say that the bomb blast is once again an indication of power struggles within the military.

June 1997. Burma is admitted as a full member of ASEAN. The military junta hope that this will increase foreign investment in Burma; pro democracy activists hope membership of ASEAN will encourage SLORC to enter into dialogue with ethnic and democracy leaders.

June 1997. The military junta arrests at least 316 senior members of the NLD, including elected Members of Parliament, so as to prevent them from meeting with Daw Aung San Suu Kyi to commemorate the anniversary of the NLD election victory in 1990. Riot police are used to block roads and the headquarters of the NLD are fenced off with barbed wire.

June 1997. SLORC forms a new committee in a bid to stem the crashing of the national currency, the kyat. The committee is called the Monetary Stabilization Committee and it is headed by military intelligence chief, Lieut. Gen. Khin Nyunt.

August 1997. Canada imposes economic sanctions on Burma.

August 1997. The military junta sentences three of Daw Aung San Suu Kyi's relatives to ten-year prison sentences. They are accused of accepting money from foreign pro-democracy activists and passing it on to the NLD.

August 1997. Four prominent dissidents are arrested and sentenced to long prison terms for high treason. It is believed that these arrests are the result of intelligence gathered using the military's new 'cyber warfare centre', a high tech information warfare centre that is part of the Directorate of Defence Services, Intelligence. The multi-million dollar centre and training for its staff are supplied by a Singaporean company and the centre allows military intelligence to be able to track and trace satellite calls, faxes, telephone calls and e-mail.

October 1997. A member of Daw Aung San Suu Kyi's NLD Party dies in jail. Kyaw Din, 58, dies in a prison hospital while serving a two-year jail sentence.

November 1997. Democracy leader Daw Aung San Suu Kyi is again locked in her home. Riot police barricade an office of the NLD and fifty members of the party are taken into custody.

15 November 1997. The State Law and Order Restoration Council (SLORC) renames itself the State Peace and Development Council (SPDC). The council is made up of nineteen members including regional military chiefs, the top generals of the Burmese military and the head of each of the army, air force and navy. Only the Chairman of the SPDC, General Than Shwe, maintains a position as a minister. Other ministerial positions are filled by senior military figures although some deputy-minis-

ters are taken from civilian ranks. It is said that Military Intelligence chief Lt. Gen. Khin Nyunt is largely behind the reshuffle and as a result a number of long-term military incumbents are 'retired' on grounds of corruption. It is suggested that perhaps he is stacking the SPDC against his rival, head of the Burmese army, Gen. Maung Aye.

17-19 November 1997. The European Union (EU) cancels an EU/ASEAN joint meeting in Bangkok because ASEAN insists upon Burma being allowed to be present.

March 1998. The military arrests forty students alleging that they are linked to the NLD and that they have been planning to attack public buildings and assassinate national leaders. Soon after, 1988 student leader Aung Tun is sentenced to fifteen years in prison for writing a history of the Burmese student movement.

April 1998. As part of the its annual dry season offensive against the Karen, military junta-backed soldiers once again enter Thai territory and raze a Karen refugee camp to the ground. Thailand's response is nominal and perhaps reflects its desire to get rid of its refugees which are seen as both an economic burden and a diplomatic nuisance in its relations with the military in Rangoon.

April 1998. Former student leaders Ko Thein and Khin Hlaing, are tried and sentenced to death in a secret military court in Burma on charges of terrorism, possession of explosives, and plotting to assassinate military leaders. It appears, however, that their actual crime is that they try to forward a letter on human rights abuses in Burma to a special United Nations Investigator.

April 1998. Pro-democracy activist San San is sentenced to 25 years imprisonment for giving an interview to the BBC.

14 April 1998. The United Nations Commission on Human Rights adopts a motion on Burma which expresses concern at abuses including extra judicial executions, the use of torture, suppression of political opposition, and repression of ethnic and religious minorities.

22 May 1998. The International Monetary Fund stresses that without comprehensive political and economic reforms Burma's prospects for economic growth and exports will only worsen.

May 1998. Aung Kyaw Moe, a thirty-eight-year-old NLD member dies in prison. He and six other political prisoners began a hunger strike because they had not been released from prison after serving the full term of their jail sentences. Aung Kyaw Moe was repeatedly beaten by soldiers on the day of his death.

June 1998. Two members of the NLD are sentenced to fourteen years imprisonment for distributing copies of a letter from the rebel Shan State Army leader to Lt. Gen. Khin Nyunt.

June 1998. Restrictions on the movement of regional members of the NLD are imposed. Many are not allowed to leave their towns or villages. The military junta also implements a policy of forcing members to resign from the party.

July 1998. The SPDC refuses to grant an entry visa to a special envoy of the UN. His mission would have been to encourage political dialogue between the military regime and the democratic opposition.

July 1998. The NLD demands that the military junta convene parliament as elected in 1990, by 21 August 1998.

July 1998. Lt. Gen. Khin Nyunt blames internal subversive elements for the failure of Visit Myanmar Year to attract the desired number of tourists.

July 1998. Eleven leading members of the NLD are arrested. They are accused of trying to plunge the country into violence.

24 July/August 1998. In the lead-up to the tenth anniversary of the 8/8/88 massacres, Daw Aung San Suu Kyi is stopped on a bridge in her car whilst travelling to a party meeting thirty kilometres from Rangoon. It is the third time that month that the military has physically intervened when Daw Suu has attempted to leave Rangoon. On this occasion, however, she refuses to return and the ensuing stand off lasts eighteen days. During this time the military erects barbed wire road blocks on the road and leaves armed personnel to make sure no one leaves or approaches the bridge. Local villagers are not permitted to provide Daw Suu with food or drink. Daw Suu, Hla Pe (also from the NLD), and their two drivers live on bread, chocolate and water. Ultimately the military forcibly returns Daw Suu to her residence on University Drive.

8 August 1998. The tenth anniversary of the massacres of 8/8/88. Daw Aung San Suu Kyi calls for the immediate and unconditional release of political prisoners in Burma, the convening of parliament as elected in the general elections of 1990, and respect of basic human rights by the SPDC. In Rangoon, eighteen foreign nationals are arrested for distributing business cards bearing the message "8888 don't forget, dont give up". They are held for six days and then sentenced to five years imprisonment. After diplomatic negotiations they are deported to Bangkok.

18 August 1998. The military junta tries to create a rift in the NLD when it announces that it will enter into dialogue with anyone except Daw Aung San Suu Kyi.

24 August 1998 . The first street protests in two years in Rangoon. The first takes place when one hundred students stage a sit down protest near Rangoon University and the second occurs in the evening outside the Rangoon Institute of Technology.

2 September 1998. The military junta announces that it will reopen universities for a short period of time to allow students to sit exams. Over one thousand students protest because they are given only one week of tuition prior to being allowed to sit the exams.

6 September 1998. In anticipation of the NLD trying to convene a people's parliament, the SPDC sweeps through NLD ranks arresting 110 party officials and MPs elected in the 1990 election. Later in the month the NLD convenes the Committee Representing the People's Parliament (CRPP). It is supported by the majority of members elected in the 1990 general election. Daw Suu asks the UN and the International Community to recognize the authority of the CRPP.

September 1998. The International Labour Organization (ILO) accuses Rangoon of allowing systematic and widespread use of forced labour. The labourers, it is reported, are victims of theft, neglect, assault, rape, torture and murder.

September 1998. It is alleged that fifteen military officers (twelve colonels and three majors) are arrested for attempting to open negotiations with NLD leader Daw Aung San Suu Kyi.

October 1998. Another twenty-nine members of the NLD are rounded up and arrested because of their involvement with the party. Since May, 882 members of parliament and NLD officials have been arrested, constituting the largest crackdown on the party since the early 1990s.

October 1998. A planned meeting between ASEAN and the EU is again called off because of Burma's membership in ASEAN and the failure of the SPDC to address human rights violations occurring in Burma.

November 1998. The number of pro-democracy activists arrested in Burma in the last six months reaches one thousand as military round ups continue.

November 1998. The military release ninety-five members of the NLD. The military announces that the members had not in fact been arrested but had instead been invited to 'government guest houses' so as to facilitate an exchange of views. NLD reports say that its members had been taken into custody and coerced into resigning their membership.

December 1998. The Human Rights Commission for the United Nations General Assembly adopts a resolution deploring 'the continuing violations of human rights in Burma, including extrajudicial and arbitrary executions, rape, torture, inhuman treatment, mass arrests, forced labour and forced relocation'.

December 1998. The military announce that 467 members of the NLD have voluntarily revoked their membership from the party. A number of these have recently been released from prison suggesting that thei release was dependent upon their resignation.

Late 1998. The Burmese military is offered US$1 billion in aid if it undertakes dialogue with the pro-democracy opposition. The military refuses and SPDC foreign minister Win Aung announces that any movement towards democracy will only be possible if the money is handed over first.

26 January 1999. Talks scheduled between ASEAN and the EU are again postponed because of Burma's human rights record.

February 1999. Ma Thida, a close associate of Daw Aung San Suu Kyi is released from prison after serving six years of a twenty-year sentence for distributing pro-democracy leaflets. Ma Thida is pardoned on humanitarian grounds because of the deterioration of her health whilst in prison.

February 1999. It is announced that Burma will host the 13th ASEAN Labour Ministers' Meeting, the first ministerial level gathering to be held in the country.

23 February 1999. Interpol holds an International Police Conference on heroin in Rangoon. The conference is boycotted by Britain, Denmark, the Netherlands, Belgium and Luxembourg because of the Burmese military's tolerance of both drug traffickers and the practice of laundering of drug money into legitimate national industries. These countries also query Burma's refusal to join UN programmes for drug eradication. Countries attending, on the other hand, make no issue of the fact that two of Interpol's most wanted drug dealers, Loh Hsing-han and Khun Sa, enjoy residence within two kilometres of the Rangoon conference centre.

April 1999. Daw Aung San Suu Kyi announces that in excess of 150 members of the parliament elected in 1990 are still in prison at the hands of the Burmese military.

May 1999. The EU votes to continue the sanctions that it first imposed on Burma in 1996. These sanctions include a suspension of humanitarian aid for Burma, a ban on the granting of visas into Europe for senior military officials and their immediate families, and the imposing of an arms embargo on the country until such time as the military junta takes steps towards restoring democracy and stops human rights violations.

June 1999. At the annual conference of the ILO, it is reported that "The attitude and behaviour of the junta are grossly incompatible with the conditions and principles governing membership of the organization."

June 1999. The International Committee of the Red Cross (ICRC) regains permission to visit Burmese prisons. The military regime will allow the ICRC to visit forty-eight out of its 900 prisons. The Red Cross had withdrawn from Burma early in 1995 because of the restrictions that had been placed on it by the military regime.

August 1999. UK and Australian National, James Mawdsley, is arrested for handing out leaflets in Burma calling for peaceful political change. He is tried and convicted for terrorism and sentenced to seventeen years imprisonment. He is beaten whilst in prison although the Burmese military claim that his injuries are self inflicted. He is released on 20 October 2000.

October 1999. The military round up and imprison 120 pro-democracy activists in the lead up to 9/9/99, a date seen by some to be an auspicious date on which democracy could once again come to the fore in Burma, as it had on the 8/8/88.

1 October 1999. Twelve armed men calling themselves the Vigorous Burmese Student Warriors raid the Burmese Embassy in Bangkok and take thirty-eight hostages including thirteen Burmese officials and several foreign nationals. The dissidents responsible demand the release of political prisoners in Burma and meaningful dialogue between the military junta and the Committee Representing the People's Parliament. The siege is resolved peacefully when the Burmese activists are flown by helicopter to Mae Sot and then released over the border. It is suggested that part of the negotiations leading up to this resolution involves the dissidents handing to Thai authorities documents seized in the Burmese Embassy which give information about Burmese intelligence agents in Thailand and also Burmese dealings in the Golden Triangle. The hostages are released unharmed and both Thai and Western hostages freely express their support for their captors and the democracy movement in Burma.

November 1999. The World Bank reports that economic prosperity is impossible in Burma without political and human rights reforms.

28 November 1999. Japanese Premier, Keizo Obuchi, meets with head of the military junta, Gen. Than Shwe. This is the first meeting between a senior world leader and a top Burmese military official since the 8888 massacres. Mr Obuchi says he will help rebuild Burma's economy if the military agree to economic and democratic reform. It is suggested that concern over China's influence in Burma may be the motivation behind Japan's initiatives.

January 2000. The Burmese military relocates 50,000 hill tribe villagers from opium-producing areas. The military claims that this is part of its tackling of the drug problem. Independent sources, however, suggest that the relocation is part of the continuing oppression of the Shan people and that the cleared land is to be made available to the Wa drug barons who enjoy friendly relations with the Burmese military regime.

24 Jan 2000. The God's Army, a group fighting for the rights and autonomy of the Karen people, take over a hospital in Thailand's Ratchaburi Province. It is retreating after having come under heavy artillery fire from both the Burmese military and, allegedly, the Thai military. Upon taking the hospital its members demand that the Thai Government send doctors to treat Karen people injured in the offensive. Heavily armed Thai police surround and later storm the hospital. No Thai police or hostages are injured but all ten members of the God's Army are killed. Later reports from some of the hostages suggest that they had surrendered but were then undressed, bound and shot in the back of the head. In an official statement, the Burmese military praises the Thai Government for the decisive way in which they handle the hospital siege.

March 2000. Because of the gross nature of the abuses involved, an ILO report on the use of forced labour in Burma is referred directly to the ILO annual conference. The military junta denies the ILO report and says that the world "is ignoring the fact that the entire population (of Burma) is enjoying peace, stability and better living standards for the first time in their life".

11 May 2000. Burmese Prime Minister, Gen. Than Shwe, Chairman of the SPDC, sends a letter to the nineteen-member council intimating his intention to resign from

his post. This increases speculation that there will be a power struggle between rivals Gen. Maung Aye (army commander) and Lt. Gen. Khin Nyunt (head of military intelligence).

27 May 2000. The tenth anniversary of the NLD's unfulfilled election victory.

May 2000. The EU and ASEAN Nations meet for the first time since Burma's admission into ASEAN.

June 2000. For the first time in its history, the ILO votes in favour of invoking section 33 of its charter against a country - Burma. Section 33 approves sanctions against a member state and means that the ILO will actively enlist the support of member states, the UN and national governments to review their dealings with Burma to ensure that by their involvement they are in no way contributing to the perpetuation of human rights abuses in that country. The ILO gives the military junta until 30 November to redress the situation.

June 2000. The Australian Government, in association with the Burmese military junta, funds a human rights training programme in Rangoon. The programme is attended by fifty Burmese delegates all of whom are hand selected by the military junta. The initiative attracts criticism from national governments, human rights organizations, and Daw Aung San Suu Kyi. It is feared that the programme will only add legitimacy to the military junta.

7 June 2000. Aye Tha Aung, head of the NLD's ethnic minority branches, is sentenced to twenty-one years in jail.

June 2000. In its annual report, the World Health Organization rates Burma as providing the second worst medical health care to its citizens of the 161 nations assessed. The UN also estimates that there are one million children suffering from malnutrition in Burma.

June 2000. A report from the Burmese Border Consortium, a group of non-government organizations operating along the Thai/Burmese border report that 123,000 Karen, Mon, Shan and Karenni refugees are living in sixteen camps along the border. These refugees are fleeing forced labour, forced relocation, crop destruction, arbitrary execution, rape, torture, and the destruction of their villages by the Burmese military.

7 July 2000. The Burmese Deputy Minister for National Planning and Economic Development, Brigadier General Zaw Tun is forced to resign after presenting a seminar in which he describes the failure of the military's economic policies and the gross and deliberate exaggeration of official economic data.

July/August 2000. Some of Burma's tertiary institutions are reopened for the first time since December 1996. For students to attend, both students and parents must sign undertakings that they will support the military. Furthermore, institutions are relocated beside military installations outside urban centres, and offices for military intelligence are opened on campuses.

24 August 2000. Daw Aung San Suu Kyi is stopped and barricaded on a road by the military when she tries to attend a meeting with an up-country youth wing of the NLD

September 2000. The NLD announces that it will begin to take measures to draw up a new Burmese Constitution.

22 September 2000. Daw Aung San Suu Kyi tries to travel to Mandalay by train. Military officials seize her and place her and eight NLD central executive committee members under house arrest. Up to a further eighty supporters of the NLD are also taken to prison

September 2000. The Burmese military rejects a proposal from ASEAN that Vietnam act as an intermediary in dialogue between the junta and the NLD.

October 2000. United Nations Human Rights Commission expert on Burma, Rajsoomer Lallah, reports that the human rights situation in Burma is deteriorating with the military taking particular efforts to suppress all opposition political activity. In particular there is evidence of military policies and directives aimed at completely eliminating the NLD through intimidation, coercion, threats and the imposition of jail sentences.

19 November 2000. The ILO votes in favour of imposing sanctions on the Burmese military junta because of the continuing use of forced labour in Burma. The sanctions come into effect on 30 November 2000.

13 December 2000. An Amnesty International report on torture and detention in Burma estimates that there are 1,700 political prisoners currently in jail in Burma.

December 2000. Thai narcotics intelligence officers estimate that, with the help of the Burmese military junta, the United Wa State Army has relocated people into border areas that formerly came under Shan control. The narcotics agents say that this has led to an extra 3,000 hectares of land being used for opium fields.

January 2001. In its annual summer offensive against the Shan and Karen people, an estimated 30,000 Karen villagers are displaced from their homes, which are burnt by the Burmese military.

January 2001. Daw Aung San Suu Kyi and head of Military Intelligence Lt. Gen. Khin Nyunt meet secretly for talks. It is only the second time that military leaders have met with Daw Suu and the first since 1994. No details are released and within Burma there is no public acknowledgment of the dialogue. With the retirement of Gen. Than Shwe imminent, it is suggested that Lt. Gen. Khin Nyunt is prepared to negotiate with Daw Aung San Suu Kyi and the NLD in order to obtain the support that he will need to take over from Gen. Than Shwe.

February 2001. Lt. Gen. Tin Oo, second-in-command of the Burmese army and the fourth most powerful man in the military junta, participates in strategic talks with regional commanders concerning the annual offensive against the Karen people. On his journey back to Rangoon the helicopter in which he is flying crashes. The official press blames mechanical problems. Lt. Gen. Tin Oo, however, had been tipped to take over the Burmese military if Gen. Maung Aye were to take the reins after Gen. Than Shwe's retirement. As such, military rivalries are suspected to have played a role in the death of Lt. Gen. Tin Oo.

ABOUT THE AUTHOR

Timothy Syrota first visited South-East Asia with his backing-packing mother as a child, spending time in Sulawesi, Java, Bali, Thailand, Malaysia and Singapore in the late 1970s. Evidently this left a positive impression and from University age onwards he has returned to the region whenever the opportunity has presented itself. This has sometimes been as a traveller and sometimes in the capacity of freelance photographer, writer, and video producer.

Tim's first visit to Burma was at the end of 1997 and he is the first to admit that he doesn't really know why he felt the need to go. If pressed, a discourse on fate is likely to follow although another explanation might be that he was going to the country in South-East Asia about which he knew the least. Originally intending only to travel through the country, Tim was struck not only by the beauty of Burma and its people, but also by the oppressive nature of the military regime and the dearth of information available concerning Burma's ongoing predicament. It has been in response to the later that Tim has written his first book, 'Welcome to Burma.'

Whilst writing the book, Tim has spent time in the Thai-Burmese border towns of Mae Sot, Sangklaburi and Mai Sai and in 1998 he produced a video documenting the tenth anniversary of the massacres in Burma in August 1988. He has also returned to Burma on two occasions, most recently in May and June 2001 in order to film a documentary about life in the country. During this last trip the military, not surprisingly, took exception to Tim's work and he had to make a hasty and unceremonious exit.

Tim continues to work with Burmese communities both in Thailand and Australia in the belief that the dissemination of information about the country is essential if the international community is to take a positive and supportive role in seeing a peaceful and hasty transition to civilian government. Tim is currently the Vice-President of the International for Society for Human Rights, Australia.